Labour orators from Bevan to Miliband

Manchester University Press

Labour orators from Bevan to Miliband

Edited by
Andrew S. Crines and Richard Hayton

Manchester University Press

Published by Manchester University Press
Altrincham Street, Manchester M1 7JA, UK
www.manchesteruniversitypress.co.uk

British Library Cataloguing-in-Publication Data
A catalogue record for this book is available from the British Library

Library of Congress Cataloging-in-Publication Data applied for

ISBN 978 07190 8980 0 hardback

First published 2015

The publisher has no responsibility for the persistence or accuracy of URLs for any external or third-party internet websites referred to in this book, and does not guarantee that any content on such websites is, or will remain, accurate or appropriate.

Typeset by Out of House Publishing
Printed in Great Britain by
CPI Group (UK) Ltd, Croydon, CR0 4YY

Contents

Contributors

Judi Atkins is Research Fellow in British Politics at the University of Leeds, and the author of *Justifying New Labour Policy* (Palgrave Macmillan, 2011).

Hilary Benn is the Member of Parliament for Leeds Central and a leading figure in Labour Party politics. He served in the Cabinet as Secretary of State for International Development (2003–7) and Secretary of State for Environment, Food and Rural Affairs (2007–10). He is currently Shadow Secretary of State for Communities and Local Government.

Mark Bennister is Senior Lecturer in Politics at Canterbury Christ Church University, and specialises in the study of political leadership. He is the author of *Prime Ministers in Power: Political Leadership in Britain and Australia* (Palgrave Macmillan, 2012).

Andrew S. Crines is a teaching fellow in British Politics at Liverpool Hope University, and specialises in the study of political communication. He has published in leading academic journals such as *British Politics, Political Quarterly, Representation* and *Politics*. He is also the author of *Michael Foot and the Labour Leadership* (Cambridge Scholars Publishing, 2011). He tweets at @ AndrewCrines.

Mark Garnett is Senior Lecturer in Politics at Lancaster University. Amongst numerous other publications he has authored acclaimed biographies including *Keith Joseph: A Life* (Acumen Press); *Splendid! Splendid! The Authorised Biography of Willie Whitelaw* (Jonathan Cape); and *Alport: A Study in Loyalty* (Acumen Press).

Richard Hayton is Lecturer in Politics at the University of Leeds, and the author of *Reconstructing Conservatism? The Conservative Party in Opposition, 1997–2010* (Manchester University Press, 2012). He tweets at @Richard_Hayton.

Timothy Heppell is Associate Professor of British Politics at the University of Leeds and the sole author of four books including, most recently, *Choosing the*

Labour Leader: Labour Party Leadership Elections from Wilson to Brown (I.B. Tauris, 2010).

Michael Hill is a tutor in British Politics at the University of Leeds. He has published in leading academic journals including *British Politics, Political Quarterly* and *Political Studies Review*.

Keith Laybourn is a leading authority on British Labour history. He has published more than 70 journal articles and is the author or editor of more than 40 books including *A Century of Labour: A History of the Labour Party 1900-2000*. He is a Fellow of the Royal Historical Society and Honorary Fellow of the Historical Association.

Thomas McMeeking is a PhD student in the School of Politics and International Studies at the University of Leeds.

Stephen Meredith is Principal Lecturer and Subject Leader for Politics at the University of Central Lancashire. He is the author of *Labours Old and New: The Parliamentary Right of the British Labour Party 1970-79 and the Roots of New Labour* (Manchester University Press, 2008).

David S. Moon is Lecturer in Politics at the University of Bath.

Robin Pettitt is Senior Lecturer in Comparative Politics at Kingston University, London.

David Stewart is Course Leader and Lecturer in History at the University of Central Lancashire. He is the author of *The Path to Devolution and Change: A Political History of Scotland under Margaret Thatcher, 1979-1990* (I.B. Tauris, 2009).

Foreword

Of the eleven Labour politicians featured in this book, I have had the privilege of hearing nine of them speak in person; the other two (Nye Bevan and Hugh Gaitskell) I have seen on film. Although they all represent different traditions within the Labour family, each of them had a capacity to make an argument, to move an audience, to win over hearts and minds, and to lift our spirits in a way that transcended a moment in time and space.

Bevan was famed for his ability to inspire those who heard him speak, and at the sixtieth anniversary service to mark the founding of his, and Labour's, greatest achievement – the NHS – Westminster Abbey filled with the sound of a scratchy recording of Bevan explaining how the NHS would work. It brought our celebration to life.

Gaitskell is best remembered for his great 'fight, fight and fight again to save the party we love' speech at the 1960 Labour Party conference. He showed great passion on that occasion and I remember the enormous sense of loss and sadness felt by my parents when news of his untimely death was reported just three years later.

I heard Harold Wilson speak a number of times, the first being in Bristol when I was still at school. I recall the excitement, the force of his reasoning, and the wit and ease with which he dealt with hecklers. Indeed, he relished their challenge such was his confidence.

Barbara Castle was always passionate and utterly determined. Her memorable speech to the 1999 Labour Party conference – a spellbinding ten minutes in which she excoriated the government for its treatment of pensioners – showed that she remained true to her principles until the end of her remarkable life.

Jim Callaghan's oratory was different in character. Not for him exuberance, but he was just as powerful in his own way. He had a reassuring presence and an authority – forged by his life experience – that commanded respect and won listeners over.

Michael Foot was a spellbinding orator. His voice – indeed his whole being – would swoop up and down as he railed against injustice, tore into hypocrisy and inspired many to follow him. He, and his successor as Labour leader, were the last of the era of thundering oratory.

In full flow, Neil Kinnock was a force of nature. Passionate, tremendously funny – his fund-raising turn at the Tribune Rally every year was not to be missed – and able to rouse a hall with power and conviction. His courageous 1985 conference speech denouncing Militant laid the foundation for Labour's 1997 election victory.

John Smith brought a sharp wit and great wisdom to his speeches. He commanded the chamber with his debating skill and his charm, and like Gaitskell before him, his untimely death was keenly felt as we mourned the great future that had been taken from us.

Tony Blair was a tremendous performer whether in the Commons or the television studio, and his conference speeches were masterly in their construction and delivery. He commanded the hall just as he commanded politics for a decade which saw him become the first Labour leader ever to win three consecutive general elections.

Gordon Brown was indeed a son of the manse, and two speeches stick in my memory. One was in a church in Brighton where his argument of the moral case for fighting global poverty inspired and visibly moved the large audience. The other was his address to Citizens UK a few days before the 2010 general election which electrified those listening.

I have left Tony Benn until last for obvious reasons. Apart from my late dear mother, my siblings and I probably heard my father speak more often than anyone else. I have seen him hold small rooms and vast halls in the palm of his hand, speaking with passion, eloquence and conviction. It's hard for me to sum him up, so I will quote someone else: 'One of the great orators of the post-war period'. Above all, he always encouraged those who heard him, as he always encouraged me.

Oratory is first and foremost about communicating, and in the age before amplification and television, it was the only way the human voice could reach an audience and put a case. Now, there are lots of different ways in which we can do so – the politicians in this book had a wide variety of styles – but I somehow doubt that in years to come someone will publish a work on 'Great Political Tweets'! This reminds us that – for all these changes – the power to move us is a rare gift, and nothing moves us more than a great speech. And for the Labour Party and our tradition, the ways in which we have helped to transform the lives of people have sprung from our beliefs, the way in which they have found expression in speeches, and the action these words have inspired.

Rt Hon Hilary Benn MP
House of Commons

Acknowledgements

This edited book grew out of a conference on Labour Oratory held at the University of Huddersfield in November 2011, and we are grateful to that institution for supporting the event. We would like to thank all the contributors for taking part in the conference and for working with us to bring this project to fruition. We would particularly like to thank Tony Mason for supporting this idea from its inception, and owe a debt of gratitude also to the anonymous reviewers for their thoughtful comments and timely feedback. Finally we would like to thank the Rt Hon Hilary Benn MP for kindly providing the foreword for the volume. The foreword was completed before the decision was taken, somewhat late in the day, to add a chapter on Ed Miliband to the volume.

Andrew S. Crines and Richard Hayton

Abbreviations

BBC	British Broadcasting Corporation
CBI	Confederation of British Industry
CLP	Constituency Labour Party
CND	Campaign for Nuclear Disarmament
EEC	European Economic Community
EMU	Economic Monetary Union
EU	European Union
GDP	Gross Domestic Product
ILP	Independent Labour Party
IMF	International Monetary Fund
LPACR	Labour Party Annual Conference Report
LSE	London School of Economics
MP	Member of Parliament
NATO	North Atlantic Treaty Organization
NEC	National Executive Committee
NHS	National Health Service
NUS	National Union of Seamen
OMOV	One Member, One Vote
PLP	Parliamentary Labour Party
PMQs	Prime Minister's Questions
SDP	Social Democratic Party
TGWU	Transport and General Workers Union
TUC	Trades Union Congress
UN	United Nations

Introduction

Analysing oratory in Labour politics

Andrew S. Crines and Richard Hayton

Introduction

The British Labour Party has been blessed – or perhaps, in some cases cursed – by a succession of commanding orators, many of whom have used the power of their speech to become highly influential figures within the movement. More broadly 'oratory has long been a highly prized political skill, regarded as an almost essential prerequisite for political advancement in modern liberal democracies' (Leach, 2000: 1). Since its foundation Labour has been committed to parliamentary democracy, and the achievement of its ends through evolutionary change rather than revolutionary action. The party also has a long tradition of internal (often fierce) debate about its direction, policies and ideology. The capacity to persuade others within the party and the Labour movement more generally, and indeed voters beyond it, has consequently always been a vital and valued skill for Labour politicians.

Oratory is therefore not only an attribute common to successful politicians, but a key mode of engagement and debate in a democratic society. This has long been recognised, with the art of oratory being admired, analysed and taught since the age of Athenian democracy. In modern times great orators such as Abraham Lincoln, Winston Churchill and Martin Luther King, to name but a few, have been similarly lauded not only for their oratorical skills, but also for their ability to inspire followers and effect political and social change through the power of their words. In spite of this, the study of oratory by political scientists, particularly in the UK, has been limited. As discussed below, a small (but growing) number of scholars have energised the study of rhetoric in British politics, and brought it more mainstream attention in the discipline. However, even this work – which this volume takes inspiration from and seeks to add to – has perhaps underplayed the oratorical dimension of the study of rhetoric. This book therefore aims to shift the focus of our analysis to a selection of leading political figures in post-war Labour Party politics. By focusing on each as individual orators, the volume concentrates on the analysis of speech, both in terms of what is said, and how it is said. In this sense oratory is conceptualised simply as the art of public speaking, while the emphasis on oratory means that we are particularly interested in the style of delivery employed, as well as the rhetorical content of the speech itself. In the traditional canons of rhetoric, 'style' and 'delivery' (i.e. how something is said) have been distinguished from 'invention' and 'arrangement', which are concerned with what is being said. In practice, however, it is near impossible to divorce how something is said from its rhetorical content. Consequently, each chapter will utilise the three primary modes of persuasive appeal identified by Aristotle, namely *ethos* (appeal based on one's character); *pathos* (appeal to emotion); and *logos* (the appeal to reason/logic). This acts as a common analytical thread throughout the volume, and is discussed in greater detail in 'The study of oratory and rhetoric in British politics' section below.

This book examines the use and impact of oratory in Labour politics through case studies of twelve key figures in the party in the post-war era. Each chapter considers how the politician in question used their oratorical skills in relation to three key audiences: 1) the Parliamentary Party; 2) the wider party membership; and 3) the electorate. These audiences relate to three important oratorical arenas, namely 1) Parliament; 2) party conference; 3) public and media engagement (the electoral arena). As such the volume assesses how political rhetoric has been deployed in an effort to advance competing ideological positions within the party, and the role of oratory in communicating Labour's ideology to a wider audience. Through this case-study approach, the book argues that oratory remains a significant feature of Labour politics in Britain, and analyses how it has changed over time and in different contexts.

Labour Party politics in historical context

The academic study of Labour history is a well-trodden road. To name but a few Steven Fielding (2003; 2007; 2010; Fielding and Tanner, 2006), Andrew Thorpe (2005; 2006; 2008; 2009), and Keith Laybourn (2008; 2009; 2011a; 2011b) represent something of a vanguard in the field of Labour history. Scholars such as these have advanced a range of interpretations that aims to better understand the political and intellectual significance of socialism, and with it the growth of the British Labour Party. These historical studies tend to revolve their interest around trade unionism, ideological theory, and issues such as the growth and disintegration of the Independent Labour Party. Our focus, however, is on the distinctive contribution of leading orators to such debates. Consequently the focus of this volume is on the style of communication of leading Labour figures, namely Aneurin Bevan, Hugh Gaitskell, Harold Wilson, James Callaghan, Barbara Castle, Tony Benn, Michael Foot, Neil Kinnock, John Smith, Tony Blair, Gordon Brown and Ed Miliband. Utilising carefully crafted rhetoric, each has contributed to key debates about the direction and ideology of the Labour Party.

Given Labour was founded by a range of groups such as the Social Democratic Federation and various trade unions it can be little surprise that disagreements over the ideological objectives of the Parliamentary Party would emerge (Thorpe,

2012). In the post-war period many of these divisions were expressed through two dominant ideological traditions: the social democratic right and the broadly moderate left (Crines, 2011; Jones, 1996; Kogan and Kogan, 1982; Thorpe, 2008). There was, of course, the much larger but less cohesive group of 'centrists' who tended to avoid entanglement with either the left or right traditions (Crines, 2011). Ideologically each faction eschewed revolutionary approaches to socialist change in favour of the parliamentary route (Morgan, 2007b; Radice, 2010). Only Benn's flirtations with the radical left during the 1970s and early 1980s represent a significant shift in favour of extra-parliamentary action (Powell, 2001). As a result the orators analysed in this volume tended to frame their rhetorical arguments against their internal and external ideological enemies whilst seeking to attract greater support from the 'centrists'. For example, Gaitskell at Stalybridge in 1952 attacked the moderate left by suggesting they hid a more Soviet-inspired interpretation of socialist theory (Brivati, 1999: 103). Indeed, he also argued a number of Communists had infiltrated the party for the purpose of radicalising it towards revolutionary action. Many on the left rejected this, with Michael Foot seeing it as a British form of McCarthyism (Morgan, 2007b). However by making such a passionate and confrontational speech Gaitskell was able to present himself as a patriotic anti-Communist. In so doing he solicited the all-important support of more centrists as well as the Transport and General Workers Union, which was on Labour's right (Brivati, 2008; Crines, 2011). Conversely the speech irritated many of Bevan's ideological allies (Saville, 1980). Gaining the support of the centre was particularly important to Gaitskell given there was a growing suspicion that Clement Attlee may step down as leader thereby precipitating a leadership election in which both he and Bevan would be important players (Bernstein, 2004). In the event, Attlee would go on to contest the ill-fated election in 1955 after which Gaitskell defeated the ageing Herbert Morrison and Bevan for the leadership (Bernstein, 2004). However by striving to appear more moderate and considered Gaitskell was better positioned than his competitors for the leadership.

The divisions between the social democrats and the moderate left in this period established much of the ideological heat of contention for the coming decades as a form of tribalism (Hassan, 2009). In 1963 Harold Wilson sought to present a new direction for the Labour Party during his 'white heat' conference speech. He argued that the divisions between the Bevanites and Gaitskellites were holding the party back electorally. Moreover, by embracing a new conception of scientific socialism Labour would be better suited to capture the rhetorical value of the new technological age for the progressive majority (Wilson, 1963). By doing so he characterised the Tories as backward-looking, whilst simultaneously implying the same for some in his own party who may reject the need to renew (Wilson, 1963). He also suggested that higher education, abolition of the 11-plus, and investment in science would enable Britain to compete with the dominant global powers of the United States and the Soviet Union. However, to achieve this it would be necessary for

Labour to move beyond a mindset that was stuck in the age of heavy industry and embrace the technological future (Crines, 2013b). Wilson was consequently able to position his leadership above the two ideological factions of the 1950s, adopt a more pragmatic approach to socialist theory, and to simultaneously make Labour appear forward-looking and dynamic (Walden, 2006). It was, put simply, a performance aimed at the electorate which was designed to sell Labour as a united political force of moderates. Although it only helped secure Labour a majority of five, it was partly successful in cooling the longer running ideological battles. As Roy Jenkins argues, these were also tamed by having a (lukewarm) Bevanite as prime minister with a team of Gaitskellites dominating his Cabinet (Jenkins, 2009).

During the 1980s the Labour Party faced a cataclysmic explosion of ideological division because radical groups such as the Socialist Campaign for Labour Victory and the Militant Tendency had begun infiltrating the party since the abolition of the Proscribed List in 1973. They rose to prominence through the Campaign for Labour Party Democracy and the Rank and File Mobilising Committee (Fielding and Tanner, 2006; Kogan and Kogan, 1982: 15; McCormick, 1980: 381). Without the Proscribed List individuals that were affiliated to radical groups were able to join the Labour Party at constituency level and begin radicalising the membership (Crines, 2011). After the 1979 election defeat sufficient numbers of radicals existed at constituency level for an ideological battle to take place at the conference(s) (Thorpe, 2008). This battle was between Benn's characterisation that the Labour leadership were, essentially, 'closet Tories' (BBC, 1995) and Michael Foot's argument that Labour was, and always had been, a democratic socialist party of non-revolutionary moderates (Morgan, 2007). This debate publicly dominated conferences and party meetings for a number of years, tainting the public's perception of the party at a time of economic change (Kavanagh, 2011). However, the Bennite faction ultimately went into remission after Denis Healey defeated Benn for the deputy leadership in 1981, precipitating a right-wing backlash (Heffernan, 1992). After 1983, a sizable majority of moderate social democrats and the moderate left recognised the need to renew the Labour Party which required a process of ideological change. This was accelerated by Kinnock's powerful attack on the Militant Tendency and the radicals at Liverpool council at the 1985 conference (Clifford, 2012). This speech sent the clear message that Labour was not a radical party and that militant elements were not welcome (Blackledge, 2013). It also solidified the loose bond between the moderate factions and helped lay the foundations for the emergence of New Labour ten years later (H. Smith, 2010).

Kinnock's speech and subsequent modernisation agenda were not sufficient to secure office, and following the 1992 election defeat his successor Smith argued that Labour's closeness to the trade unions was damaging its electoral image (Hyman, 2005). In an effort to counter the perception that the trade unions had too much influence over the party leadership Smith reformed Labour's constitution to end the trade union block vote and replace it with One Member, One Vote (OMOV).

However, when Tony Blair became leader he argued Smith's reforms lacked sufficient impact with the electorate and that reforming Clause IV would send a clearer message that Labour had modernised (Riddell, 1997). This was predicated on Blair's argument that the old Clause IV did not reflect the needs and values of the electorate and that it represented a hostage to fortune that Labour's opponents could use to undermine its credibility. Indeed, he strongly argued that Labour should 'say what we mean, mean what we say' (McSmith, 2006). As a result Blair's modernisation strategy substantially accelerated the earlier attempts to reform Labour as a moderate and united party through articulating a case for ideological transformation and unity of purpose. Underpinning this change was the move beyond traditional left-wing adherences and social democratic theory and more towards Third Way Revisionism (White, 1998). This shift placed greater emphasis on the role of the individual in society and that, although the state would provide certain services, individual responsibility would play a stronger part in a new social contract.

After Blair stood down as Labour leader, Brown sought to define his leadership by articulating a coherent narrative of Britishness. He argued that a greater sense of national identity would produce 'a clearer understanding of the common core of rights and responsibilities that go with British citizenship' and that these 'will help build our sense of shared identity and social cohesion' (Brown and Straw, 2008: 193). However this failed to resonate because his credibility and character were undermined by ideological infighting at the heart of New Labour (Heppell, 2008) and his premiership was soon overtaken by events in the form of the global financial crisis.

In sum, Labour's transformative journey has been substantially shaped by the delivery of powerful speeches at key moments in the party's history. Specifically, Gaitskell (revisionism), Wilson (white heat), Kinnock (renewal), Blair (Clause IV), and Brown (Britishness) have each sought to articulate new roadmaps for Labourism that attempted to change elements of Labour's ideological narrative and, as a consequence, its image with the electorate. Others such as Bevan (moderate left), Benn (radical left) and Foot (liberal left) each found themselves on the opposing side of such ideologically driven debates, yet what unites them all is the ability to deliver rousing speeches to both their supporters and the centrists.

The study of oratory and rhetoric in British politics

The academic study of the art of oratory has received relatively little attention from scholars interested in British politics. This is somewhat surprising given its clear linkages to burgeoning areas of the discipline such as the study of party leadership and ideological controversies. The study of rhetoric, however, has received an upsurge of interest amongst analysts of British politics in recent years, with significant contributions being made by academics such as Judi Atkins, Max Atkinson, Jonathan Charteris-Black, Alan Finlayson, John Gaffney, James Martin and Richard Toye.

Collectively this developing body of scholarship has shed new light on the nature of political communication in the UK.

Toye's (2013) introduction to rhetoric concisely summarises historical and contemporary approaches to the study and execution of communication. He rightly starts by reminding the reader that 'the idea of rhetoric as a distinct branch of knowledge had its origins in Athens in the second half of the fifth century' (2013: 7). He continues by highlighting the longevity of the study of rhetoric by reminding the reader that it was developed by the Sophists, Protagoras, Gorgias, Prodicus, Hippoas and Thrasymachus (2013). It was amongst these early philosophers that the study of rhetoric first developed and gained influence. Famously, Aristotle identified the core modes of persuasion which continue to be studied today. Aristotle suggested that 'Of the modes of persuasion furnished by the spoken word there are three kinds. The first kind depends on the personal character of the speaker; the second on putting the audience into a certain frame of mind; the third on the proof, or apparent proof, provided by the words of the speech itself' (Aristotle, 2004: 8). These modes are condensed by Aristotle into ethos, pathos and logos. For Toye, 'Aristotle's treatise was a remarkable effort to deal systematically with the problem of rhetoric, and the categorization he devised was to have a long influence' (2013: 14). Toye rightly argues that the study of rhetoric can produce valuable insights into the nature of political arguments, but that an appreciation of context is also vital as 'rhetoric is a social phenomenon, and its reception depends on the norms in operation in the society in which it is delivered' (2013: 109). By drawing upon specific modes of persuasion the rhetorical actor may prove more influential with one audience than with another: 'however good the effect on the immediate listeners, it is impossible to tell how a speech will travel and with what effects' (2013: 109). This caution rightly suggests that a written speech can be (and often is) reinterpreted after delivery which may result in unintended changes of emphasis in the political message.

To demonstrate the contemporary value of the academic study of rhetoric Toye explains the power of John F. Kennedy's rhetorical assault on global Communism, and discusses Ronald Reagan's striking performances in the presidential debates against Jimmy Carter (2013). Like most of the literature on rhetoric, Toye's embrace of the classical philosophies often draws inspiration from the more developed study of rhetoric in the United States. In the United States the study of political rhetoric is considerably more advanced 'because of the emphasis, in reality and in political science, on acutely personalized leadership itself (from Franklin D. Roosevelt onwards) as an agency of political change' (Gaffney and Lahel, 2013: 484). Yet the growing personalisation of politics in post-war Britain has led to a greater awareness of how political elites use rhetorical techniques.

Finlayson and Martin, for example, use the study of rhetoric to 'underscore the importance of speech as a form and mode of political action in its own right and highlight how the study of political speeches is of importance and interest for a range of concerns within British political studies' (2008: 446). As they note, 'political rhetoric offers a rich seam for those seeking both to interpret and explain the interplay of tradition, innovation, ideology, action, performance, strategy and rationality in British politics' (2008: 466). For them the study of rhetoric enables distinctive analyses and interpretations of debates and divisions to emerge. Furthermore Atkins and Finlayson acknowledge that although 'there is not yet a single, systematic overarching research programme focused on political speech in Britain speeches are often an object of analysis and scholars are becoming more methodologically self-conscious about how best to use them in the study of political ideas, ideologies and actions' (2013: 162). Finlayson also highlights that political rhetoric allows us 'to think about how to bridge the gulf between what we "know" to be the case and what we think others imagine it to be' (2012: 758). This is because the ideology of a political actor informs the kind of rhetoric they are likely to deploy. Indeed, as Finlayson notes, 'ideologies provide actors with a series of locally established "commonplace" arguments which must be adapted to the demands of the situation' (2012: 760). Thus the needs of the audience, the ideology of the rhetorical actor, and an appreciation of what is politically expedient may be challenges for the speaker and will likely texture their arguments. Moreover for Martin an audience can also be persuaded of an uncomfortable argument by demonstrating a logical (logos) need to embrace it whilst striving to protect core values (2013). For example, when attempting to convince the Labour conference of the need for modernisation, Blair 'invited his audiences to perceive modernisation as the timely adaptation to a perpetually changing world, yet also securely anchored to enduring "Labour values" such as "progress" and "justice"' (Martin, 2013: 2). By approaching the argument in this manner Blair successfully persuaded a sceptical audience of the need for ideological change that reflected the changing world. Successful persuasion of this kind can be made possible by employing specific rhetorical devices and oratorical techniques.

Presenting a credible and likable persona is a highly significant aspect of producing convincing rhetoric. By developing a political character the rhetorician may gain credibility (ethos) for their arguments. As Gaffney suggests, political rhetoric is used to construct or indeed undermine political personas and identities. For example, in the case of Miliband, both his Conservative opponents and the media rhetorically attacked Miliband's persona in an attempt to undermine his credibility, variously describing him as 'Red Ed' and comparing him to Wallace from the animated comedy *Wallace and Gromit*. However, Gaffney and Lahel argue that Miliband was able to use the 2012 party conference 'to modify his political identity as party leader, and to restore his political authority and status. By bringing "himself" centre stage, Ed also screened David Miliband out of the political narrative and out of contention as a potential rival' (2013: 497, 498). To do this he gave an interview on the *Andrew Marr Show* before the conference which acted as 'a prelude to the central issue that would dominate the conference: the character of the leader' (2013: 490). He also invited Professor Michael Sandel from Harvard to give a lecture to the conference which developed his earlier arguments on economic 'predistribution', thereby soliciting endorsement from an economic expert (2013: 491). Miliband also spent time attending and contributing to events taking place on the conference fringe ahead of giving his keynote speech. Gaffney argues this rhetorically constructed personal image enabled Miliband to fit effortlessly within a larger 'discernible structure ... of performances' which solidified his political authority over the party (2013: 498).

As well as the importance of the political persona, the rhetorician may also use anecdotes or metaphors to connect with their audience. These short 'stories' are brought into political speeches to use their own or other's experiences to support their argument. These 'witnesses', as Aristotle described them, are designed to give credence to a rhetorician's speech. Atkins and Finlayson note that the use 'of anecdote[s] in political speech has recently become more extensive' within British politics (2013: 161). This is because of a shift in audience expectations where narratives and experiences can be used to emotionalise arguments. Moreover, such anecdotes enable the speaker to avoid rhetoric that may appear overly politically abstract or dominated by logos. Instead they tell a story which they can claim was drawn from the experiences of real people. By doing so they seem more human and strive to show they appreciate the concerns of their audience. Atkins and Finlayson suggest this shift towards anecdotes and metaphors can partly be attributed to 'a populist shift in the "rhetorical culture" of contemporary British politics' (2013: 162). This enables the political actors to use such experiences as evidence to justify an argument they are striving to advance. Certainly this allows the rhetorician to claim greater authority as the anecdote carries 'force because of its presumed reality: the source confers authority, and the actuality of the events enables a conclusion about reality to be drawn' (2012: 164). This enables the political actor to enhance their authority by the virtue of their awareness of 'the real world', because such an awareness enables the actor to grow their credibility (ethos) as someone who can genuinely relate to the electorate.

For Charteris-Black metaphors embody a key part of speechmaking because they represent a significant technique that the speaker can use in persuading the audience of their case. As he notes, 'voters make decisions based on their judgements of the honesty, morality, and integrity of politicians' (2011: 1). Political rhetoric can thus be seen as a positive force that contributes to the essential lifeblood of politics because it enables parties to function by connecting politicians to the electorate. As a consequence how a rhetorical actor communicates with their audience will affect how the political process functions. Classical 'rhetoricians such as Aristotle and Quintilian recognised that different contexts required different methods of persuasion: influencing political decisions would not require the same methods as arguing legal cases or commemorating fallen heroes' (2011: 7). Charteris-Black continues: 'metaphors are very effective' in that process 'because they provide cognitively accessible ways of communicating politics through drawing on ways of thinking by analogy' (2011:

321). As a rhetorical technique, metaphors enable the speaker to construct complex arguments in a relatable fashion given the need to keep the attention of their audience. Indeed, as Atkinson argues 'the speaker who proves himself to be incapable of holding the attention of live audiences stands little chance of winning their approval' (Atkinson, 1984: 9). Such devices contribute towards keeping the attention of the audience. However Atkinson also suggests that the speaker may use applause as a barometer to measure their effectiveness in retaining the attention and approval of the audience by monitoring their responses. 'Depending on whether they are greeted by frequent bursts of applause, heckling or complete silence, they will be deemed to have had a rapturous, hostile or indifferent reception' (1984: 13).

The ability to enrapture an audience is a prized skill that serves to enhance an orator's reputation. Atkinson argues however that this is not simply a matter of possessing an innate gift, rather speakers can learn techniques to elicit support such as laying a 'claptrap' (1984: 48). Through careful timing and phraseology 'claptraps' are carefully crafted sentences where an audience is expected to respond in a specific way. As Atkinson explains, a speaker:

> has to communicate with his audience in much the same way as a conductor communicates with an orchestra or choir. A single movement of the hand, arm, head, lips or eyes is unlikely to be enough to get musicians to come in on time ... but if he waves his baton, nods his head, and mouths the word 'now', synchronizing them all to occur at the same time, the chances of everyone spotting at least one of them are greatly increased. In the same way an effective claptrap must provide audience members with a number of signals which make it quite clear both that they should applaud and when they should start doing so. (1984: 48)

For the politician, these can be boasts about prior achievements, condemnations of political opponents or insults directed at political enemies. The speaker may also purposefully stress specific words or phrases through using carefully timed delivery so that the audience will respond to the speaker in the desired manner.

Dennis Glover confirms the validity of rhetorical techniques by arguing that 'the best orators are those who understand the needs of their audience and employ the right combination of logic, character, and emotion to convince, charm and sway' (2011: 56). For him, the political rhetorician needs to know their audience before being able to successfully apply any rhetorical devices. Glover also warns of the potential harm of an ineffective speech delivered to the wrong audience: 'the sudden disappearance of a forum can spell the end for a faltering politician. Like the sand rushing through an hourglass, an audience making for the exits usually signals that a leader's time is up' (2011: 63). To avoid this he argues that the strongest speeches use classical devices to keep an audience engaged. Successful speeches are delivered by those who 'combined the rules of rhetorical style – ethos, pathos, and logos' (2011: 74). Succinctly, the rhetorical devices are used interdependently by politicians but can be distinguished from each other analytically. Glover also agrees with Atkinson that the meaning of words can be changed by their delivery, which the classical theorists divided into *tropes* (changes to an accepted meaning of a word) and *schemes* (rearranging the delivery of words to make them more appealing) (2011: 91). He rightly argues that these techniques remain relevant in analysing contemporary politicians. For example the electorate witnesses politicians using *tropes* and *schemes* 'every day when we watch the evening news: using the same word with double meaning; employing overstatement and understatement; asking a question and sometimes answering it; balancing a statement with its opposite; using the same words but in a different order; and repeating words, clauses and sounds' (2011: 95). These rhetorical techniques are, for Glover, hidden in plain sight. Indeed, 'watch a good or even moderate speaker in a political meeting or on television and you will notice that the applause tends to follow the use of these rhetorical devices' (2011: 95). The personal style of the speaker, their form of delivery, their passion and relationship with the audience are highly significant when evaluating communication, thereby suggesting that the study of oratory, which is inextricably linked to the growing field of rhetorical study, is also very important.

Structure

The following twelve chapters are dedicated case-study analyses of leading individuals during post-war Labour politics, drawing on the analytical tools discussed above. They have been selected for their noteworthy contributions to the development of Labour politics within their generational contexts. The twelve featured are Aneurin Bevan, Hugh Gaitskell, Tony Benn, Harold Wilson, James Callaghan, Barbara Castle, Michael Foot, Neil Kinnock, John Smith, Tony Blair, Gordon Brown and Ed Miliband.

In the first chapter, Andrew Crines and Keith Laybourn assess one of the most renowned Labour orators, Aneurin Bevan. They argue that although his fiery oratory and role as standard-bearer for the Bevanites informed his reputation as a divisive agitator, Bevan's powerful rhetoric was primarily anti-Conservative rather than aimed at fermenting intra-party ideological disputes. In Chapter 2, Timothy Heppell and Thomas McMeeking evaluate the man who defeated Bevan in the 1955 leadership election to succeed Clement Attlee as Labour leader, Hugh Gaitskell. As they point out, Gaitskell was not regarded as a great political orator and in many ways was the antithesis of Bevan, and he could also not match the communicative skill of the Conservative Prime Minister Harold Macmillan. As their analysis reveals, Gaitskell's oratorical dependence on *logos* limited his capacity to appeal to the emotions of his audience, leaving him reliant on attempting to educate and persuade listeners through rational argument. By contrast, in Chapter 3, Michael Hill notes how Gaitskell's successor, Harold Wilson, could employ varied forms of oratory to appeal to different audiences and frequently drew on pathos and a romantic style. Wilson, Hill suggests, was able to articulate a new vision for Britain (encapsulated in his 'white heat of technology' speech) which for a time captured and helped define the zeitgeist of the age. Chapter 4 profiles one of the most acclaimed female orators in British Labour history, Barbara Castle. As David S. Moon discusses, Castle developed a rousing oratorical style which conveyed her fervently held beliefs and socialist politics, and drew on her gender and reputation as a 'fiery redhead'.

In Chapter 5, Stephen Meredith considers the more laid-back communication style of the fourth Labour leader to become prime minister, James Callaghan. Although displaying very different attributes to 'Labour firebrands' such as Castle or Bevan, Callaghan's oratory was, Meredith suggests, both effective and a key factor in his personal popularity, despite the problems his government faced in office. Callaghan's successor, Michael Foot, was already a renowned public speaker and parliamentary debater by the time he became Labour leader in 1980. In Chapter 6 David Stewart examines the development of this reputation from his election to the House of Commons in 1945, and argues that Foot's oratory has primacy over that of his peers in upholding Labour's liberal socialist idealism. Tony Benn is the subject of Chapter 7 where Mark Garnett characterises Benn's oratorical style as reflecting the tradition of nineteenth-century dissenters, and explores how in spite of his undeniable skill as a public speaker Benn was ultimately an unsuccessful radical orator. In Chapter 8, David S. Moon argues that Neil Kinnock had the consummate blend of oratorical attributes to defeat the Militant movement and shift Labour away from the hard-left towards electability. However, Moon also suggests that the very same characteristics ultimately impeded his appeal to the wider electorate. The chapter therefore offers a fascinating case-study of how oratorical skill and style can be powerful mobilisers of political change and also have far-reaching unintended consequences.

As Robin Pettitt argues in Chapter 9, John Smith's experience as a barrister lent itself to the confrontational nature of the Commons, and his success in that arena was key to his rise through the ranks of his party. Like Gaitskell, he based his oratory primarily on reason and logic, which occasionally led to the charge that he lacked ideological conviction. Smith's untimely death meant that his ability to connect with the electorate as a party leader at a general election was never tested, and the mantle passed instead to Tony Blair. As Mark Bennister contends in Chapter 10, Blair was an undeniably gifted communicator and in many ways redefined the standard for the modern British politician. However, as Bennister suggests, Blair did not come from, or become part of, a tradition of Labour oratory, but had a highly personalised form of political communication which rested on his own character and credibility. This was undermined in his later years in office as his power to persuade waned, but he remained an impressive orator. In Chapter 11 Judi Atkins evaluates the oratory of Gordon Brown, who after Blair himself was the dominant figure in New Labour politics. As Atkins suggests, Brown's impressive ability to deploy statistics and factual evidence was central to his successful oratory as Chancellor of the Exchequer, but as prime minister he lacked the broader ability to develop a winning rapport with the electorate.

Finally in Chapter 12 Andrew Crines examines Ed Miliband's political oratory with particular reference to the emergence of rhetoric surrounding One Nation Labour. He argues that Miliband's style of communication is often effective in moments of political crisis (such as the phone-hacking scandal) or internal renewal, however more generally his oratorical abilities are held back by appearing uncertain during media encounters and, more particularly, Prime Minister's Questions.

Conclusion

In conclusion it is certainly evident that the academic study of rhetoric in British politics has received an upsurge of interest in recent years. This can be attributed in part to the growing personalisation of politics and the 'presidentialisation' of political leadership (Foley, 2000), and also to interest in analysing the role of individuals in the advancement of ideological positions. The personalisation of politics has placed greater onus on the character of individual speakers and the arguments they sought to make. As a fundamental the character of a speaker determines whether the audience is more or less likely to be persuaded by their argument. Throughout Labour history the character of the speaker has depended upon their ideological drive to advance their interpretation of socialism whilst attacking socialist traditions of rivals. These moments of disunity led to a tradition of oratory emerging that then became the mechanism through which ideological battles were fought. Indeed, the ideological discontent in the Labour Party was partly enabled by the oratory of those who sought to advance their conception of socialism. For example Gaitskell and Bevan both had very different understandings of socialism yet both used oratorical and rhetorical techniques to promote their ideas, thereby causing an ideological splintering.

The relatively recent upsurge of interest in rhetorical analyses demonstrates the twin importance of evaluating oratory and rhetoric. However thus far the focus of the literature in this introduction has been more upon the record of words (rhetoric) rather than their delivery (oratory). This focus risks overlooking some of the other major elements that can lead to effective communication. These may include their personal style, the persona of the speaker, passion, and their relationship with the audience. Of course, the tradition of powerful oratory in the Labour movement is generally recognised in those we have considered in this volume. Yet the academic study of Labour politics has also resisted focusing upon oratory itself. In part this is because it has emphasised the importance of collective action and internal ideological movements. The role of individual speakers tends to be subsumed by a more generalised approach to the study of Labourism. In fact, the advancement of ideological traditions is traditionally seen to be the result of collective action rather than individual communicators. We would contend, however, that a more balanced approach reveals the duality of these causal factors and that communication played a significant yet overlooked role in such ideological battles. As a consequence this volume serves to fill this gap in the literature by analysing the oratorical and rhetorical techniques of twelve leading orators who have affected the evolution of Labour Party politics in the post-war period, and by doing so we demonstrate the important role of oratory.

1

The oratory of Aneurin Bevan

Andrew S. Crines and Keith Laybourn

Introduction

We have been the dreamers ... we have been the sufferers ... now we are the builders.
(Bevan, 1945)

As fundamentals, the mastery of effective political communication derives from both rhetoric and oratory. These are inextricably linked, thus a consideration of both is a necessity for efficacious analyses of political communication by politicians. As shown in the short extract above, like most effective orators, Aneurin Bevan possessed a communicative ardour for rhetorical imagery. In his case, he utilised this capacity to demonstrate aspiration, pain and ultimately the triumph of his conception of social democratic socialism. The question remains – how?

Bevan's more noteworthy rhetorical orations straddle a twenty-year period between 1940 and 1960. These include memorable speeches made in the Commons, at public meetings, and to the party conference. Consequently these are the focus of this chapter. In order to fully demonstrate his communicative impact during these more prominent years of his career, this chapter will evaluate eight indicative speeches from the three arenas spanning this period. By adopting this approach, it becomes possible to appreciate how Bevan's communicative significance can be measured over the course of his post-war career. In terms of the theoretical basis established by the Introduction, Bevan's appeals to pathos, whilst tying in a certain logos to his rhetoric, enabled him to deploy ethos-driven deliberative oratory. This emerged as the dominating characteristic of his oratorical style, and is the focus of this chapter. It is important to acknowledge, however, that his background was highly significant in extending his oratorical ethos.

Bevan's oratorical character derived from the values and beliefs gifted upon him by his upbringing in Wales. He had a strong 'support for Wales, the Welsh language, Welsh culture and Welsh identity' (Andrews, 2008). His values, based on ethical socialism and social justice, enabled him to oratorically confront the complacency of the conservative establishment by drawing upon these beliefs in his rhetoric. Moreover, Wales stood apart from the rest of the UK because 'she has a language of her own, an art and a culture' which Bevan articulated through passionate oratory and a strong belief in social justice and equality (Andrews, 2008). He drew from this conception of Welsh identity to frame his oratory, whilst also using it as a means of promoting those hard-working values his father taught him. His identity also framed his political character, enabling him to distinctively argue for socialist values with a manner to which only Neil Kinnock and David Lloyd George can be justly compared. David S. Moon scrutinises a particular mode of Welshness as an oratorical form in Chapter 8, developing *hwyl* as a linguistic characteristic of Welsh Labour politics which can justly be ascribed to Bevan also. This national identity helped set him apart from most other Labour orators, ensuring his speeches attracted attention from political friends and foes alike. Across the arenas Bevan's Welshness textured his orations, enhanced his credibility as a speaker, providing his arguments with a forceful delivery that either enlivened or enraged his audiences.

The first arena for consideration is the Commons, where Bevan's reputation for effective oratory was consolidated by his ability to deliberate and ignite controversy where required. The second arena represents his engagements with the broader electorate through public meetings. Here, he utilised a range of rhetorical emphases to inform and influence the party activists of the rightness of Labour's claim to social democratic reform. Importantly, these gatherings enabled Bevan to extend his message to the broader electoral audience, given the reporting of such meetings in the national press provided a more extensive assemblage. The final arena for consideration is the conference, where Bevan is most noted for two particularly memorable speeches. The first on renouncing unilateralism, the second on the role of public ownership and the need for unity. This chapter will conclude that Bevan's rhetoric and oratory largely reflected audience expectations in each specific arena, however his advocacy for party unity behind broadly defined egalitarian values was ever present.

Parliamentary performance

Bevan's effectiveness as a parliamentary orator can be illustrated by three examples, which demonstrate how he utilised his communicative skills towards advancing positions and perspectives that he regarded as requisites. The first of these speeches concerned issues regarding Winston Churchill's strategic competence in his conduct of the Second World War. The second concerned Bevan's legitimising arguments for the formation of a National Health Service (NHS), whilst the third example evaluates his strong hostility to Anthony Eden's position on the Suez Crisis. These speeches demonstrate Bevan's performance in the Commons, enabling an appreciation of his parliamentary engagements to emerge, linked to forms of oratorical delivery and rhetorical content.

Partly as a result of his position on the back benches, Bevan's ethos as a leading figure grew during the Second World War. Often this is a position which ambitious individuals seek to leave as a matter of some urgency in favour of the front bench, however for Bevan it afforded him an opportunity. Moreover, at a time when the Labour Party had joined the wartime coalition government, national unity was key, although, in terms of parliamentary engagement, he advanced challenges to the national government.

> Bevan kept up his role of Parliamentary rebel throughout the war, never ceasing to attack the government's sometimes shaky direction of the war effort even after Labour entered the national government in 1940. (BBC, 1998b)

It would be facile to suggest Bevan sought to challenge the life of Churchill's government, given he recognised the need for consensus against the foes threatening Britain's survival. Indeed, in this regard Bevan complimented the wartime prime minister as 'the unchallenged leader and spokesman of the British people' (Wrigley, 2002: 60). However despite this clear necessity, Bevan endeavoured to ensure the convention of constructive opposition to the national government was retained. By retaining a degree of distance from the leadership of his own party, Bevan was able to enhance his ethos as a de facto opposing force to the seeming monopolistic leviathan of parties that constituted the government. He was also able to draw upon his distinctive Welsh identity as the outsider, to challenge the English Westminster elite across the ideological divide and to ensure his opposition to the national government included challenging those in his own party, where required.

Throughout the war, Bevan advanced the charge that Churchill was ineffective as a leader, whilst inversely proving more effective as simply a propagandist. This point was advanced by Bevan for an article written for the left-wing organ *Tribune*. Entitled 'The Problem of Mr Churchill', his article critiqued Churchill for his propensity for grandiose speeches, arguing 'if speeches could win a war then we have as good as won' (Foot, 1962: 323–324). Consequently Bevan's oppositional stances in the Commons led to Churchill describing him as 'a squalid nuisance' for providing an unwelcome thorn in the side of the wartime leader. This helped to inversely grow Bevan's reputation amongst parliamentary colleagues as an ethos-driven agitator. It is this capacity which defined Bevan's parliamentary contributions in the war years.

Bevan's critique against the wartime government centred on its ineffectiveness in providing necessary resources for the front-lines. Advancing these arguments, Bevan drew passionately upon his Welsh character, enhancing his credibility both as a critic and an orator. As an example, Bevan delivered a highly effective yet damaging performance on the conduct of the war to the Commons on 2 July 1942. In this speech, Bevan highlighted the apparent inability of the government to provide the armed forces with the necessary weaponry.

> It seems to me that there are three things wrong. First, the main strategy of the war has been wrong; second, the wrong weapons have been produced; and third, those weapons are being managed by men who are not trained in the use of them and who have not studied the use of modern weapons. As I understand it, it is strategy that dictates

> the weapon and tactics that dictate the use of the weapon. The Government have conceived the war wrongly from the very beginning, and no one has more misconceived it than the Prime Minister himself. (*Hansard*, 1942)

Bevan's use of logos aimed to inspire pathos; to draw out an injustice against the forces by highlighting three key failures of the execution of the war. The necessity to appeal to an emotional injustice aims to prompt an outrage, striving towards forcing a logos-driven change of policy. Importantly, Bevan directs the thrust of his critique firmly towards Churchill himself, thereby laying the central charge of incompetence at the door of the prime minister and not the armed forces themselves. This enables Bevan to attribute these failures to Churchill's decisions, presenting the prime minister with a clear expectation of a shift of policy, whilst demonstrating support for the defensive military action.

Furthermore, by framing his analysis of the war as a *loyal* critic, Bevan was able to communicate what he saw as his realistic appraisal of how Churchill was conducting the war, using emotional and logical arguments to ensure his arguments were both credible and effective. Bevan's use of logos can be located in these practical issues facing the armed forces. For example, the absence of appropriate weapons presents a clear and logical case for a change of policy, whilst also appealing to pathos through an allusion to 'something wrong'; a moral judgement designed to stir an emotion, striving to create an impetus for change from all sides of the Commons. Combined, these enabled Bevan to communicate an effective critique. To advance this critique, it was necessary for him to draw from his distinctive ethos by presenting himself as an alternative perspective, whilst simultaneously presenting the case that more effective fighting tools were required by the armed forces. Bevan's deliberative (considered) oratorical style was also tied to an epideictic (performative) approach, ensuring his rhetorical ethos was advanced further. Indeed, by communicating his critique in this manner, his audience may better understand the full brevity of Bevan's argument, enhancing the possibility of a change of policy.

Beyond this role as a wartime critic, Bevan's social democratic values framed his peacetime rhetorical content and oratorical delivery. His subsequent parliamentary engagements enabled him to advance these ideological positions as a maturing member of Clement Attlee's government. These attitudes underscored his epideictic oratory with an emotional propensity that alluded to the wrongness of social evils, whilst simultaneously texturing his rhetoric with a strong logos-based belief in equality, egalitarianism and social justice. These carried with them an ethos derived from his own experiences of the inverse vis-à-vis social inequality.

Following the war and Labour's subsequent electoral victory in 1945, Bevan was granted an opportunity to advance these ideological perspectives as a member of Attlee's government. As Minister for Health, he was able to enact sweeping reforms towards progressing social justice. Bevan most memorably advanced this desire for equality in the sphere of healthcare and the subsequent formation of an NHS.

For Bevan, the argument for a nationalised health service was rooted in pathos. It was an emotional struggle for an equal healthcare system that derived from the death of his father from a preventable disease. Although it must be acknowledged that Bevan's drive had this emotional undercurrent, he framed his arguments in the Commons logically, making it harder for those opposing his positions to dismiss them. Bevan argued against the 'abstract principles' of political philosophy, preferring to focus more upon 'the concrete requirements of the actual situation as it exists' (*Hansard*, 1946a). This ensured he was able to emphasise the logos of an equality-focused system of healthcare drawn from real world manifestations of perceived social injustice. This also ensured he was able to avoid accusations of being a *moral crusader*. Linking his logos with pathos, Bevan argued:

> the first reason why a health scheme of this sort is necessary at all is because it has been the firm conclusion of all parties that money ought not to be permitted to stand in the way of obtaining an efficient health service. (*Hansard*, 1946a)

Given money had frequently acted as an obstacle for the poor accessing efficient healthcare, the logos of making access free appeared designed to guarantee greater encapsulation of all the population. Bevan also emphasised the broad consensus in the Commons on this key point, thereby aiming to capitalise on the largely agreed logos of this approach. As a first standard of practice, Bevan also argued this would ensure 'a person ought to be able to receive medical and hospital help without being involved in financial anxiety' (*Hansard*, 1946a). Critiquing the status quo, Bevan sought to illustrate the incompatibility between connecting an individual's ability to pay with the delivery of healthcare. Since the death of his father was partly the result of financial impediments, this logos incorporates a high degree of pathos, which when combined grew his ethos as a social democratic reformer.

Moreover, the justification for the nationalisation of the health service stems from Bevan's logos-based rhetoric that care in preceding years had been 'unevenly distributed over the country and indeed it is one of the tragedies of the situation, that very often the best hospital facilities are available where they are least needed' (*Hansard*, 1946a). Taking into account these inequalities, Bevan's core argument for nationalisation stemmed from the belief that healthcare should be equally provided regardless of regional variation. His logos, therefore, for a state-led provision derives from his critique of these regional variations, which for Bevan could only be alleviated by state management, given it was the only structure available to administer such a scheme on the scale required.

Furthermore, Bevan highlighted the absence of appropriate care for those with mental health difficulties, inadequate dentistry, opticians, and hearing difficulties. By bringing these together within the NHS, Bevan argued: 'there shall be no limitation on the kind of assistance given – the general practitioner service, the specialist, the hospitals, eye treatment, spectacles, dental treatment, hearing facilities, all these are to be made available free' (*Hansard*, 1946a).

Bevan's core argument was for complete consolidation of healthcare provision under the administrative authority of the state. It was partly possible for Bevan to advance this argument because of the wartime socialism Michael Foot identified (Crines, 2011) and the ethos the state had gained through the national mobilisation. Given the state had proven effective in organising the war effort, the premise and expectation emerged that it could prove equally effective as a social reformer. As a result, this contextualised Bevan's case for a nationalised health service, free at the point of use, and equally provided across the UK.

Yet it would be superficial to argue Bevan's argument benefitted from united support from across the Commons. Indeed, the Joint Chairman of the Conservative Housing and Health Committee, Richard Law, led the opposition to the proposed scheme, arguing that 'the workers, the poor people of this country, have an enormous affection for their own hospitals and they are very proud and glad to be able to contribute' through charity (Crines, 2011: 45). This more conservative conception of healthcare sought to demonstrate the cogency of a hospital system supported by those who exploited its services. However, since the mood of the Commons and the broader country did not favour this classic position, Bevan successfully convinced the Chamber of the logic of his arguments through his rhetorical appeals to greater social justice.

As a minister, his capacity for further pathos-driven speeches became less pronounced, given the realities of ministerial responsibility. Nevertheless, upon Labour's return to opposition in 1951, Bevan was able to orate more freely. Increasingly, as a 'wildcard' of the pathos-driven legitimate left faction within the Labour Party, he gained enhanced ethos with those holding such ideological perspectives. During this time, his reputation as an agitator was consolidated because of his increasing association with the antagonist label within the Gaitskellite/Bevanite axis. However, under the leadership of his ideological enemy, he returned to more moderate positions on matters of international relations, such as in relation to the Suez Crisis, the final topic under consideration here.

Such was Bevan's moderation following two general election defeats that he was appointed Shadow Foreign Secretary in 1956. In this capacity, Bevan's parliamentary performances again drew from pathos linked to logos, simultaneously utilising an epideictic form of oratory. Indeed, his performance concerning the Suez Crisis drew from a distinctive display of discontent against the Conservative prime minister, Eden. During the years preceding the Suez Crisis, Bevan had increasingly critiqued higher defence expenditure along with the resistance of the Conservative Party to recognise the decline of the imperial age and to embrace the emerging modern age. In this modern age, war had evolved to include weapons of mass destruction, making it no longer a 'bargaining tool' between states, but rather a potentially apocalyptic endeavour that, for Bevan, had increasingly alarming consequences.

Yet central to Bevan's parliamentary critique of the Conservatives' approach to the Suez Crisis was to highlight the perception of ineptitude in their case for the intervention. By highlighting repeated inconsistencies in the stated objectives, Bevan argued Eden had wholly failed to outline the rationale for the intercession in Egypt. He argued Eden's objectives shifted over short periods of time, revealing that 'there is, in fact, no correspondence whatsoever between the reasons given today and the reasons set out by the Prime Minister at the beginning. The reasons have changed all the time' (*Hansard*, 1956). The basis of Bevan's strong critique was rooted firmly in logos, highlighting the necessity for clear objectives in times of conflict. This is an argument he repeated against the Eden government by drawing in pathos-driven rhetoric linked to a strong logos for strategy. He argued that:

> In the history of nations, there is no example of such frivolity. When I have looked at this chronicle of events during the last few days, with every desire in the world to understand it, I just have not been able to understand, and do not yet understand, the mentality of the Government. If the right hon and learned Gentleman wishes to deny what I have said, I will give him a chance of doing so. If his words remain as they are now, we are telling the nation and the world that, having decided upon the course, we went on with it despite the fact that the objective we had set ourselves had already been achieved, namely, the separation of the combatants. (*Hansard*, 1956)

The provocative characterisation of Eden's governing frivolity sought to undermine the position of both the prime minister and the Conservative government, whilst simultaneously highlighting Bevan's own ethos as a cognisant critic. Furthermore, Bevan attributes the intervention as a means of enabling Nasser to shield from his own 'faults', highlighting that international critiques would be targeted towards Britain rather than the Egyptian regime: 'What has deeply offended us is that such wrongs as Nasser has done and such faults as he has have been covered by the bigger blunders of the British Government' (*Hansard*, 1956).

By making this case, Bevan attributes Eden with the blame for the potential isolation of Britain internationally, whilst simultaneously arguing that the transgressions of Nasser's administration may be overlooked by the international community given it emerges as a victim of British imperialism. Indeed, such was the ill-advised intervention, that Bevan went on to argue potential British isolation extended to those who Britain economically and politically depended on the most. In fact, he argued Eden had:

> [O]utraged our friends, after having insulted the United States, after having affronted all our friends in the Commonwealth, after having driven the whole of the Arab world into one solid phalanx, at least for the moment, behind Nasser. (*Hansard*, 1956)

This damning critique of the intervention succinctly highlighted foreign policy failures that were incompatible with the post-imperial age. This enabled Bevan to demonstrate his own ethos by connecting himself with a modern social Britain:

The social furniture of modern society is so complicated and fragile that it cannot support the jackboot. We cannot run the processes of modern society by attempting to impose our will upon nations by armed force. (*Hansard*, 1956)

Characterising Eden's position as incompatible with the social conditions of 1950s Britain, Bevan's critique proved devastating in its political impact whilst growing his own ethos as an individual in touch with 1950s society.

In fact, such was the reception of this speech that it came to be regarded as one of his most effective orations in the Commons. The speech straddled pathos and logos, rooting the pejorative critique in logical examples and indicators of maladroitness. Drawing upon his own ethos as an impassioned parliamentary orator, Bevan utilised deliberative and epideictic oratory to showcase both his own position and that of the broader Labour Party. This enabled him to demonstrate how Eden had mismanaged the execution of the intervention, whilst striving to connect the endeavour to an outdated conception of British society.

In terms of legacy, the speech is well remembered by both supporters and critics. Selwyn Lloyd remarked that it was Bevan's greatest parliamentary performance, affirming that 'it was at my expense, because as foreign secretary, it had been my duty to speak before him and put the government's case' (Dalyell, 2007). Although the speech did little to shift the policy position of Eden's government, it must be viewed as a noteworthy example of Bevan's parliamentary oration. The speech extended further his ethos as an advocate of international peace, whilst simultaneously proving devastating against a government he sought to portray as incompetent.

In summary, across these three indicative examples it can be concluded that Bevan's parliamentary oratory was rooted both in pathos and logos. The logos derives from the need to engage deliberatively in the Commons, however this does not detract from his clear performance technique. As the most prominent opponent to the wartime government, as the advocate of an equal healthcare system, and the promoter of international peace, Bevan emerged as a convincing parliamentary orator. His ethos amongst the rank and file was in part derived from his flirtations with the left-wing group that took his name, however in the Commons that ethos was more located in the mainstream. This broader appeal enabled him to advance social policies likely to prove beneficial, whilst the narrower focus of his mainstream logos enabled him to present himself as a credible parliamentary performer. In so doing, Bevan's impact can be seen as a promoter of core ideological values held by the legitimate left of the broader party, whilst simultaneously possessing a realistic conception of moderate social democracy.

Public performance

The second arena for consideration is public engagement, namely Bevan's addresses to the electorate, trade union organisations, and party meetings. These illustrate his ability to directly engage with the core supporters of the Labour movement.

Contrasting the first arena, an alternative style of oratorical delivery and rhetorical emphasis was required. Rather than the deliberative delivery utilised in the Commons, Bevan adopted a stronger form of epideictic oratory. The more informed style of this oratorical approach ensured the audience granted him their attention. It would be inadequate to suggest Bevan's rhetoric became less considered as a consequence, however the less deliberative nature of these arenas required a more performative manner in order to advance his rhetorical message. On a more personal level, this style was aided by his propensity to play upon his quiff, thus enabling him to connect rhetorically with his chosen audience.

To demonstrate this approach, we evaluate orations to the National Federation of Building Trades Operatives, the local constituency office of the Liverpool Labour Party, and the Eastern Regional Labour Party in Cambridge. These different forms of public arena necessitated distinctive oratorical approaches. The trade union audience expects rhetoric on preserving its industry, the local constituency office expects instruction on electoral strategies, whilst the regional office sought a degree of intellectual engagement about the future of British social democracy. Each of these public audiences had varying expectations, each requiring a specific message. Consequently, Bevan deployed contextualised rhetoric with an oratorical style suitable to convey his message.

The first speech, delivered in 1946, emphasised the necessity of a post-war house building programme that combined the need for reconstruction with the twin issue of combating social injustice. Within the pathos-driven dimension to his speech, Bevan ascribes such policy failures to previous Conservative governments. To make this national requirement a partisan argument, Bevan combined both logos and pathos forms of rhetoric in his argument:

> At the end of the last war, no houses *at all* were being built. Yet we have got, as I said, across the country as a whole, not only to replace the consequences of the destruction of war, not only to put up the houses that Hitler's bombs blew down, not only have we got to repair the houses that were damaged, not only have we to make up the arrears of six years of lack of housing maintenance, but in addition to that, in addition to what the enemy did to us, we have also got to try and make up for the arrears of housing left by 50 years of Tory misrule. (Bevan, 1946)

By contextualising the necessity for a house building programme against social indecision following the First World War, Bevan draws upon quantifiable logos to demonstrate the rationale behind following a more interventionist policy. He also aims to demonstrate that following an inverse position would be inconceivable owing to the scale of required house building. To illustrate this, Bevan frames his argument emphasising that a house building plan must be seen as a national requirement, and that its origins can be located not only from the consequences of war, but also to the longer perception of Conservative 'misrule'. The logos of this approach enhances his ethos with the union audience, bearing in mind their natural propensity towards the Labour position. For Bevan, this enables him to demonstrate his own ethos given his established political reputation as a logos-driven orator. Ineluctably, Bevan's ethos both derives and grows from the positive response of the audience reaction, subscribing to his persuasive analysis.

Continuing in his speech to the Federation, Bevan further drew from his credibility as an established advocate of collectivisation by connecting the necessary house building programme with socialist economic theory:

> Before you can start building on any skill, every single industry in society has got to be organised and stimulated into production. A house, a modern house, is the most complex economic production. Every single industry is a contributor. Not only the simple building materials of bricks and mortar, and cement and plasterboards, and slates and chimneys, but every single component and all the furnishings of a house may contribute upon *every* conceivable industry. And therefore before we start houses going up in any great numbers all these industries have got to be manned and organised. (Bevan, 1946)

To ensure the house building programme proved effective, Bevan argues the major industrial sectors of the economy must be subjected to planning and organisation in order to remedy the legacies he previously alluded to. Indeed, Bevan roots this analysis in logos-based argument that house building is more than simply materials, but rather the state must play an active role in the organisation of that programme in order for it to prove effective in providing homes for those in need. Moreover, this programme would become more compatible with his conception of a socialist society. To make this part of his argument, Bevan's aim is to convince the audience of the logos of the appropriateness of socialist economic theory. However the advocacy of collectivisation requires a more abstract appreciation of the conception of state ownership amongst his listeners. To do this, Bevan draws upon his capacity for pathos to deliver the collectivist aspect of his argument using epideictic oratory. Combined together, Bevan's speech convincingly argues that the government must not follow the same free market mistakes of previous Conservative administrations, and that the solution is to follow a more socialist route. By doing so, Bevan argues a more effective building programme would emerge. Therefore, the emotional dimension of Bevan's oratory proved effective in convincing the audience of his case for a more collectivist approach to reconstruction.

The second public speech under consideration took place in the context of the 1950 general election. It was delivered to the Liverpool local party headquarters at the start of the campaign and was designed to motivate local activists to ensure they canvassed successfully against the opposition. For this speech Bevan adopted an even stronger pathos-driven form of rhetoric which aimed to *redeem* the Conservative leader in the eyes of his audience, attempting to divorce Churchill from those he had previously described as *vermin*. To do this, he sought to claim a higher level of familiarity with the Conservative leader that went beyond partisan hostility. In reference to the pre-war political career of the former wartime leader, Bevan recollected that:

[I]n those days when he was an outcast, I was on quite friendly terms with him. Being a member of a downtrodden nation, I have a warm spot for outcasts, and therefore when I speak about Mr Churchill you must always remember, when we are having a public controversy, he is a man for whom I have quite considerable respect, and who in 1940 said things in a way that was unmatched, and did great service to this country. That is why I deplore the miserable mob he has got among (Bevan, 1950)

Politically, the logos of this approach would enable the local activists to critique the Conservative opposition whilst acknowledging the longer service of its leader to the survival of the nation. Importantly this necessity derived from Churchill's remaining positive profile, which was contextualised against Attlee's declining economic record. The electoral benefits which gravitated to Attlee in 1945 had less potency after five years of Labour rule, especially when contextualised against the Conservative reform programme since 1947. Furthermore, Bevan alluded to Wales as a downtrodden nation, highlighting his own sympathies with those in such a position. When discussing the specifics of the electoral strategy, Bevan continued to root his rhetoric in logos, arguing that:

[S]upreme though Mr Churchill is, it is not good enough in Great Britain to ask the people to elect a whole Government on the basis of the qualities of one man. After all, he is not even a young man, and if you elect a Conservative majority because of the virtue of Mr Churchill – suppose he is run over by a bus – even Mr Churchill is not immortal – and if all the Conservatives have got is Mr Churchill and they do have a majority, which I do not think they will get, will they promise to have an immediate general election? (Bevan, 1950)

Central to Bevan's logos-based argument is that the Conservative Party's perceived over-reliance upon its high profile leader may render the remainder of the party lacking in terms of governing competence. Moreover, by claiming a longer acquaintance with the Conservative leader, Bevan's strategy of guiding the attack more towards the local Conservative parliamentary challengers emerges, divorcing such attacks from the wartime victor. As a strategy to motivate local activists, this rhetoric may prove convincing, providing them with a clear message on this issue. Given the setting of this forum, Bevan also incorporated elements of pathos rooted in humour to ensure he connected the central thrust of his message to the audience emotionally. Bevan concluded his speech by attributing the policies of the Attlee government with economic success. Specifically, he argued that 'if the Labour Party had not nationalised the mines in 1945 there would have been no industrial recovery in Great Britain' (Bevan, 1950: 3). In so doing, this speech provides local activists with an electoral strategy and argument, whilst retaining the affection for Churchill's unarguable wartime accomplishments. The prevailing technique of this speech, therefore, was logos, given the necessity of the electoral process and subsequent motivation of local activists with a clear strategy, although it also utilised moments of pathos.

The third speech concerned the arguments within the Labour Party during the early years of opposition in the 1950s. Following on from Labour's electoral defeat, divisions within the party pivoted around Hugh Gaitskell and Bevan. Although as individuals they did not fully embrace the complete analysis of those who claimed their names, both did engage in public disagreements on the direction of social democracy. Gaitskell combated the perception of increasing radicalism on the fringes of the movement, informing an audience at Stalybridge in the north of England that 'I was told by some observers that about one-sixth of the constituency party delegates appear to be Communist or Communist-inspired' (Mallalieu and Gaitskell, 1952: 1). This accusation led to an infusion of discontent amongst some moderate constituency offices, as well as a defensive reaction from those ideologically aligned to the legitimate left.

In an attempt to restore a degree of normalcy, Bevan sought to re-emphasise the need for unity across the movement. He utilised deliberative oratory combined with pathos-led rhetoric in order to strongly appeal for unity. Addressing the annual rally of the Eastern Regional Labour Party in Cambridge, he argued that:

> What I want this movement to do is to have all the unity that we can possibly get, but unity behind activity, not passivity. We always speak about the Labour movement, and by that we mean movement, we don't mean paralysis. We decided at Morecambe to try to get the British Labour movement united once more, on another programme, analogous to that of 1945. (Bevan, 1952a)

Evident in Bevan's emotional appeal is a strong case for unity. Given the importance of his belief that the Labour movement requires unity in order for it to be an effective challenger to the Conservatives, this is unsurprising. However, his retreat from Gaitskell's central thesis implies a resistance to engaging on a public platform with those issues. Rather, Bevan's audience is the broader, moderate activist, who roots her conception of social justice more in Bernstein rather than Marx. The logos of this approach ensures he resists directing his hostility to either those Gaitskell calls *Communists* or, indeed, the messenger himself. This also enables the legitimate left to avoid misguided associations with any radical fringes which Gaitskell identified, by remaining with the moderates. This propagates the overarching requirement for unity, central to Bevan's conception of effective socialism.

In terms of public engagement, Bevan's oratory and rhetoric shifted in emphasis depending upon the context in which he was orating. For the unions, a more grassroots focus was required, whilst for the constituency office Bevan sought to provide a motivational assessment of Labour's governing success, and for a more intellectual audience Bevan emphasised unity over division. These engagements demonstrate Bevan's capacity to shift his rhetorical message depending upon the audience. Given this ability, the impact of his message was enhanced. These three examples also illustrate his ethos with the various sections of the movement. Bevan's ethos derived from his reputation as a principled actor, demonstrable by prior achievements, and the expectation of future success.

Conference performance

In terms of direct engagement with the members and viewpoints of the Labour movement, the most influential arena was the conference. At the time of Bevan's prominence, its importance derived from the unique role it played in enabling members from across the various sections of affiliated groups to come together and debate the policy framework of the political wing of the movement vis-à-vis the Labour Party. In order to showcase prospective policies to the delegates, an elite orator demonstrated their aspirational compatibility with the egalitarian ambitions of the movement. Such delegates would also propose resolutions likely to resonate with supporters of such social democratic traditions.

It is important to note that it was not Bevan's most impelling arena. In fact, Bevan preferred the Commons chamber or direct public engagement. The conference was an infrequent affair, and one to which he rarely contributed noteworthy orations. That is not to say he did not deliver high impact speeches to the conference, but rather his reputation was developed more when addressing those outside the conference chamber. Despite this preference for the other arenas, he delivered a small sampling of memorable speeches to the conference arena. His most memorable conference engagements occurred in the latter years of the 1950s, at a time when he had journeyed further towards more mainstream positions, distancing himself from some of his earlier left-wing associations. It is important to note, however, that despite this moderation, he remained a committed advocate of nationalisation. Despite the divisive nature of such a position, oratorically he sought to emphasise the importance of party unity.

Two indicative conference speeches are attributed with generating substantive impact. The first concerns his position on nuclear disarmament and the future direction of Labour's position in respect of international relations. The second concerns his position towards Gaitskell's divisive modernisation agenda. Each had the capacity to prove factious for the Labour movement, the first in opposition to the ideological left and the second to the ideological right. In each Bevan demonstrated his oratorical ability, contextualised by the rhetorical significance of the speeches in shaping Labour's ideological direction of travel. It is important to note, however, that such impact rarely extended beyond the movement given their clear internal relevance.

On the matter of nuclear disarmament, in order for Britain to retain a place at the negotiation table between the United States and the Soviet Union, Bevan believed it was necessary to renounce the epicurean romanticism of unilateral nuclear disarmament. His adoption of a more realist position gained greater ethos with advocates of more moderate positions. At the conference, Bevan strove to convince the delegates of the logos of his opposition to unilateralism by arguing the conference should not 'decide upon the dismantling of the whole fabric of British international relations' (Bevan, 1957a: 10). For Bevan, the issue of how Britain related to the major power blocs was not an issue for the conference to dictate, arguing 'it is not in your hands to do it' (Bevan, 1957a: 10). By questioning the rationality behind the Norwood resolution, he was striving to demonstrate the importance of the issue, and its potential longer term impact. For Bevan, such a decision was outside the remit of the conference, and despite its importance to the movement, the conference was not entitled to dictate international relations policy. The logos of his position did little to convince the audience of his argument, but it further enhanced his ethos with social democratic moderates. Furthermore, Bevan argued that should the resolution prove successful in its journey through the conference it would isolate Britain entirely from the international community. 'I would like to have the opportunity of exerting influence upon the policies of the United States and the Soviet Union' (Bevan, 1957a: 10), thereby ensuring that Britain had an opportunity to promote multilateral movements towards disarmament. Inversely unilateralism risked reducing Britain's influence to that of irrelevance. Through such appeals to logos, Bevan's argument utilised his ethos as a deliberative orator. Moreover, Bevan argued the international community 'will be polarized between the Soviet Union and the United States' leaving the 'little nations running to shelter with Russia or the United States' (Bevan, 1957a: 10) should Britain retreat from its global responsibilities. Further appealing to logos, Bevan's argument continues to highlight the realism of the conference retreating from the unilateralist position, whilst attempting to connect the consequences of British disengagement internationally with the emergence of a bipolar global structure over which Britain had no control. Indeed, given Britain's senior Commonwealth role, Bevan argued it had a responsibility that went beyond the self-interest of the Labour conference, appealing to his ethos outside of the conference chamber.

The consequence of this shift towards the logos-driven Gaitskellite position stunned those on the left, simultaneously enabling him to showcase his ethos as a potential foreign secretary. As evidence of his growing credibility with such moderates, Bevan was supported in this position by the former Secretary of State for War John Strachey, and Philip Noel-Baker, the Nobel Peace Prize winner and long-standing campaigner for multilateral disarmament. However, their contributory support led to an outpouring of heckling from the conference floor, who shouted 'you are talking your way out of it' and 'you've sold your past' (Bevan, 1957a: 10). These pathos-driven distractions incensed Bevan's sentiments, who described the unilateralist position as an 'emotional spasm'. Despite this lapse into pathos, the speech concluded with a reaffirmation of logos, with Bevan appealing to the conference not to disarm the Foreign Secretary 'diplomatically, intellectually and in every other way before he has a chance' to follow 'a workable policy' (Bevan, 1957a: 10). Central to Bevan's logos-driven argument was the importance of Britain remaining a significant player between the United States and the Soviet Union (Bevan, 1957a: 10).

This speech confirmed his ethos as a potentially credible figure of a future Labour government, whilst simultaneously subverting those on the left. Whilst it would be facile to argue the left was terminally impacted by Bevan's speech, it would be duplicitous to disregard the damage inflicted upon the left and its credibility.

Bevan's perceived move beyond classic left-wing perspectives must not be overstated. Granted, his moderation on disarmament positioned him within a Gaitskellite orientation, however on matters of economic policy, he remained firmly located on the left. Nonetheless, as previously demonstrated, most importantly was the need for continued unity and conciliation. In fact, at the 1959 conference Bevan argued that:

> Hugh Gaitskell and Barbara Castle and myself would not be doing a service to this movement if we did not make our individual contributions to its variety, but making the contributions to its variety and to its diversity without mortally injuring its unity. (Bevan, 1959: 152)

Despite the emergence of discontent in relation to Gaitskell's post-defeat reform agenda, Bevan clearly sought to emphasise again the requisite of unity. Indeed, given healthy division is an essential characteristic of European social democratic parties (Crines, 2011), Bevan rightly argues that such divisions could contribute to the richness of political and intellectual debate. However by 1959, Gaitskell's modernisation agenda had aggravated some on the left, with selected supporters of Bevan calling for a leadership challenge (Jones, 1996: 50). Clearly Bevan's agitation did not extend to such displays of outward disloyalty. Indeed, for his second noteworthy conference speech, Bevan combined a review of Gaitskell's modernisation agenda with a calm conciliatory tone (Foot, 1973a; Jones, 1996).

In the context of a third general election defeat, the revisionists were accelerating their emphasis on Labour renewal. For such reformers, this renewal process necessitated the abandonment of public ownership as a core commitment of any current or future Labour government. Using logos, Gaitskell argued the commitment to public ownership 'lays us open to continual misrepresentation. It implies that the only precise object we have is nationalisation, whereas in fact we have many other socialist objectives' (Gaitskell, 1959: 107).

This position enlivened the enmity of the left, threatening party disunity. Bevan's conciliatory contribution to the debate aimed to focus on both his own emotional ties with the Labour movement, and Gaitskell's argument to reform the party. To the conference, Bevan (1959: 107) argued that in a 'modern complex society it is impossible to get rational order by leaving things to private economic adventure. Therefore, I am a socialist. I believe in public ownership'.

This reaffirmation of his core socialist values seeks to connect his own values with those of the audience using pathos, re-legitimising his ethos as a socialist. This position laid careful foundations for the subsequent logos of his speech, in which he agreed 'with Hugh Gaitskell yesterday: I do not believe in a monolithic society. I do not believe that public ownership should reach down into every piece of economic activity, because that would be asking for a monolithic society' (Bevan, 1959: 29).

It would be facile to argue that Bevan overtly supported the modernisation agenda to the extent to which the revisionists sought to advance, however through deliberative oratory and pathos-driven rhetoric, Bevan was able to provide assuasive perspectives to a seemingly contentious debate. The logos of this position can be found in the need to avert internal conflict given its propensity to swiftly become overtly ideological, with such splintering divisions favouring neither faction. In terms of his approach, by using logos Bevan was able to enhance his ethos with the chosen audience that enabled him to calm left-wing agitators. It is important to note, however, that he later privately remarked to Michael Foot that he opposed the substance of Gaitskell's reform agenda (Foot, 1973a). This does not belie Bevan's clear effort to use his rhetorical and oratorical style towards nullifying potential division through logos-driven deliberative oratory, yet it does indicate his ideological opposition to the thrust of the modernisations.

In summary, Bevan's main conference orations sought to position the Labour Party more towards the mainstream. Bevan's advocacy for multilateral disarmament and the necessity for a conciliatory approach is broadly indicative of a logos-driven deliberative orator from the social democratic tradition. His ethos derives from both his logos and pathos, however these are framed by longer contributions to both the social democratic and left-wing traditions which enables him to appeal to both ideological factions. The examples above demonstrate Bevan's rhetorical and oratorical moderation, despite any superficial perceptions of ideological dogmatism.

Conclusion

The examples discussed in this chapter demonstrate that Bevan's oratorical delivery had a propensity towards both deliberative and epideictic forms of engagement. Rhetorically, these drew from logos and pathos in order to construct effective and unifying arguments. His ethos derived from both his Welsh identity and a long association with the Labour Party, which importantly never flirted with the more radical elements of Marxist revolutionary change. Indeed, both his ideological and policy rhetoric indicates a socialism based on social democratic moderation linked strongly to unity. Although his reputation can appropriately be described as an agitator, his communicative approaches imply a stronger propensity towards resisting divisive conflicts, such as those around the nuances of socialist theory. In fact, Bevan's rhetoric was notably anti-Conservative rather than perpetuating factional divisions within the Labour Party.

Some political commentators have commented upon his communicative legacy. Despite the apparent preference for unity, Bevan's name did become associated with a faction within the movement which splintered his own reputation amongst his political peers. Although Bevan did not claim to be a Bevanite, this association coloured that reputation. As John Campbell remarked: 'Bevan was one of the best loved and at the same time most bitterly hated figures in British politics this century, a man of deep humanity and generous anger, the most compelling orator of his generation' (Campbell, 1987: 431).

Although to describe Bevan as 'the most compelling orator of his generation' is potentially overstating the tribute, he certainly did garner significant praise for his rhetorical content and oratorical delivery. In part, this was because he ensured they reflected the expectations of his audience. This was possible due to the ethos he developed with his chosen audience, matching his oratorical style to the requirements of the moment, enabling him to develop the noteworthy reputation to which Campbell alludes.

2

The oratory of Hugh Gaitskell

Timothy Heppell and Thomas McMeeking

The Labour leadership of Hugh Gaitskell between 1955 and 1963 was defined by three intra-party disputes – over Clause IV, unilateralism and the Common Market – and three speeches on these three seismic issues at the Labour Party annual conferences of 1959, 1960 and 1962 respectively (Minkin, 1978). His rhetoric in challenging the party constitution over Clause IV, and then his refusal to abide by the will of conference which had advocated unilateral nuclear disarmament, showcased his revisionist credentials. It explains why he is positioned as a leading thinker of the old right within the Raymond Plant, Matt Beech and Kevin Hickson typology of Labour thought (Plant *et al.*, 2004). His advocacy of a revisionist position in the 1950s, which ran counter to the instincts of the expansionist left, contributed to the perception that Labour was a factional party and that Gaitskell was a 'factional leader' backed by a 'hard core of supporters' – the Gaitskellites (Rose, 1964: 40; see also Haseler, 1969). Michael Foot wrote in *Tribune* in October 1960 that Gaitskell can 'neither unite the party, nor lead it to power' and this feeling contributed to two challenges to his leadership of the party – by Harold Wilson in 1960 and Anthony Greenwood in 1961, both of whom secured backing from the left (Heppell, 2010: 26–30). Gaitskell may have survived the challenges, defeating Wilson 166 to 81 and Greenwood 171 to 59 in parliamentary ballots, but 'much blood was left along the way' (Morgan, 1987: 221).

However, what makes Gaitskell really intriguing was the speech that he provided to conference on the Common Market in 1962. Here the 'great confrontationist' used the Common Market to 'ironically' blur those 'factional divisions' (Howell, 1980: 235). Gaitskell marginalised the minority pro-Common Market revisionists with the Parliamentary Labour Party (PLP), many of whom had been his principle allies in the battles of the previous two years. In alienating his revisionist friends, and siding with the left on a major policy issue, Gaitskell was motivated by a desire to bring the party together to secure a level of unity not previously seen during his leadership (Gaitskell, 1962a). As Lewis Minkin noted Gaitskell had 'helped to heal the breach within the party which he himself had done so much to create' and in doing so he 'strengthened his position as leader' making him 'independent even of the faction which had protected him' over Clause IV and unilateralism (Minkin, 1978: 232).

His rhetoric on the Common Market highlighted how it did not cut down the clear left–right continuum of Labour's political thought, and that it divided the revisionist and 'so-called' Gaitskellite grouping (Meredith, 2008: 2).

When assessing the political thought of the Labour Party the legacy of Gaitskell is therefore clearly significant. His brand of politics became a reference point against which academics sought to interpret New Labour – with 1950s revisionism being seen to represent the 'old right', as compared to the modernised 'new right' of the Third Way (Beech, 2004: 89). Moreover, his leadership methods have been used within comparative evaluations of how the 'effective' Tony Blair was able to address the Clause IV issue in 1995, and why the 'ineffective' Gaitskell was unable to in 1959 (Heppell, 2012: 34; Jones, 1996: 41–64; 139–47).

Having identified the significance of Gaitskell to the political thought of the Labour Party this chapter therefore will be broken into four sections. First, it will assess how he used parliamentary debate; second, it will consider his conference oratory; third, it will examine his public oratory in terms of wider media appearances and electioneering; and finally, it will evaluate his rhetorical methods and the extent to which he drew upon logos (the appeal to reason and logic), pathos (the appeal to emotion) and ethos (an appeal based on one's character).

Gaitskell and Parliament

By the norms of his time Gaitskell made progress up the ministerial ladders remarkably quickly. Promoted to junior ministerial ranks within a year of entering Parliament, he spent three years as the Minister for Fuel and Power before entering the Treasury as Minister of Economic Affairs in early 1950, whereupon he replaced Stafford Cripps as Chancellor of the Exchequer in October 1950. Such advancement was a product of establishing a reputation as a gifted administrator and 'efficient Minister' but also a 'very effective parliamentarian' (Williams, 1979: 139). Whilst his parliamentary style may have been 'dull' there was a widespread acknowledgment that he was good at:

> measuring his statements, marshalling his facts and his arguments, taking note as he goes along of his opponent's viewpoint, answering it dispassionately, and all of the time taking the listener to the conclusion *he* thinks is the right one. He never batters or bullies an opponent in argument, but rather meets him halfway and then leads them gently along the Gaitskell path. (Williams, 1979: 140)

His greatest parliamentary challenge whilst at the Treasury was to be the controversial April 1951 Budget, where increases to defence expenditure alongside the imposition of NHS charges levied on false teeth and spectacles, would contribute to the resignations of Aneurin Bevan and Harold Wilson (Campbell, 1987). Whilst in *content* terms it offended the left (*Tribune* derided it as 'contemptible', 'timid' and 'squalidly inadequate' and accused Gaitskell of 'deserting Socialism at the moment of crisis'), Gaitskell did receive plaudits for its *delivery* (Williams, 1979: 249–58). For example, Joan Mitchell later described it as a 'tour de force in analysis and exposition' which 'stood out from those before', and when replying on behalf of the opposition Winston Churchill praised Gaitskell for his 'lucidity' and 'evident lack of hatred and malice' (HC Debs, 12 April 1951, cols. 879–92; Mitchell, 1963: 100).

One of the greatest parliamentary challenges that Gaitskell would experience would be the Suez Crisis. By this stage Gaitskell had become Leader of the Opposition. Here he was to gain both critical acclaim (initially) and significant criticism for his parliamentary interventions (later on). Before the crisis broke Gaitskell initially received relatively positive press reactions to his parliamentary contribution to the unfolding situation in the Middle East (*The Times*, 1956a; 1956b). By August 1956 Gaitskell informed Parliament of the clear threat that the seizure of the Canal could imply. On the struggle he noted that 'our friends desert us because they think we are lost, and go over to Egypt' he warned, before noting that 'it is all very familiar … it is exactly the same that we experienced from Mussolini and Hitler in those years before the war' (HC Debs, 2 August 1956, vol. 557: 1613). However, Gaitskell also warned that the government could not use force

> in breach of international law or, indeed, contrary to the public opinion of the world. We must not, therefore, allow ourselves to get in a position where we might be denounced in the Security Council as aggressors, or where the majority of the Assembly were against us … while force cannot be excluded, we must be sure that the circumstances justify it and that it is, if used, consistent with our belief in, and our pledges to, the Charter of the United Nations and not in conflict with them. (HC Debs, 2 August 1956, Vol. 557: 1609–17).

As Leon Epstein notes, whilst these latter observations were significant, there was reason to believe from the 'bulk of the speech' that Gaitskell's emphasis was on the 'seriousness' of the seizure of the Canal, and thus that his 'initial reactions reflected as much indignation as Eden's' (Epstein, 1960: 204). Thereafter it was felt that there was movement in his parliamentary rhetoric (Epstein, 1960). A belief would emerge that his rhetorical movement reflected his view that the Suez Crisis had provided an opportunity to 'score political points against the Conservatives' (Ramsey, 2004: 476). In October, Gaitskell informed the House that 'we cannot support the action they have taken and that we shall feel bound by every constitutional means at our disposal to oppose it'. He was at pains to stress the word 'constitutional' and emphasised that Labour would seek 'through the influence of public opinion, to bring every pressure to bear upon the Government to withdraw from the impossible situation into which they have put us' (HC Debs, 31 October 1956, vol. 558, col. 1462).

However, by selective interpretation of his oratory, critics made a series of negative assumptions about Gaitskell. First, there was the accusation that his oratory and positioning was unpatriotic (Epstein, 1960). His critics argued that as Leader of the Opposition he 'had a duty to hold his peace and support the government when British troops were going into action', irrespective of his 'own doubts' (Williams, 1979: 437). In Parliament on 7 November 1956, Gaitskell even attempted to repudiate that charge, arguing: 'we have different views as to what constitutes the honour and interests of Great Britain … the law of the jungle has been invoked by the British Government … and there are much more dangerous animals wandering about than Great Britain' (HC Debs, 7 November 1956, vol. 560, cols. 25–39). Second, and tied to the above criticism, came the accusation that Gaitskell had 'put his own political ambitions, both to unite his party and to defeat the government, ahead of the good of his country' (Epstein, 1960: 209). In particular the Conservative press suggested that Gaitskell had initially supported Eden and his proposed use of force, only to change rhetorical tack later due to a revolt within his own party (Braddon, 1963). However, it should be noted that an analysis of his parliamentary speeches demonstrates that 'he never hinted that either Labour might support seizing the Canal by force, or that he personally favoured doing so' (Williams, 1979: 424; see also Epstein, 1964 and Bowie, 1974 which also question that myth that Gaitskell had supported the Eden policy of using force).

Ultimately, however, Labour failed to gain from the Suez Crisis (Williams, 1979). The damage done to the credibility of the Conservative Party was largely addressed by the replacement of Anthony Eden with Harold Macmillan, who was to be widely praised for the 'inspirational' leadership that he displayed in immensely challenging political circumstances (Ramsden, 1998: 362). The change of prime ministerial leadership neutralised the issue, leaving Gaitskell with limited parliamentary options. Periodically Gaitskell would use Parliament to demand a Committee of Inquiry, but 'there was no way for Labour to force an inquiry on an unwilling government' (Epstein, 1960: 214). Gaitskell was left frustrated as he could only argue that the 'truth could not be known without an inquiry' and that by refusing to agree to one, Conservative elites were 'concealing their own discreditable roles' (Epstein, 1960: 214). By the time of the 1959 general election it was a less significant issue, although Gaitskell did 'melodramatically' (according to Epstein) reassert the need for an inquiry by arguing: 'I believe that the guilty men are sitting on those benches. It is time that they were brought to trial' (Epstein, 1960: 214; HC Debs 620, 16 March 1959, cols. 123–5).

Gaitskell clearly suffered when Eden was replaced by Macmillan (Williams, 1979). He struggled against Macmillan in Parliament, especially in the 1957 to 1960 period (Hennessy, 2000). During the course of parliamentary debates Macmillan's mocking manner towards Gaitskell, and the accompanying jeering and heckling that this provoked amongst Conservative back benchers, made its impact. On occasions during debates it 'made Gaitskell wonder if he should continue' (Williams, 1979: 293, 302). The co-ordinated barracking from the Conservative back benchers ensured that he was frequently interrupted during the course of his parliamentary contributions. There was genuine concern within the PLP that his parliamentary performances were so 'poor' that it was 'impairing' his effectiveness as Leader of the Opposition (Williams, 1979: 439). Indeed, until the Macmillan administration began to degenerate in the 1961 period onwards, there was anxiety that Macmillan was 'tactically superior' and, as Richard Crossman noted, this was damaging to morale within the PLP (Morgan, 1981: 742; Williams, 1979: 474).

However, Alderman suggests that against Macmillan Gaitskell undermined his own capacity for effectiveness by using 'over-lengthy questions'. Commenting upon how both adapted to the formal introduction of Prime Minister's Questions (PMQs) in 1961 he noted that not only were Gaitskell's longer questions 'more vulnerable to barracking and interruption by government supporters' but they also gave Macmillan 'longer to decide upon an answer' and thus made it easier for him to 'evade' (Alderman, 1992a: 73). Macmillan would later elaborate on this by arguing that Gaitskell

> made the mistake of asking several questions one of which was answerable. Without telling him a direct lie I soon learned that you only answer the easy ones … If he had asked *one* question which I knew I couldn't give answer to truthfully, it would have been more effective. (Horne, 1989: 156)

Gaitskell was at his most effective in parliamentary terms when critiquing the appointment of Lord Home to the Foreign Office in 1961 (Heppell, 2012). He questioned whether Home was the 'best available' candidate, and implied that Macmillan had selected him for his political compliance so that he could effectively perform the role himself. If 'puppets' are to be used they should be in the House of Commons Gaitskell argued, and then concluded with 'why bother with the monkey when the organ grinder is here'. Gaitskell had used 'satire, ridicule, and straight crushing argument' to devastating parliamentary effect (McDermott, 1972: 194). Macmillan later admitted that it was 'the cleverest and most effective speech I have heard him make' (Macmillan, 1973: 232). However, there was considerable disappointment at how Gaitskell failed to fully exploit 'the Night of the Long Knives' when Macmillan dismissed six members of his own Cabinet in July 1962 (Alderman, 1992b: 243–65). Of his parliamentary questioning of Macmillan, Gaitskell was less effective and failed to make the impact that the opposition would have anticipated (Williams, 1979: 700). Here Gaitskell was unable to match the 'much remembered words' of Jeremy Thorpe who said: 'greater love hath no man than this, than he lay down his friends for his life' (Douglas, 2005: 267).

Gaitskell and conference

The introduction to this chapter emphasised how the oratorical reputation of Gaitskell was defined by his conference speeches on the internal party disputes over Clause IV, unilateralism and the Common Market. Through his conference oratory we can obtain a clear sense of how between 1959 and 1962 Gaitskell would advance a 'concept of leadership', and would use oratorical methods that did not try 'to reconcile the opposing sides' but 'to educate the party by force of argument' (Brivati, 1999: 105).

With regard to all three of these policy issues, Gaitskell was motivated by the drive for electoral appeal. In his view nationalisation and unilateralism were electoral liabilities. Moreover, he came to the view that adopting a critical position on the Common Market could create electoral opportunities for Labour against a Conservative administration destined to see their application vetoed (Jones, 1996: 60). In the Clause IV debacle Gaitskell was seeking to persuade the Labour movement to end their obsession with nationalisation as the means of socialising society but to focus explicitly on the ends (Kenny and Smith, 1997). Gaitskell argued that Clause IV was 'politically irrelevant and electorally unattractive' and it was 'not an accurate expression of the policy goals of a forthcoming administration that he would lead' (Heppell, 2012: 37). By choosing to maintain it Gaitskell feared that would allow 'the Conservatives to exploit it and engender fears surrounding the implications of Labour occupying power' (Heppell, 2012: 37). He informed the November 1959 conference that:

> We regard public ownership not as an end in itself but as a means – and not necessarily the only or the most important one to certain ends – such as full employment, greater equality and higher productivity. We do not aim to nationalise every private firm or to create an endless series of state monopolies. (Labour History Archive and Study Centre, 1959)

In challenging the constitution of the party Gaitskell emphasised how it was dated as it excluded 'race relations, disarmament, full employment or planning' before finally addressing Clause IV and arguing:

> It lays us open to continual misrepresentation … it implies that we propose to nationalise everything, but do we? Everything – the whole of light industry, the whole of agriculture, all the shops – every little pub and garage? Of course not. (Williams, 1979: 554)

Noting that the party had long ago come to accept the mixed economy he concluded by justifying his case for facing up to the Clause IV conundrum by arguing that above all else they needed to win power, and that this required the removal of obstacles to victory. In making that case he admitted that 'I would rather forego the cheers now in the hope that we shall get more votes later on' (Williams, 1979: 555). During the course of the speech he faced 'hostile interruptions' and prominent left-wingers refused to applaud at the conclusion of the speech (Williams, 1979: 555). The wider extra-parliamentary left then put up a fierce defence of Clause IV, for whom there was a huge 'symbolic' importance associated with it to the Labour movement. For all his logically constructed rhetoric Gaitskell had simply failed to appreciate that his proposals amounted to 'taking down the signpost to the promised land' (Williams, 1979: 570). Peter Shore suggested that this indicated that Gaitskell was 'not on the same wavelength as the majority of active Labour Party members' (Shore, 1993: 60).

He was then forced into a humiliating climb-down, although Clause IV would now be supplemented by supporting statements of principle, which concluded that national-isation could only be applied 'according to circumstances' (Fielding, 2007: 313).

Gaitskell revisionists also offered 'new thinking' in terms of foreign policy. They questioned the validity that 'foreign policy decisions could and should always be firmly based around socialist principles' (Haseler, 1969: 112). They rejected the left's position as 'the last refuge of utopianism' and chose to promote the 'power-political' approach, and in doing so they rejected the notion that 'ideology' should be a primary influence in foreign policy development (Black, 2001: 28, 34). These competing left–right perspectives manifested themselves in Gaitskellite condemna-tion of unilateralism, and when unilateralism was foisted upon the leadership at the 1960 annual conference, the Gaitskellites waged a successful campaign for its rever-sal at the 1961 annual conference, when a multilateralist *Policy for Peace* platform was accepted (Black, 2001).

In oratorical terms Gaitskell would be best remembered for his speech to the 1960 annual conference. During the course of the speech he was frequently interrupted, and on one occasion he snapped back 'I have been subject to some criticism and attack and I am entitled to reply' (Williams, 1979: 611). He then provocatively argued:

> Supposing all of us, like well behaved sheep, were to follow the policies of unilat-eralism, what kind of an impression would that make upon the minds of the British people? ... What sort of people do they think we are? Do they think that we can really accept a decision of this kind? Do they think we can become overnight the pacifists, unilateralists and fellow travellers that other people are? I say this to you: we may lose the vote today and the result may deal this party a grave blow. It may not be possible to prevent it, but I think there are many of us who will not accept that this blow need to be mortal, who will not believe that such an end is inevitable. There are some of us, Mr Chairman, who will fight and fight again to bring back sanity and honesty and dig-nity, so that our party with its great past may retain its glory and its greatness. (Brivati, 1996: 374)

The speech was described as being 'great' by David Marquand and it was noted that although Gaitskell lost, the scale of defeat was considerably smaller than had been anticipated (Marquand, 1999: 124). His speech would contribute to the mobilis-ing of multilateralist forces that would reverse the decision a year later. As Philip Williams noted this conference speech at Scarborough was classic Gaitskell and his oratory reflected his 'commitment to intellectual honesty and clarity, to teaching his supporters that the right thing must be done for the right reasons' (Williams, 1979: 614).

The other foreign policy dimension to the Gaitskellite platform was more com-plex. On the matter of the Common Market, Gaitskell attempted to avoid commit-ting himself publicly to a distinct policy position, partly because he did not view it as an important electoral issue (Williams, 1979). This ambiguity was sustainable until the Macmillan government sought entry 'whereupon his eventual critical positioning was determined by a combination of important factors: first, his strong commitment to the Commonwealth; second, his belief that the application would be vetoed and thereby opposition would have electoral advantages given its increasing saliency; and, third, out of a desire to retain party unity' (Heppell, 2012: 36). On that latter issue Gaitskell was influenced by the alternative intra-party dynamics surrounding the Common Market (Gaitskell, 1962a). On the Common Market all sections within the movement – trade unionists; constituency Labour parties; and the PLP – were felt to be opposed to entry, that is, they adopted what was interpreted as a position identifiable with the left. When Gaitskell confronted unilateralism, his ability to argue for the position identifiable with the right (multilateralism) was strengthened by the knowledge that a majority of the PLP shared this view (Haseler, 1969). Therefore, coming out anti-Common Market was the best way to unify the party, as a pro position 'would put him on a collision course' with *all* sections of the movement (Heppell, 2012: 40).

The negative impact of such a position meant that Gaitskell would marginalise the minority pro-Common Market revisionists, many of whom had been his principle allies in the battles of the previous two years (Brivati, 1996). However, by alienating his traditional revisionist friends, and 'siding with the left' on a major policy issue, Gaitskell brought the party together and secured a level of unity not previously seen during his leadership tenure (Brivati, 1996: 418). Gaitskell knew the significance of the anti-Common Market speech before he delivered it to the 1962 conference (Broad and Daddow, 2010). This was evident from the fact that he did not even allow George Brown, his pro-Common Market deputy, to see a draft of the speech before he delivered to conference (Brown, 1971). Gaitskell spelt out how:

> We must be clear about this: it does mean, if this is the idea, the end of Britain as an independent European state. I make no apology for repeating it. It means the end of a thousand years of history. You may say 'let it end', but my goodness, it is a decision that needs a little care and thought. And it does mean the end of Commonwealth. How can one seriously suppose that if the mother country, the centre of the Commonwealth, is a province of Europe (which is what Federation means) it could continue to exist as the mother country of a series of independent nations? It is sheer nonsense. (Gaitskell, 1962b: 10–12)

When Gaitskell concluded the 'ovation was unparalleled' (Brivati, 1996: 414). Douglas Jay, who was one of the few on the right hostile to the Common Market, was fulsome in his praise of Gaitskell, describing the speech as 'unique among all the political speeches I ever heard; not merely the finest, but in a class apart' before concluding that 'It can only be described as an intellectual massacre … nobody had anything else to say … for its uniqueness rested in its ring of truth' (Jay, 1980: 286). The 'thousand years' speech was to be hugely influential in terms of the dynamics of future Labour Party politics in relation to Europe. As Matthew Broad and Oliver

Daddow note, his oratory placed a negative slant on the argument surrounding Europe. They conclude that: 'this meant that their entire rhetoric on British membership was framed for domestic audiences by an "anti-federal" doctrine, with damage to the British-Community relationship being the inevitable long-term outcome' (Broad and Daddow, 2010: 211). Furthermore there were to be huge implications in terms of the revisionist faction. Stephen Haseler, writing in 1969, noted that pro-Common Market revisionists, such as Roy Jenkins and Bill Rodgers, were reported to feel Gaitskell's rhetoric had 'reinforced the impression that a real break was imminent' (Haseler, 1969: 238).

Gaitskell and electioneering

Whilst the oratorical reputation of Gaitskell has been largely shaped by his appearances at conference, his wider impact through other means – public meetings and media appearances and electioneering – was relatively mixed. It was early in his political career that Gaitskell endured the 'most celebrated gaffe of his public life' (Williams, 1979: 150). Within the context of a winter coal budget that was projecting a 10 per cent reduction in gas and electricity by households, Gaitskell had taken to discussing fuel economy within his speeches. At a public meeting in 1947 at Hastings he was to deliver a line that he would later claim was a joke to 'liven things up'. He suggested:

> It means getting up and going to bed in cold bedrooms. It may mean fewer baths. Personally, I have never had a great many baths myself and I can assure those who are in the habit of having a great many baths that it does not make a great deal of difference to their health if they have fewer. And as far as appearance goes – most of that is underneath and nobody sees it. (Williams, 1979: 150)

Such a gaffe was ruthlessly exploited by Churchill in Parliament, with references to the government 'getting increasingly into bad odour' (HD Debs, 28 October 1947, 443, col. 709). The reputation that Gaitskell acquired for this took time to overcome – for example, when he delivered a ministerial broadcast on petrol rationing, *The Economist*, whilst praising his performance, felt that he had 'served the government well – [and] *on previous form, astoundingly well*' (Williams, 1979: 151).

The remainder of his ministerial career passed without his courting any further negative comment about his rhetorical delivery of government policy. The transition to opposition, and the internal wrangles that the Labour Party then became engulfed in, ensured that Gaitskell's public profile would remain high. The 1952 Elections to the National Executive Committee (NEC), in which Gaitskell was defeated alongside departing members Herbert Morrison and Hugh Dalton (replaced by Harold Wilson and Richard Crossman), provoked one of Gaitskell's most infamous public speeches outside of Parliament or conference. Fearing that the Bevanites were using the NEC elections as an organised factional campaign to discredit the parliamentary leadership, Gaitskell delivered what he intended to be an 'unusually violent speech

... a call to battle' (Williams, 1979: 304). Using intemperate language (alleging that one in six delegates were Communists or Communist-influenced), he denounced the rejection of Morrison which he felt was an 'act of blind stupidity' given that Morrison was in his view the 'principal architect of efficient organisation and realistic policy' (Williams, 1979: 304). In his 'Stalybridge speech' (October 1952) went on to assert that Constituency Labour Parties were being misled by the Bevanites and accused them of a

> stream of grossly misleading propaganda with poisonous innuendos and malicious attacks on Attlee, Morrison and the rest of us ... Because of our distaste for public rows inside the party, we have endured it for the most part in silence. But it is now quite clear that we were wrong ... [to reply was not] ... endangering the unity of the party. For there will be no unity on the terms dictated by *Tribune*. Indeed [their] vitriolic abuse of the party leaders is an invitation to disloyalty and disunity. *It is time to end the attempt at mob rule by a group of frustrated journalists and restore the authority and leadership of the solid sound sensible majority of the Movement.* (Williams, 1979: 305)

Gaitskell's intervention prompted Clement Attlee into action. He attempted to 'get a grip' by carrying a resolution banning all unofficial groupings inside the party (Jefferys, 2000: 82). His denouncement of such unofficial groupings went hand in hand with a plea with the PLP to end the 'personal attacks on colleagues' (Brookshire, 1995: 232). The dramatic nature of the Gaitskell intervention at Stalybridge was to be reflective of his tendency towards recklessness in defence of his commitment to his logically constructed arguments. This was again to be evident in his public comments on Suez outside of Parliament. He utilised the opposition's right to a public broadcast in response to Eden's at the height of the crisis. Here his central pitch in condemning the policy of Eden and his administration was to state that a new prime minister and new government would be needed. Some critics felt that at a time when British troops were in battle such partisanship seemed virtually treasonable (Braddon, 1963). If his objective was to encourage dissident anti-Suez Conservatives to abandon Eden then his intervention was counter-productive – for them the prospect of a general election or even a Labour government would be a betrayal to their party. Thus Gaitskell inadvertently pushed them back to Eden and party out of necessity (Williams, 1979).

Suez was not to be a significant issue in the general election campaign of 1959, with Labour choosing not to stress the issue in case the 'unpatriotic' label was attached to it again (Butler and Rose, 1960: 64). However, once again Gaitskell was to make a significant miscalculation during the course of the campaign. There was tremendous focus on him as the party leader during the campaign – in the thirteen-day period leading up to Election Day he delivered an amazing fifty-three speeches and not surprisingly 'fatigue' became increasingly apparent during the filming of Party Election Broadcasts (Butler and Rose, 1960: 54, 86). Normally Gaitskell had attempted to win hearts 'not with emotional gestures and cries, but with economics and figures', but when speaking in Newcastle on 28 September he committed what was described as the 'tax gaffe' (Brivati, 1999: 107; Butler and Rose, 1960: 59). He stated that: 'there will be no increase in the standard or other rates of income tax as long as normal peacetime conditions continue' (Butler and Rose, 1960: 59).

This provided Macmillan with the political ammunition that he needed to confirm the central message of the Conservative campaign – that is, that the Labour Party were financially irresponsible and that Gaitskell was engaging in electoral bribes, whereupon greater scepticism was evident amongst voters and Labour lost their 'momentum' (Fielding, 2007: 311). Exploiting Gaitskell's tortuous relationship with Bevan and the left, the prime minister fired back with: 'it was his addiction to figures on which he built what seems now a false reputation, that led Mr Bevan to describe him as a desiccated calculating machine ... That is now only a half-truth ... I think he is still rather desiccated, but his reputation as a calculator has gone with the wind' (Butler and Rose, 1960: 62).

The 1959 general election was a watershed election as the impact of television changed the dynamics of party projection and increased the emphasis on the party leader and image (Rowland, 1960). Gaitskell was aware of this. He recognised the decline in the importance of public meetings as a means for party projection, and he encouraged his party that the best means of reaching out to, and appealing to, affluent voters was through the press and television (Fielding, 2007). To aid this he welcomed in the advice of advertising specialists and sought to utilise public opinion research more extensively (Haseler, 1969). He paid particular attention to image projection through television. Williams noted that 'he saw that mastering television technique was now indispensable for a politician and patiently spent many weary hours in rehearsal' (Williams, 1979: 382).

However, writing in the *Political Quarterly* shortly after the 1959 general election, Christopher Rowland noted the dominance of Macmillan over Gaitskell on television. He felt there was a certain irony that it was the aristocratic and older Macmillan who was adapting to this new technique of political communication. Noting that an 'image of Macmillan pruning his rose garden is worth half a dozen solid speeches by Gaitskell' he concluded that:

> He [Macmillan] has shown himself much more adaptable than Gaitskell, who by virtue of his personal experience and the nature of the party he leads, should really be much more in touch. The difficulty is that Gaitskell's high mindedness and moral honesty, and his genuine belief that the electorate responds mainly to reasoned argument, have made him temperamentally unsympathetic to showmanship. (Rowland, 1960: 358)

That Gaitskell placed such importance on trying to make the Labour Party more electorally appealing made the impact of the defeat in 1959 more profound (Haseler, 1969). It created an environment in which, according to Marquand, Gaitskell felt that he 'had nothing to lose', and as such 'he *would* now pursue truth ... [and]

putting his faith in the power of reason, he *would* try to persuade his party to see the light' (Marquand, 1999: 135). However, by doing so 'he breathed new life into the internal schism which had begun in the closing years of the Attlee Government' (Marquand, 1999: 135). Such an attitude would fuel the collisions that he would have with his own party in the 1959 to 1962 period. For example, Clause IV demonstrated that 'once he was committed to a course of action, his relentless application of intellectually honesty forced him on to take events to their logical conclusion, even if this was unpalatable, or damaging to his own interests' (Brivati, 1996: 421).

Gaitskell's oratory showed, for example, that he was 'fed up' with the unilateralists within and beyond their PLP, for what he considered their 'perverse, disruptive stupidity' (McDermott, 1972: 197). Whilst feeling that the amount of 'noise' made by neutralists and pacifists was 'out of proportion to their real strength in the community', he still had to confront them (Black, 2001: 51). In doing so Gaitskell would find that whenever he made a speech he would attract 'crowds and controversy' and Jay was shocked by 'the sheer hatred directed towards him ... people would spit and shout abuse, and on some occasions there was a real threat of physical violence' (Brivati, 1996: 379). He became used to being 'heckled', but he was often upset by the 'boorishness of the demonstrators' and their 'arrant refusal to consider any logic or reasoning' (McDermott, 1972: 237). Hostility towards him at public meetings was at its most profound in the immediate aftermath of the 1960 annual conference. The *Guardian* would report that Gaitskell would show 'a tough, uncompromising attitude to the noisy – sometimes hysterical – interrupters', and that he was heckled and interrupted by frequent boos and cries of 'Resign' and 'Join the Liberals' (*Guardian*, 1960a; 1960b).

Between the summer of 1961 and the summer of 1962, with the resumption of nuclear testing and the Cuban Missile Crisis, the Campaign for Nuclear Disarmament (CND) and the far left once again felt emboldened and their target remained Gaitskell. Once again they proved to be a thorn in his side at public meetings. This was despite the 1961 annual conference endorsing his stance on defence by an overwhelming majority (Williams, 1979). The atmosphere was particularly rowdy at the 1962 May Day rally in Glasgow: 'in a noisy clash with demonstrators who drowned his speech, Mr Gaitskell called on "Communists down there" to go to the Kremlin with their placards and ask Mr Krushchev to ban his bomb.' Gaitskell once again remained defiant in the face of such opposition, telling the demonstrators:

> The time has come when we have to say this to them – either they choose to go on wrecking our chances, in which case they ought not to be in the Labour Party at all, or they must agree to accept the official policy of the party, even if they may disagree with certain parts of it, and do their best to get a Labour Government into power. (*Guardian*, 1962)

If nothing else, at Glasgow, Gaitskell once again showed his political courage and defiance of the opposition within the party, a leitmotiv of his speeches. The *Guardian* 'complimented Mr Gaitskell for refusing to be put off' and the editor concluded that 'never in my political life of over forty years have I seen such an example of political courage' (*Guardian*, 1962). The *Guardian* noted that Gaitskell kept 'his temper through some extremely trying scenes' but a later biographer, Brian Brivati, would comment that 'giving speech after speech in such circumstances must have been soul destroying and exhausting' (Brivati, 1996: 379; *Guardian*, 1960b).

Gaitskell and oratorical methods: *logos, pathos and ethos*

The consensus view would be that Gaitskell was not a top rating orator. During the height of his political importance the parliamentary sketch writer, Bernard Levin, used his column to ridicule him for his seriousness (Hoggart, 2008). That seriousness reflected the fact that his preferred oratorical method was to appeal to logic and reason or logos. His style was one which was heavily dependent on the use of factual evidence with an emphasis on policy detail. This was partly seen as a reflection of his temperament. For example, during the 1959 general election he proudly informed the *Daily Mail* that: 'I am a rationalist ... I like to think that in a mature democracy people reach their conclusions mostly on the basis of actual evidence and argument' (Butler and Rose, 1960: 29). More famously he informed Jean Monnet, the chief architect of the concept of a common Europe: 'I don't believe in faith. I believe in reason and you have not shown me any' (Brivati, 1996: 412). Gaitskell therefore viewed the function of leadership oratory as a means to 'persuade' rather than to 'manipulate', and as such Minkin concluded that 'no British party leader since Gladstone has staked so much on his capacity to change men's minds by the sheer force of rational argument' (Minkin, 1978: 325).

With this emphasis on rational argument in mind, it is worth considering the observation of Haseler, who noted that Gaitskell used socialist rhetoric far less than previous Labour leaders: 'his speeches lacked reference to much of the visionary aspects of socialist doctrine' and 'when he departed from practical issues his political sentiments were often expressed more in terms of human values than the quasi-religious idealism' that many within the Labour movement wanted and expected to see deployed (Haseler, 1969: 156). This view reflects the limited use of pathos, or the use of emotion, within Gaitskell's oratorical style. Or more specifically it reflects the limited way in which he sought to appeal to the emotional instincts of the Labour movement – i.e. their prejudices – through his oratory. Where emotion was clearly evident in his speeches – for example the 'fight, fight and fight again' speech or at Stalybridge – it was often within the context of an internal party feud or when he felt that his leadership and his character were under attack from within the movement itself. In this context many of his conference speeches were delivered to a relatively hostile and fractious movement. Here we can argue that his 1959 and 1960 speeches, on nationalisation and unilateralism respectively, involved Gaitskell seeking to educate the party through his oratory. Gaitskell was thus basing his appeal not on the approach that may be most worthy or good – i.e. *dignitas* or *bonum* – which is how many within the movement view nationalisation and unilateralism; rather he is basing his appeal on what is most useful or advantageous to the party – i.e. *utilitas* (Corbett and Connors, 1999).

Ultimately, however, the reliance on logos (factual evidence) at the expense of pathos, and then within this the reliance on utilitas (what is good for us), demonstrated that Gaitskell could allow his sense of 'rationality' to triumph over 'common sense'. This creates the conundrum in which his over-commitment to rationality meant he completely misjudged the emotionality of the movement that he was leading (Morgan, 1987). This demonstrates the importance of the interrelationship between personality, policy and oratory. All forms of literature on Gaitskell have similar assertions. He is accused of 'arrogance', 'rigidity', 'intolerance', 'stubbornness' and of being 'blunt', 'insensitive' and 'uncompromising', by his critics on the left, although his admirers on the right emphasised his 'courage' and 'determination' (Brivati, 1996: 425; Marquand, 1999: 136). Whilst on the Common Market, Roy Jenkins, who had experience of being both with and against Gaitskell on these divisive issues, admitted of 1962 that: 'I inevitably felt a little more sympathy with those who had differed from him in the past! Courage can be interpreted as inflexibility and an aggressive respect for rationality as a tendency to equate little points with big ones' (Campbell, 1983: 72).

When considering the oratorical distinctions of Dennis Glover (2011), we can legitimately define the Gaitskell approach as realist rather than romantic, with a strong reliance on factual evidence to support the arguments that he was attempting to make, although emotionalism often came to the surface when the movement could not accept the logic of his argument. What Gaitskell did little of within his oratory was appeal to ethos and seek to draw upon his own character to buttress his arguments. His neglect in this dimension was perhaps a reflection of the political times and the culture of Labour for whom there remained residual scepticism about the personalisation of politics and granting too much power and focus in the hands of one individual – here the legacy of Ramsay MacDonald continued to matter.

Conclusion

Gaitskell was not viewed as a top ranking political orator. His reliance on logos and within this the extended focus on *utilitas* as a rhetorical method came at the expense of pathos and ethos. His rhetorical methods and style were also a by-product of his times and his own personality. He suffered from comparisons in both intra- and inter-party terms – i.e. he was compared unfavourably with Bevan within the movement, who was the primary romanticised and passionate orator, and then with Macmillan in terms of party competition. Moreover, his oratorical capability was undermined by the fact that he found that he could not always hide his awkwardness in public settings, both at party rallies and in front of the camera. He was normally at his happiest one-to-one rather than on the public platform when it came to persuading others during his time as leader. Against Macmillan the contrast was stark, particularly on television – Macmillan outshining Gaitskell 'as a lighthouse does a glow-worm' in the new medium (*Sunday Express*, 1958). The same was true in Parliament, Gaitskell's starchiness being exploited mercilessly to the joy of Conservative back benchers (Williams, 1979). But in the febrile atmosphere of Labour politics, Gaitskell was in policy, ideology and oratory seen as the antithesis to Bevan. Richard Hornby captures this by arguing that:

> There is no orator in the Commons today quite like Bevan; nobody with quite the same cadence of voice, or quite the same joy in the selection of words, sometimes spilled out in a prodigal torrent and sometimes chosen and spoken more slowly, as if each was a gem selected with loving care ... there is nobody who when angry can lean forward across the dispatch box as he did, and spit his accusations full in the face of the government. He was an artist, and one is happy to have heard him. Gaitskell, too, made fine speeches. But with him it was the range and the orderliness of his thinking rather than the oratory which commanded attention. A Gaitskell speech was a parade of his well-stored mind. It stated the situation, it posed all the right questions, and then it proceeded to his criticisms of the government ... but ... sometimes it seemed that his intellectual vigour encouraged him to develop lines of argument much further than it was wise to do. (Hornby, 1963: 244–5)

3

The oratory of Harold Wilson

Michael Hill

Introduction

Harold Wilson was first elected to Parliament in 1945 and enjoyed a meteoric rise through the government ranks, becoming President of the Board of Trade in 1947 at the age of thirty-one, making him the twentieth century's youngest Cabinet minister. He led the Labour Party for a little over thirteen years from February 1963 until his resignation in April 1976. During this time he had two spells as Leader of the Opposition (1963–64 and 1970–74) and served twice as prime minister (1964–70 and 1974–76). Despite this long career within the higher echelons of the Labour Party, Wilson's ideological beliefs and position within the party have always been hard to pin down and still remain the subject of great debate. As Clive Ponting noted, 'It is impossible to find out what Harold Wilson really believed, as opposed to what he said and did, about the policy issues the government had to face' (Ponting, 1989: 402).

Wilson carefully cultivated his public image and 'wore his roots like a badge' (Pugh, 2011: 321). He deliberately contrasted his social background as a working-class Yorkshireman who'd bettered himself through hard work to that of Harold Macmillan and Sir Alec Douglas-Home. He often talked of his love for Huddersfield Town and told the *Daily Express* that, 'If I had a choice between smoked salmon and tinned I'd have it tinned. With vinegar'. He always smoked a pipe in interviews and public appearances, but smoked cigars in private (Sandbrook, 2010). By contrast Macmillan and Douglas-Home were portrayed as the sons of privilege who had attained their position through their family connections rather than by their talent and diligence. A recurring theme of Wilson's rhetoric was that Macmillan and Douglas-Home were the embodiment of their party: they belonged to a bygone aristocratic era, were out of touch with the modern world and lacked the skills to govern Britain in the space age. By contrast Wilson and Labour were modern, dynamic and would harness the skills of all social groups in the national interest (Fielding, 1997).

Macmillan's view of his new opponent was that, 'Wilson is an able man ... He is good in the House and in the country and so I am told on TV' (Macmillan,

1973: 396). Wilson was seen by his supporters as a skilful and pragmatic politician, whilst his critics, especially within his own party, saw him as slippery, unprincipled and only interested in short-term solutions. Denis Healey said that Wilson 'rarely looked more than a few months ahead' (Healey, 1989: 336; Heppell, 2010: 165). Labour's deputy leader and Wilson's great rival, George Brown, likened him to the fictional fantasist Walter Mitty. 'I would have said that if the film of Walter Mitty hadn't come first, Harold Wilson must have been the prototype ... His fantasies are endless. The roles he allots himself are breathtaking' (Roth, 1977: 46). In a similar vein Healey wrote that Wilson had 'a capacity for self-delusion which made Walter Mitty seem unimaginative' (Marquand, 1999: 162). Dominic Sandbrook highlighted Wilson's optimism, his 'unflagging self confidence and good cheer' that sustained him through difficult times (Sandbrook, 2010: 26–7). Whilst this optimism could be an asset, Wilson's colleagues often believed it was dangerously overstated: Crossman referred to the 'interminable self-defeating optimism of Harold Wilson' and Barbara Castle once noted in her diary, 'That optimism again. It could be fatal' (Castle, 1984: 297; Crossman, 1976: 332; Ziegler, 1993: 42). However, Wilson's record has been defended by Richard Coopey *et al.*, who argue that: 'those who have sought to condemn Wilson have often wildly exaggerated their case ... It is at least possible that the Prime Minister's endless manoeuvring was because he confronted exacting foes on difficult terrain' (Coopey *et al.*, 1993: 6). He has also been defended by his biographer Ben Pimlott, who argues that there were issues, such as the defence of sterling and trade union reform where Wilson stuck rigidly to his principles, even though his stance aroused fierce opposition and damaged his reputation (Pimlott, 1993).

Having established the nature of Wilson's character and the debate over the 1964–70 Labour government I will now examine Wilson's oratorical methods and his use of the devices of ethos, pathos and logos. I will then assess how Wilson deployed his oratorical skills in Parliament, at the Labour Party conference and examine his use of public meetings and the media. Although Wilson had a long political career, this chapter concentrates on Wilson's oratory during the period between him becoming Labour leader in 1963, to when he left office in 1970, as it was in this period that his political reputation was made and then broken.

Wilson's oratorical style: ethos, pathos and logos

Epideictic, or ceremonial speeches, such as those to party conferences, allow speakers to outline their political vision and thus establish a virtuous ethos for themselves, through the use of praise and blame (Olmsted, 2006). Wilson's 1963 conference speech, whilst essentially setting out a vision of the future, also blamed the incumbent Conservative government for being privileged, amateurish and complacent, whilst praising the Labour Party for being meritocratic, professional and dynamic. Wilson again used praise and blame in his speech opening the parliamentary debate on the Profumo affair. Although the speech initially lays out a factual sequence of events, Wilson uses these to praise the conduct, both of himself and his party: 'We did not canvass or propagate rumours about personal conduct' and 'rightly or wrongly, we did everything in our power to prevent this becoming a matter of public discussion' (HC Deb, 17 June 1963, vol. 679, cols. 34–176) and then contrast this with the conduct of Prime Minister Macmillan and the Conservatives, 'the indolent nonchalance of the Prime Minister's attitude to this: the attitude of "what has this to do with me?"' (HC Deb, 17 June 1963, vol. 679, cols. 34–176). Again this device is used to establish Wilson's virtuous ethos, whilst undermining that of his opponent, Macmillan, who will follow him in debate.

Pathos is the appeal to the audience's sympathies and imagination as well as their emotions, so that an audience will identify with the speaker's point of view. Wilson used pathos to establish his working-class credentials in a speech he made in Birmingham in 1948, in which he told his audience that 'half the children in my class had never had boots and shoes on their feet' (Pimlott, 1993: 122). Wilson's 1963 'white heat' speech is full of pathos, which was reinforced by the passion in his delivery. Wilson took his audience on a journey into the exciting future of a Britain forged in the white heat of the technological revolution where ministers would 'think and speak in the language of our scientific age' – clearly encouraging his audience, both at conference and in the media, to dream of a brighter, more affluent future. This theme was continued in Wilson's public speeches during the election campaign of 1964 where voters were told they had 'a chance to change the face and future of Britain' (Wilson, 1964: 10). In the summer of 1966 Wilson used pathos rather differently and to much less acclaim to rally the nation in the face of economic austerity: 'This is your country and our country. We must work for it'. Wilson repeated this style in November 1967 after the devaluation of the pound: 'We are on our own now. It means – Britain first'.

Wilson's speech to Parliament over the Profumo affair perhaps best demonstrates his use of logos to build a case against the Conservatives: he deployed facts to show how he had dealt with information that had come into his possession, detailing the occasions on which he had spoken to Macmillan, the contents of his letters and Macmillan's replies to those letters. In the course of laying out these facts Wilson not only showed himself to be knowledgeable about his subject and thus made it more difficult for Macmillan to argue against him, but also as we have seen above portrayed himself positively, whilst painting Macmillan in a negative light, thus enhancing his ethos. A further, although less successful, example of Wilson's use of logos is his broadcast on the devaluation of the pound. In this he stated (correctly) that imported goods would be more expensive, but that British exports would be more competitive (Sandbrook, 2010). However, Wilson's use of the ill-judged attempt to argue that 'the pound in your pocket' had not been devalued was widely disbelieved, undermining Wilson's virtuous ethos.

In Parliament

When Wilson was first elected, he showed very little talent for parliamentary debate: his maiden speech was interrupted on four occasions and it was three months before he spoke again. The *Spectator*'s David Watt noted that 'Mr Wilson is a terrible speaker' and that, 'He builds cliché on statistic on cliché on mountainous sandwiches of tedium' (Ziegler, 1993: 52). However, over time, Wilson developed into a skilled parliamentary performer, who could command the Commons with his presence and charisma: James Griffiths, the first Secretary of State for Wales, described Wilson as 'the most accomplished parliamentarian of them all ... a superb politician and a master of the debating forum' (Griffiths, 1969: 185; Ziegler, 1993: 162). Griffith's view was shared by Members of Parliament (MPs) on the other side of the House: William Whitelaw, Edward Heath's chief whip in the 1960s, also acknowledged Wilson's abilities, saying that 'People feared what he would do in Parliament and they were right to fear it. He was a very powerful parliamentary figure' (Hennessy, 1997: 246). Wilson consistently bested Heath in their confrontations across the dispatch box. John Campbell noted that, 'Time and again Heath, trying doggedly to make a serious point on some important issue would be tripped up by Wilson's lightening agility and clever use of ridicule' (Campbell, 1994: 193). Richard Crossman thought that Wilson was 'the master of parliamentary gamesmanship', so easily did he outmanoeuvre Heath (Crossman, 1976: 301). Heath's successor fared little better. Although Margaret Thatcher would later develop into a formidable parliamentary debater in her own right, she was consistently outclassed at Prime Minister's Questions (PMQs) by Wilson (Campbell, 2000: 352).

Wilson's first opponent after he became leader of the Labour Party was Macmillan. Macmillan had himself been an impressive parliamentary performer, but by 1963 was tired, dispirited and contemplating retirement. The parliamentary debate over the Profumo scandal in June 1963[1] offered Wilson and the Labour Party a chance to severely damage the Macmillan government and is an excellent example of Wilson's prowess in debate. Wilson opened the debate for Labour. He was careful to state that the question was not one of morals: rather he argued that by sharing a mistress with a Russian spy Profumo had endangered national security. Wilson's second line of attack was the conduct of government ministers: Macmillan had staunchly defended Profumo until it became clear the latter had lied to the House (Pimlott, 1993). As Wilson stated:

> What concerns us, also, is whether a man in a position of high trust, privy to the most secret information available to a Government, through a continuing association with this squalid network, imperilled our national security or created conditions in which a continuing risk to our security was allowed to remain: We are not here as a court of morals, though the nation as a whole cannot escape the responsibility so to act. But questions affecting national security, questions affecting the duty of Ministers to this House, must be pressed and probed today, and this debate, in one form or another,

must continue until the truth is known so far as it can ever be known. (HC Deb, 17 June 1963, vol. 679, cols 34–176)

Wilson also defended the Labour Party's conduct during the time the scandal was unfolding, stating that Labour had behaved in an honourable fashion and had refrained from leaking any embarrassing information to the press:

> We did not canvass or propagate rumours about personal conduct, but where security questions were raised, and, later, where there was a question of the inaccuracy of statements made in this House, we felt that we had a clear duty, and any other Opposition would have had that same duty. (HC Deb, 17 June 1963, vol. 679, cols. 34–176)

Wilson then tied the scandal to the decadence of some parts of society that had developed under the Conservatives. Remarking on newspaper reports that Keeler had been offered a £5,000 a week job as a nightclub 'hostess' he stated:

> I say to the Prime Minister that there is something utterly nauseating about a system of society which pays a harlot 25 times as much as it pays its Prime Minister, 250 times as much as it pays its Members of Parliament, and 500 times as much as it pays some of its ministers of religion. (HC Deb, 17 June 1963, vol. 679, cols. 34–176)

He concluded his speech by linking the Conservative Party to the privilege, corruption and immoral behaviour of a small minority who belonged to the past. The future would belong to the decent majority, who would be inspired by Labour's leadership. Having gone out of his way to state that the issue for debate was not one of personal morals, Wilson's conclusion suggests that morals were important after all: it was the ideological immorality of Conservatism and unfettered capitalism that were at fault for what the Profumo affair revealed about some sections of British society:

> What we are seeing is a diseased excrescence, a corrupted and poisoned appendix of a small and unrepresentative section of society that makes no contribution to what Britain is, still less to what Britain can be … The sickness of an unrepresentative sector of our society should not detract from the robust ability of our people as a whole to face the challenge of the future. And in preparing to face that challenge, let us frankly recognise that the inspiration and the leadership must come first here in this House. (HC Deb, 17 June 1963, vol. 679, cols. 34–176)

The speech was a devastating indictment of the government. When Macmillan rose to reply he was visibly shaken (Sandbrook, 2008: 662). Crossman wrote in his diary: 'Harold made an absolutely magnificent speech, the best I've ever heard him make, better than I thought possible. It was really annihilating, a classical prosecution speech, with weight and self control' (Morgan, 1981: 1001). In the short term the speech was judged to be a resounding success: Wilson came across as a serious, thoughtful politician and crucially a potential future prime minister (Ziegler, 1993: 146). In the long term the characterisation of the Conservative Party as a class ridden sectional party that was both obsolete and out of touch with modern meritocratic

Britain set the tone for Wilson's subsequent attacks in the run up to the 1964 general election and during the campaign itself.

Three years after Wilson's broadside against the Macmillan administration he rose to attack not the Conservatives, but other members of the labour movement – the leaders of the National Union of Seamen (NUS). In May 1966 the NUS went on strike in a dispute over pay and working hours: the claim amounted to a pay rise of 17 per cent, far above the government's 3.5 per cent target (Sandbrook, 2010). The strike threatened to severely impede British exports, the value of the pound came under intense pressure on foreign exchanges and the Bank of England had to intervene to maintain the currency's value. By June Wilson's patience with the NUS had run out. The strike he claimed was being run by a

> tightly knit group of politically motivated men who, as the last General Election showed, utterly failed to secure their views by the British electorate, but who are now prepared to exercise back-stage pressures, forcing great hardship on the members of the union and their families, and endangering the security of the industry and the economic welfare of the nation. (HC Deb, 20 June 1966, vol. 730, cols. 38–54)

Wilson's clear implication, although he did not say it, was that the 'politically motivated men' he referred to were Communists. As Pimlott points out Wilson accused individuals of intimidation, but did not name them and implied that the striking seamen were gullible dupes of the union leadership. In addition the speech 'suggested that "political motivation" was something to be ashamed of, as if political motivation had never entered the Prime Minister's head' (Pimlott, 1993: 407). The speech caused a great deal of disquiet within the parliamentary party. Tony Benn agreed with Peter Shaw that Wilson 'was completely bonkers' (Benn, 1988: 436). Ian Mikardo asked: 'Why shouldn't trade unionists be politically motivated?' (Ziegler, 1993: 251). A month later Frank Cousins resigned from the Cabinet and returned to his post as secretary of the Transport and General Workers' Union (TGWU) in protest over the government's incomes policy (Laybourn, 1992). The speech also damaged Wilson's reputation in the wider labour movement: trades union leaders who had previously reserved judgement on Wilson now regarded him with deep suspicion. Jack Jones later said that Wilson's standing with the union movement had been 'greatly weakened by his silly remarks' (Pimlott, 1993: 407–8). Wilson's reputation also fell with Labour members and sympathisers (Sandbrook, 2010).

Historians have noted that after Labour's defeat in the 1970 general election Wilson's oratorical skills seemed to wane, and that by the time he returned to power in 1974 he could no longer command the House in the same way as he could at the height of his powers and that he began to find PMQs much more stressful (Hennessy, 1997; Pimlott, 1993; Ziegler, 1993). Phillip Ziegler believes that Wilson's health was declining and, having seen off Edward Heath,[2] Wilson had lost much of his relish for politics (Ziegler, 1993). In Pimlott's words, 'Wading through the shit had taken its toll'. However, a study by Paul Garrard has suggested that during his second spell as prime minister Wilson may have been suffering with the early stages of Alzheimer's disease. Garrard analysed vocabulary trends in transcripts of Wilson's performances during PMQs throughout his two terms of office. The study looked at Wilson's speech patterns and the number of times he used certain words, and compared these to the speech of his fellow MPs. Garrard found that there were significant differences between the ways in which Wilson spoke compared to his parliamentary colleagues. However, these differences were much smaller during the months leading up to his resignation – a sign that he was losing his distinctive oratorical voice and a possible sign of the earliest stages of Alzheimer's (BBC, 2008a).

At the party conference

Alan Finlayson and James Martin argue that the leader's speech to the party conference should be seen as an attempt not only to 'influence news agendas and market the party to a national media audience' but also as an 'affirmation and reaffirmation of party culture and identity' (Finlayson and Martin, 2008: 448). Wilson's most famous conference speech was the leader's address he gave to the Labour Party conference at Scarborough in October 1963, in which he talked of the 'white heat of the scientific revolution'. The speech was Wilson's first distinctive contribution to Labour's strategy and linked the need for a science-led modernisation of British industry to state-led planning. However, Labour's interest in science as a political issue was not new, nor did it originate with Wilson (Fielding, 2007). The roots of 'white heat' lay in the reaction of Labour's leadership to the 1959 election defeat. This was believed to be a result of the growing affluence of British society, which had altered the political attitudes of crucial sections of the electorate. In particular, groups of affluent working-class voters were adopting middle-class values and abandoning Labour in favour of the Conservatives. Consequently, the party needed to change its message to the public and adopt a more aspirational tone (Fielding, 1995: 30–1). In 1960 Morgan Phillips, then Labour's General Secretary, wrote a policy document called *The State of the Party*, in which he linked Labour to science and modernisation. Phillips hoped that this would divert members from arguing over Clause IV and prove the party's contemporary relevance. The document was presented to the National Executive Committee (NEC) in July 1960 and was even debated at the party conference that year, although it was overlooked because of the row over unilateralism (Haseler, 1969). However, the document eventually evolved to become *Signposts for the Sixties* and then expanded to become a series of pamphlets, *Labour in the Sixties*, before finally forming the basis for the 1964 Labour election manifesto (Fielding, 2007).

Despite Labour's championing of the cause of science Wilson did not decide to use it as the major theme of his speech until the night before he was due to speak and then only at the suggestion of Marcia Williams (Pimlott, 1993). The speech he delivered the next day was an oratorical tour de force that linked planning, science and economic modernisation to socialism (Jones, 1996). Wilson's main argument was that an unfettered free market economy was not the most effective or equitable means of delivering technological and scientific innovation. Therefore a future Labour government would introduce economic and social planning to ensure that modernisation was both efficient and fair (Horner, 1995). The speech argued for better education and the end of selection, and for the need to train more scientists. These measures, Wilson promised, would help to establish a second industrial revolution creating millions of new jobs:

> Planning on an unprecedented scale to meet automation without unemployment; a pooling of talent in which all classes could compete and prosper; a vast expansion of state-sponsored research; a completely new concept of education; an alliance of science and socialism. (Ziegler, 1993: 143)

He concluded by saying:

> In all our plans for the future, we are re-defining and we are restating our socialism in terms of the scientific revolution. But that revolution cannot become a reality unless we are prepared to make far-reaching changes in economic and social attitudes which permeate our whole system of society.
>
> The Britain that is going to be forged in the white heat of this scientific revolution will be no place for restrictive practices on either side of industry … In the Cabinet room and the boardroom alike those charged with control of our affairs must be ready to think in the language of our scientific age.
>
> For the commanding heights of British industry to be controlled today by men whose only claim is their aristocratic connection or the power of inherited wealth or speculative finance is as irrelevant as would be the continued purchase of commissions in the armed forces by lordly amateurs. (Quoted in Pimlott, 1993: 304)

The forty-five minute speech kept the Labour delegates, a potentially difficult audience, spellbound (Ziegler, 1993). Crossman noted in his diary that Wilson 'spoke beautifully, completely collectively carrying the whole conference with him' and that Scarborough was 'The most successful Labour Conference I've attended' (quoted in Morgan, 1981: 1025–6). Crossman also understood the significance of the speech for the Labour Party, noting how it allowed the party to move on from the factional feuding that had marked the Gaitskell years:

> In fact of course he had provided a revision of socialism and its application to modern times which Gaitskell and Crosland had tried and completely failed to do. Harold had achieved it. (Quoted in Morgan, 1981: 1026)

'White heat' was greeted with rapturous approval by both the left and the right of the party. The Gaitskellite *Socialist Commentary* argued that Wilson had 'struck the essential theme of the times' (Coopey *et al.*: 1–9) and appealed to the wider electorate 'in terms capable of gripping the imagination'. Similarly the Bevanite *Tribune* thought the speech was 'an historic utterance which established Labour unchallenged as the Party of Britain's destiny' (Fielding, 1995: 29). The speech not only gave Labour an idea around which they could unite, but also attacked the Conservatives for being unwilling and unable to modernise Britain as they acted in the interests of those who made money through financial speculation, rather than through hard work. Wilson's characterisation of British boardrooms being controlled by those with aristocratic connections and worldly wealth drew clear parallels with Macmillan's Conservative Party that was in the process of choosing a fourteenth earl as its next leader (Fielding, 2007).

At the same time the speech 'bypassed rather than resolved ideological arguments that had long divided the party' (Ponting, 1989: 11). In Tudor Jones' words:

> Wilson's approach to ideological revision by means of the flexible concept of the scientific revolution was both indirect and highly ambiguous, designed to convert Labour into Britain's natural party of government without openly breaking with its traditional aims and symbols. (Jones, 1996: 85)

Nevertheless, the Labour-supporting *Daily Herald* argued that the speech showed that Wilson 'will not just be a good Prime Minister, he may well be a great one' (Ziegler, 1993: 144). Even *The Times* praised the speech, noting that Wilson had 'firmly denied his rank and file revolutionary socialism but has shown them another revolution they cannot escape' (*The Times*, 1963). This view was echoed, although as criticism rather than praise, by a few on the left. David Coates argued that the speech redefined socialists, not by their opposition to capitalism, but rather as professional technocrats opposed to the amateurism of the Conservatives (Coates, 1975).

Despite the misgivings of a few, there is no doubt that the speech was in the short term a triumph both for Wilson and for the Labour Party. Not only had the speech enthused the party and helped it bury its old differences over Clause IV and unilateralism, but it had revised the party's ethos and so appealed to a swathe of the electorate who were offered a vision of a dramatic rise in their prospects and living standards under a Wilson administration (Dell, 2000). Moreover, it set the tone for Labour's successful 1964 general election campaign, during which the party aligned itself to the cause of 'modernisation' and to the needs of the affluent society (Fielding, 2007: 321). However, looked at in the longer term 'white heat' should serve as a warning to politicians about the dangers that lofty rhetoric can pose to their reputation. 'White heat' led both Labour members and the wider electorate to expect far more than a government, operating in the economic context of the mid-1960s, could deliver. Productivity, gross domestic product (GDP) and annual growth all rose between 1964 and 1970 and compare favourably to other post-war administrations. Nonetheless, these gains still lagged behind France and Germany and were nowhere near the targets Labour had publicly set for itself (O'Hara, 2006). Consequently, just as Wilson's character has been criticised, so too the Labour governments of 1964–1970 have not been remembered kindly and have become a byword for 'failure and demoralisation, broken promises and dashed hopes, not just for Labourites, but for a large section of the wider population' (Thorpe, 2001: 145). A second problem was that because 'white heat' only suppressed, rather than cured, Labour's doctrinal and policy disputes, 'those internal strains and the deeper doctrinal tensions underlying them, resurfaced, sharply and divisively, during the 1970s and early 1980s' (Jones, 1996: 86–7).

Public appearances and the media

Wilson was just as comfortable speaking at a public meeting as he was speaking in Parliament or to conference. In the days before such events became tightly controlled and open only to party members, Wilson was a master at dealing with hecklers. Indeed he often used to encourage heckling, which he used to feed his quick wit. At one election meeting at the Glasgow Playhouse Wilson responded to heckling by delivering 'fifteen minutes of pure music hall farce'. Wilson said afterwards that though the meeting was a success, the speech had been poor: 'It was the heckling and the reaction that made it' (Howard and West, 1965: 183). Because short clips of these public meetings were often shown on the evening television news, public meetings informed the perceptions of a much wider audience: Wilson's performances at these events therefore had an important role in enhancing Labour's electoral appeal. Wilson's style contrasted well with that of Conservative leader, Sir Alec Douglas-Home, who was very poor at dealing with heckling, which easily threw him out of his stride leaving him unable to react quickly enough to regain control of the situation (Dutton, 2006).

In January 1964, Wilson began a speaking tour of the country and his speeches were collected into a volume entitled *The New Britain: Labour's Plan Outlined by Harold Wilson*. These continued and developed the themes that Wilson first outlined in his 'white heat' speech. The first and last speeches were general overviews of Britain in the 1960s, the other seven were on specific areas of policy such as housing and foreign policy. On his first engagement at Birmingham Town Hall he talked of Labour's aspiration to create a new Britain and began to build on the ideas outlined in Scarborough the previous year. Wilson argued that the country was 'living in the jet-age but we are governed by an Edwardian establishment mentality' (Wilson, 1964: 10). The 1964 election offered the British people:

> A chance for change … A chance to sweep away the grouse-moor conception of Tory leadership and refit Britain with a new image, a new confidence. A chance to change the face and future of Britain. (Wilson, 1964: 10)

On his final engagement four months later in London Wilson talked about 'Our National Purpose', promising Labour would revitalise the nation's economic and social purpose and restore Britain's standing in the rest of the world (Wilson, 1964: 125–32). The tour was a great success for Wilson who had 'established himself in the public eye as a serious reformer with a fluent knowledge of economics, housing and education' (Howard and West, 1965: 123). Throughout his tour Wilson emphasised the theme of modernisation, of both the economy and of political institutions, and argued that it was only Labour that could achieve these aims as the Conservatives were still stuck in the past. In another attempt to portray himself as a forceful moderniser he made a conscious effort to imitate J.F. Kennedy and promised voters his government would embark on 'one hundred days of dynamic action' (Hennessy, 2000: 287). The overall message was well received by the electorate, in part because of the growing perception of decline and the realisation that Britain was being outperformed by its economic competitors (Ponting, 1989). Nonetheless, it should be said that Wilson could have his 'off days'. For example, his performance at the opening event of Labour's 1964 election campaign was somewhat underwhelming as 'he lacked the basic material of a good orator: a good text' (Howard and West, 1965: 143).

Whilst public meetings were still an important form of political communication, television was rapidly growing in importance. Wilson understood that television allowed him to bypass the largely Conservative supporting press and speak directly to the electorate (Ziegler, 1993). However, Wilson was not as comfortable with the calmer atmosphere of a television studio as he was with the rough and tumble of Parliament and public meetings. Nevertheless, he managed to adapt and discovered a way to counter Robin Day's aggressive interview style, by using Day's Christian name. By calling him 'Robin' Wilson created the impression that he and Day were really friends, making the interview seem less confrontational (Atkinson, 1984). Another device Wilson used successfully when faced with an awkward question was to pretend his pipe had gone out and relight it, this enabled him to 'blot out his interrogator, buy time for thought *and* distract the viewer while appearing human, folksy and reassuring' (Hennessy, 2000: 330). Wilson's first appearance on television was in the United States where he was interviewed on *See It Now* by Ed Murrow.[3] Opinion about the broadcast was mixed: Phillips thought it was the worst political programme ever made, whilst William Pickles from the London School of Economics (LSE) thought it was the best he had seen (Ziegler, 1993).

During his appearance on the BBC's 1964 *Election Forum* Wilson seemed to be more concerned with avoiding gaffes than with making a positive impression (Howard and West, 1965: 160). Nonetheless, a study by Jay Blumler and Denis McQuail (1968) into the impact of television on the 1964 election campaign found that Wilson was the overall favourite with the public before the campaign began and his public image improved further during the campaign itself, especially in the areas of inspiration, confidence, strength and persuasiveness. On the negative side an increasing number of voters began to see Wilson as conceited (Blumler and McQuail, 1968). Wilson's perceived conceit led the satirical television programme *That Was The Week That Was* to characterise the 1964 election contest as being between 'Smart Alec and Dull Alec' (Dutton, 2006: 66). By the time of the 1966 general election 90 per cent of homes were equipped with television, giving the medium nearly as much coverage as radio. Wilson was by now more comfortable with television as a campaign medium and appeared in two of Labour's election broadcasts. He wrote his own scripts and spoke from behind an imposing desk. He tried to avoid appearing partisan and instead project a statesmanlike image: in his broadcasts he mentioned 'Britain' forty-two times, 'government' thirty-nine times, however he never used the word 'Labour' (Harrison, 1966).

In July 1966, just four months after Labour's landslide election victory Wilson made another broadcast to the nation, this time on the fragile state of the British economy. In 1964 Labour had inherited a serious balance of payments deficit from the outgoing Conservative administration, which threatened the value of the pound. One option was immediate devaluation, but Wilson, consulting with senior colleagues, decided to avoid devaluation: partly to avoid the accusation that Labour was the party of devaluation and partly because it was believed that Labour's industrial and economic policies would make devaluation unnecessary (Dell, 2000). However, Wilson's government never really took control of the economy and as a result it was always at the mercy of domestic and international events (Morgan, 1987). Consequently, by July 1966 the pound was once more under severe pressure and Wilson was hamstrung by a promise he made to President Johnson to maintain the value of sterling in return for a large loan from the United States. Therefore, rather than devalue the pound, the government introduced a deflationary package of cuts, higher taxes and exchange controls (Woodward, 1997). Wilson went on television to announce the measures to the nation and concluded by saying that:

> We are under attack. This is your country and our country. We must work for it ... One thing the crisis has done, it has focused the eyes of the world upon us. This is our chance to show them what we are made of. (Sandbrook, 2006: 297)

Wilson's oratorical style for this broadcast has been likened to that of Winston Churchill, conjuring up an image of 'plucky little Britain' standing alone in a hostile world (Sandbrook, 2008: 296). However, sixteen months later Wilson's government was finally forced to bow to the inevitable and devalue the pound. Although Wilson had fought against devaluation since taking office in 1964, many historians now think it was a mistake not to devalue sooner: either immediately after taking office in 1964, or during the crisis of July 1966 (Marquand, 1999; Pimlott, 1993; Woodward, 1997).

Wilson announced the devaluation (from $1.80 to $1.40) at 9.30 p.m. on Sunday 19 November 1967. The announcement was timed so that the Sunday papers would not be able to report the story. However, the broadcast was a public relations disaster for Wilson and for Labour. Wilson's tone suggested that devaluation was a great victory, rather than an economic humiliation (Pimlott, 1993). *The Times* reported that viewers would have needed 'an extremely sharp ear to catch any hint of embarrassment as he explained why the government were now doing what until last month they regarded as heresy' (*The Times*, 1967). Wilson's friends were also aghast. Castle thought that Wilson's optimism had clouded his judgement and that there was 'a feeling abroad that he was too complacent by half' (Sandbrook, 2010: 431). However, the part of Wilson's broadcast that was most damaging was when he tried to explain the impact of devaluation on the electorate. He explained that imported goods would now be more expensive, but then went on to say that:

> From now the pound is worth 14 per cent or so less in terms of other currencies. That does not mean, of course that the pound here in Britain, in your pocket or purse or in your bank, has been devalued. What it does mean is that we shall now be able to sell more goods abroad on a competitive basis ... We must take with both hands the opportunity that has now been presented to us. (Quoted in Sandbrook, 2010: 431)

In Wilson's memoirs he complains, with some justification, that the phrase 'pound in your pocket' was used out of context, first by Heath and then by the press (Wilson, 1971). However, as Pimlott notes, 'Political catch-phrases plucked from the myriad words uttered by a public figure, stand as symbols' (Pimlott, 1993: 484). The speech became a symbol for everything the electorate disliked about Wilson and cemented his reputation for being devious and untrustworthy (Hennessy, 1997). Labour ratings in the opinion polls plunged after the broadcast and by December 1967 only 21 per cent of the electorate approved of the government's record, whilst 64 per cent disapproved. The Conservative lead over Labour climbed from 8 per cent in October 1967 to 18.5 per cent in December (Sandbrook, 2010).

Conclusion

Wilson believed that the party leader had to 'represent the whole party and to work with all sections' (Hennessy, 1997: 248). For this reason he tried to avoid being identified with any faction: the purpose of his oratory was therefore, first, for keeping the Labour Party united and, second, for making it the party of government. There is no doubt that Wilson was, especially between 1963 and 1970, a first-class orator, who could stir the emotions and fire the imagination of his audience. He was especially at home in Parliament, or in public meetings, where the fluidity of the situation required him to think on his feet in order to deal with interruptions and hecklers. At his best he was 'warm, knowledgeable and in touch with country' (Howard and West, 1965: 150). Wilson's oratory was inextricably entwined with his leadership style: references to 'one hundred days', whilst designed to mirror the dynamism of the Kennedy administration, also reinforced this perception of a highly personal style of government (Morgan, 1987: 256). Thus, both the successes and the failures of the 1964–1970 government were associated with Wilson personally and people compared their circumstances with what Wilson promised in his rhetoric and these comparisons were often unfavourable.

His oratorical style was also conditioned by his personality or, as Kenneth Morgan notes, his multiple personalities all competing for prominence:

> There was Dunkirk Harold in Churchillian garb, white-coated Harold caught in the white heat of the technological revolution, Walter Mitty Harold about to amaze the world with deeds that would be the terror of the earth, even World Cup Harold, appealing to popular razzmatazz, with mood as a substitute for achievement. (Morgan, 1987: 259)

Wilson's oratory was often in the romantic style and he used pathos to appeal to his audience's emotion: perhaps this should not surprise us given the characterisation, by some senior Labour politicians, of Wilson as 'Walter Mitty'. For example Wilson's speech to the Scarborough conference abounds with pathos and romantic imagery with its talk of a 'revolution in education', the establishment of a 'University of the Air' and of course the famous 'white heat' metaphor. However, Wilson did not just play to the emotions of conference, he also captured the zeitgeist of the early 1960s. 'White heat' therefore belongs with that select group of speeches such as Macmillan's 'wind of change' and Kennedy's 'ask not what your country can do for you' that Finlayson and Martin argue 'simultaneously reflected a moment and created it, giving shape to sentiments and naming a moment' (2008: 453). Consequently the speech established Wilson's ethos as a heavyweight politician who could unite the Labour Party and lead it to victory.

Wilson was capable of using different styles of oratory, depending on the audience to whom he was speaking and the subject of his speech, and was also capable of mixing the realist and romantic oratory in the same speech, as his speech on the Profumo affair demonstrates: he first used logos to build a case against the Conservatives; he deployed facts to show how the Labour Party had conducted itself competently and honourably, in contrast to the government's incompetent and duplicitous handling of the scandal. This also enabled Wilson to establish his ethos, at the expense of Macmillan, and to establish himself as an alternative prime minister and Labour as a credible alternative party of government. Nevertheless, Wilson then concluded his speech by switching to the romantic style and using pathos, in his use of the phrase 'diseased excrescence', to describe the Macmillan government and in putting forward himself and his party, together with the hard-working, decent people of Britain, as the future salvation of the nation.

Wilson deployed much of his best oratory, in this period, to attack the Conservatives. Unlike his predecessor Hugh Gaitskell, Wilson seldom used his oratory to attack his own side. Perhaps the most notable example was his speech to Parliament over the seamen's strike, for which he was roundly condemned by many within his own party. Wilson again employed pathos, making the implication that the strikers were being led by Communists who were determined to damage the national interest. Nevertheless, this assertion was not backed up by logos, at the time Wilson provided no evidence to reinforce his claim,[4] and for this he was roundly criticised by people on his own side.

The seamen's strike speech perhaps marks a change in Wilson's oratory. Once Labour took power, it was no longer enough for Wilson to attack the Conservatives and set out romantic visions of how life would improve under Labour. The realities of governing now compelled Wilson to explain and to defend the actions of his government to the electorate. This often took the form of broadcasts on television and although Wilson became a sound television performer, he was never as comfortable in a TV studio as he was speaking to a live audience. Television broadcasts were mainly realist in nature as Wilson deployed logos to outline the economic problems facing Britain, however he could also use pathos to try and win public support as in his 'Churchillian' broadcast on the July 1966 economic crisis, where he tried to reawaken Britain's wartime spirit and resolve. Nonetheless, perhaps the most memorable and most significant of Wilson's television appearances was his 1967 broadcast on devaluation, when he produced the infamous 'the pound in your pocket' sound bite. Again Wilson deployed logos to explain the implications of devaluation to the electorate: that the pound would be worth less when compared to other currencies and that imported goods would be more expensive as a consequence. However the denial that 'the pound here in Britain, in your pocket or purse or in your bank, has been devalued' proved highly damaging, as it undermined Wilson's ethos and helped reinforce his growing reputation with the electorate for being devious and untrustworthy.

The great irony, therefore, was that Wilson's oratory and his use of oratorical devices went a considerable way to both making and breaking his standing, both with the electorate and with his own party.

Notes

1 War Secretary John Profumo had been having an affair with Christine Keeler, who was also involved with Yevgeny Ivanov, the naval attaché at the Soviet Embassy. Profumo denied the affair in the Commons, but was shown to have lied and was forced to resign.

2 Heath had been Wilson's main adversary from 1965 until Heath was deposed by Margaret Thatcher in 1975: Wilson never got the same enjoyment from debating with Thatcher as he did with Heath.

3 Murrow came to prominence broadcasting for CBS Radio from London during the Blitz. He moved to television in 1951 on *See It Now*. This was a current affairs show, perhaps most famous for undermining the career of Senator Joseph McCarthy.

4 He returned to Parliament the following week and named names.

The oratory of Barbara Castle

David S. Moon

Introduction: 'battling' Barbara

Reporting on Tony Blair's speech to the 1999 Confederation of British Industry (CBI) conference, *Guardian* sketch writer Simon Hoggart (1999) gave a typically snarky description of the speechifying of the then prime minister, or as he called him, 'our very own Big Brother':

> The Big Brother smiles a lot in a self deprecating kind of way. He uses 'um' and 'well' as a rhetorical device, to convince us he's not reading out a prepared text, but needs to pause to work out exactly what he means. There is a prepared text of course but he adds to it phrases such as 'I really think' and 'you know I really have to tell you' and 'in my view'. (Hoggart, 1999)

This, Hoggart decided, was more than a peculiar quirk of Blair, and was symbolic of something which went much further:

> This is the new oratory. The old politicians told us they were right, and that there was no room for doubt, the new politician is not telling us truths, but selling us himself … His message is that you should take him on trust; you should believe him because you love him. (Hoggart, 1999)

Barbara Castle had an oratorical style quite foreign to the 'new oratory'; she was, rather, paradigmatic of the 'old politician' identified by Hoggart. As this chapter's analysis shows, Castle was a politician who believed firmly in arguing her case even in the face of fierce opposition, revelling in the fight and unafraid to state 'hard truths' to her audience, whoever they might be. Indeed, when in later years she took to the public stage to castigate the Blair government over pensions 'her quick wit and uncompromising style' was embraced by the public as 'a refreshing change from the inoffensive, conciliating manner of the new generation of politicians' (Perkins, 2003: 449).

Drawing upon the classic concepts of ethos, pathos and logos and studying examples from the three arenas of Parliament, conference and communication with the electorate, this analysis paints a particular picture of Castle. It argues that to understand her oratory it is important to also grasp her personal belief, as the title of her autobiography put it, in 'fighting all the way' (Castle, 1993). This is the figure of 'Battling Barbara'

(Martineau, 2011: 238), the Labour Party's most famous and celebrated female orator since its inception and one of its best orators full stop (Perkins, 2003).

'Fiery redhead'

Reflecting upon the oratory of Aneurin Bevan, Castle described how she had 'often watched in despair as, carried away by the intoxication of his own power over words, he threw away the chance to influence more timid souls and strained the loyalty of his friends' (1997: 36). Castle herself had an undoubted love for her own oratorical skills also, yet, arguably more than Bevan with his predilection to posture at key moments, she recognised that the primary function of oratory was functional. Beyond the rhapsodic, her rhetoric was purposefully aimed to score palpable hits within the battle of ideas – where words and argument are the only legitimate weapons – through which democratic socialist ends can only be won. Her love of words and her ferocious ability to wield them was inexorably linked to a love of this conflict, to a fidelity to the righteous cause of socialism, and an inherent belief in the power of her own arguments to convince. There was undoubtedly a personal aspect, or more precisely an aspect of personality, at play here – both in her hunger for argument and her argumentative style.

At school the young Barbara performed in plays and was a representative at inter-school compositions in prose and poetry recitals. Used to arguments with her politically active father and his friends in the Independent Labour Party (ILP), she was normally the only girl to speak in her sixth-form class debates, finding the contributions of the other girls – when they did contribute – frustratingly amateurish (Martineau, 2011). These early experiences with thespian and deliberative performance imparted valuable training in diction and projection and 'a natural flair for the dramatic', which would be vital to Castle as she 'learnt to hold and entice a sceptical, indifferent or barracking audience the hard way, on the street corners of the north' (Perkins, 2003: 73, 33).

At the heart of her oratory, however, was a sense of personal passion. This passion was well echoed in her portrayal by Miranda Richardson in the film *Made in Dagenham*, which tells the story of the 1968 Ford sewing machinists' strike and the battle for equal pay. In one memorable scene Richardson, as Castle, delivers the following speech to her incompetent civil servants in the Ministry of Labour:

> I am what is known as a fiery redhead. Now, I hate to make this a matter of appearance and go all womanly on you, but there you have it, and me standing up like this is in fact just that redheaded fieriness leaping to the fore. *Credence*? I will give *credence* to their cause? *MY GOD! Their cause already has credence!* It is *equal pay*, equal pay is *common justice* and if you two weren't such a pair of egotistical, chauvinistic, bigoted dunderheads you would realise that![1]

The trope of the 'fiery redhead', as invoked here, is a classic convention in screen writing, described by the wiki *TV Tropes* thus:

A Fiery Redhead is a red-haired character who is strong, passionate, outgoing, usually outspoken, and almost always female. She has a big personality and she's not afraid to use it. Whatever you do, don't get on her bad side, or there will be hell to pay.[2]

Undoubtedly worn though such a stock portrayal may be, by the logic of filmic verisimilitude, such scripting only works if the audience perceives a general truth within it. Certainly Richardson's ferocious performance fits the auburn-haired Castle of public imagination, the woman for whom '[t]here was scarcely an article written that did not portray her as a fiery redhead, or the red-haired conscience of the Labour Party; Red Barbara, like Red Ellen before her, red in hair and spirit' (Martineau, 2011: 123). She has, to this effect, been called 'the scarlet termagant' (Martineau, 2011: 350) and 'Labour's Red Queen' (Perkins, 2003); the *Shropshire Star* called her a 'Tigress with red hair' (6 September 1966, quoted in Martineau, 2011: 181), while amongst her compatriots, Richard Crossman bestowed upon her the title of the Labour movement's 'redhead' (Crossman, 1979: 483).

If Castle was, indeed, red in spirit as well as barnet this was not due simply to her socialism (which was, to the end, of a particularly red hue) but to a passionate temperament alluded to above. She is described, thus, at the height of her power, as a woman of remarkable energy who 'liked the volume at full blast', 'liked engagement' and 'came at everything with gusto'; as someone who 'roared ... hummed ... bristled with intensity' and was 'lustily ravenous for life, operating at her best at this high voltage and in the starring role' (Martineau, 2011: 131). By her own description she 'always admired passion in politics' (Castle, 1993: 192), a passion linked to a political 'love of combat': 'Barbara revelled in confrontation' states David Owen (1992: 237), who worked under Castle at the Ministry of Health; 'When it came, her adrenalin pumped round and she saw everything in terms of a battle that had to be won'. Described as liking 'the razor's edge', hers was a personal style, which, tied to a 'conviction of her own worth as an equal to men', made her 'the feared Amazon incarnate' (Martineau, 2011: 15–16) who would – so Ian Mikardo (1988: 189) related – throw 'clanging barrages of Amazonian bellicosity' at any who stood against her.

The 'Amazonian' portrayal was there too in Michael Foot's mock description of Castle's self-portrayal in her diaries as 'sometimes as [that of] Joan of Arc facing (and confounding) her inquisitors, sometimes almost as a new Queen Elizabeth at Tilbury,[3] rousing the troops and her country-men as no one else could do' (Foot, 1986: 47). Foot's choice of two redheaded female leaders in circumstances of conflict to describe his close friend was clearly deliberate: it also provides the perfect figurative embodiment(s) of that linkage between the personal and the political – between 'Red Barbara' and 'Battling Barbara' – which is so vital to understand Castle's oratorical style. For Castle, a personal passion for democratic socialist politics was aligned to a love of combat and a belief, both in her own ability and self-worth as a woman amongst men, and in the power of her arguments to rally and convince.

Follicly based as they so often were,[4] with each description of these sorts her position as a high profile, strong, forthright woman in a political world still dominated by men was arguably reinforced. This was a clearly frightening prospect for many of the latter and the repetitive reliance upon the 'redheaded' depiction should not be necessarily treated as a sign of admiration by those who conveyed it upon her: as Sarah Childs (2008: 141) describes, one of the 'five lurid shades' by which women politicians are symbolically represented in a gendered fashion is the 'terrifying termagant' ('but don't you just love a flame-haired hand-bagging?'), a portrayal she explicitly linked to that of Castle and Margaret Thatcher. The role of gender is key to understanding Castle's oratory and is discussed in detail below. At this point, however, the trope of the 'fiery redhead' is important to note simply in so far as it spoke to a genuine facet of Castle's personality, being indicative of the structuring girders which underlay her oratorical style and provided the basis of her favourite guiding maxim that, in politics, 'guts is all' (see Owen, 1992: 240).

'Rabble rouser'

It is understandable, recognising the above, that appeals to pathos were fundamental to Castle's rhetoric, whether speaking to the party, the public or in the Houses of Parliament. At heart Castle was a platform speaker who, in the early phase of her political career, regularly toured the country talking publicly: whether partnering with Foot in the 1930s with *Socialist League* – where together 'they would regale the downtrodden crowd with socialist possibilities' (quoted in Martineau, 2011: 36) – or as part of the *Tribune* 'Brains Trusts' public meetings in the 1950s – where, as part of a panel with fellow Bevanites such as Crossman, Harold Wilson, Jennie Lee and Bevan himself, she would battle it out in front of overflowing halls (Martineau, 2011: 108). It was through such encounters, being forced to think on her feet in the midst of argument and tailor her rhetoric to win over the crowd, that she honed the oratorical skills which underlay her particular brand of 'rabble rousing speeches' with which she would come to delight party members and supporters (Assinder, 2002).

Added to this was Castle's stage presence, of which she was greatly aware. As Lisa Martineau (2011: 33–4) describes:

> She had, and continued to have in old age, a big voice on stage, a boombox voice, rich, resonant, seemingly coming out of all sides of her, much bigger than her diminutive stature might suggest and very different from her ordinary speaking voice, which some people found grating, even shrill. And she had the X factors, star quality, charisma; the sheer force of her personality filled the stage. The words gushed out of her, wave upon wave … Barbara could feel an audience, massage it, manipulate it, cajole it.

She was indeed, as Paul Foot described, 'a tremendously inspiring speaker' who could address an audience with wit, passion and irony (Martineau, 2011: 2). As late as 1992 Castle was providing rousing speeches when, during the general election of that year her job was, as she described it:

> to wind up the proceedings with a clarion call to the faithful sitting in the ticket-only audience. I enjoyed myself, making the same punchy hard-hitting speech I would have made to a street-corner meeting in Blackburn in my earlier days. The audience rose to it, delighted to hear something unconstrained. (Castle, 1993: 584)

Part of this presence was physical. Though small in size and speaking amid pouring rain, footage from the 85th Durham Miner's Gala in 1968 shows Castle addressing her audience forcefully, her left hand held up in front of herself, balled in a fist, as with each point made she jabbed it forwards sharply in emphasis, as if to hammer home each of her points (see BBC, 1969): 'You are not the ones who theorise about the need for change in Britain' she told the crowd in a piercing voice: 'You are the ones who have to experience it. Because comrades, Britain must adapt herself, in the age of industrial change ... By definition the Labour party *is* the party of fundamental change'.

Rhetorically, she often articulated a partisan, righteous anger. For example, speaking publicly in 1966 at Sunderland Town Hall, she colourfully lamented the fact of the previous Conservative administration, since 'If only we had had a Labour Government in those 13 wasted years, we shouldn't be faced with the appalling congestion and casualties on our roads, and the traffic chaos in our towns we have today' (Castle, 1996a). The previous Minister of Transport, she attacked, for preferring 'the arid dogma of competition between road and rail which destroyed all hope of co-ordination, robbed the railways of some of their most lucrative traffic, pushed up their deficit and cumbered our roads with freight which ought to have gone by rail' (Castle, 1966a). 'Wasted', 'appalling', 'chaos', 'arid', destroyed', 'robbed', 'cumbered' – Castle was the queen of emotionally charged rhetoric and examples of rallying pathos are not hard to find in her public speeches.

Indeed, perhaps her most famous quotation – and oddly her only oratorical example in the *Dictionary of Labour Quotations* (Thomson, 1999)[5] – was emblematic of this. At the 1943 party conference, the then 32-year-old Barbara Betts took to the platform to defend the importance of the implementation of the Beveridge Report. There, drawing upon Lewis Carroll, she ascribed to the right-wing secretary of the TGWU, Arthur Deakin, the role of the White Queen who offers Alice 'jam tomorrow and jam yesterday':

> We of the rank and file ... say to the Trade Union Movement that this Beveridge issue is as axiomatic to us as the Trade Disputes Act is to them ... jam yesterday, jam tomorrow, but never jam today – that is what the government is trying to say to the people, but we want jam today! (Quoted in Perkins, 2003: 72)

This sound bite put her on the front page of the *Daily Mirror*, the most popular paper in the country. She was 'a seductive platform orator – one of the darlings of the party conference' (Marquand, 2008: 212) and it was passionate oratory of this kind, wedded to her solid left-wing politics, which meant Castle quickly became the darling of the grassroots on the National Executive Committee (NEC). In fact much of her stature within the movement came from her oratory on the conference platform, most notably her 1959 chairman's address to the Labour Party conference.

Case-study: the 1959 conference

The 1959 speech was perhaps the most powerful single oration of Castle's career. She opened strongly, telling the assembled membership: 'Last year we met in the bright hope of victory. This year we meet in the shadow of electoral defeat' and that the conference was therefore, 'in the real sense of that much abused word, an "historic" conference, for the lessons we learn from our defeat may well decide the future of social democracy, not only in this country, but the whole world' (Castle, 1959: 83). Her speech was an intervention, in the fullest sense of the term, in the debate to decide what exactly those lessons would be. Castle, therefore, through a combination of ethos, pathos and logos, attacked the policy of the Gaitskellite 'Radicals' – as she framed it – 'to abandon the attempt to take over any more industries and to use public ownership merely to ensure that the community gets a cut of the capitalist cake'. She did so on the grounds that 'it would lead us slap-bang into fallacy. That fallacy is the belief that you can separate moral issues from economic ones' (Castle, 1959: 84).

She castigated, in emotive language, a contemporary British society where '[t]he highest virtue lies in looking after No. 1 and the greatest merit is being strong enough to do it', where '[e]conomic might has become social right and the Devil has taken the communal interest' (Castle, 1959: 85). In these circumstances it was, she stated, 'chasing fantasies to imagine that we can win elections on moral issues in a democracy built on such amoral [economic] foundations' since '[a]s long as our economy depends on large accumulations of private capital, it *needs* inequality to make it work. This is the only way it can be financed and no amount of tinkering with taxation can alter it; indeed, if it did, the system would break down!' (Castle, 1959: 178).

By attacking the logos of the Gaikskellite argument, not only on economic rationale but moral also, Castle launched a withering attack upon their ethos as social reformers, summing up in her conclusion that 'Radicalism without socialism is an also-ran', noting that, after all, '[i]n a materialist society, the Tories can always beat us in an appeal to selfishness' (Castle, 1959: 180). Her answer, by contrast, was an emphatically socialist policy programme based upon extending public ownership; it was up to the party to 'convince the people of this country that they – and not a few private interests – should control their economic lives' or else they would 'shrink into an impotent appendage of the windfall state' (Castle, 1959: 180) – a phallic metaphor aimed at opponents' ethos as men (and they were almost entirely men) of strong character. In contrast to such impotence, she projected the vitality of public ownership: 'No, comrades', she told them, 'it simply won't wash to say that national-isation is fusty and out-of-date' when in actuality '[w]e can no more win the battle of nuclear power, electronics and automation on the principles of *laissez-faire* than we could have won the last war on the same principles. Nor can we win the battle against world poverty or the fight for peace' (Castle, 1959: 86). Here again was evi-dence of pathos tied to logos, as Castle's noted love of conflict found material expres-sion in her rhetoric, founded upon metaphors of combat and analogies with war.

All of this came to a head in the closing section of her speech when, having laid out the case against the Gaitskellites and for public ownership, she asked the conference:

> Do we believe that our moral aims can only be achieved by economic means? Are we prepared to affirm therefore that what Nye has called 'the commanding heights of the economy' must be publicly financed and under public control? And if so, do we agree that public ownership, either of whole industries or of key parts of them, is the most direct and effective way to bring this about? Do we believe that publicly owned indus-tries should be answerable to the public through Parliament? Let us get these basic points clear. (Castle, 1959)

This was an argument of logos, expressed in technical terms through an effective linking of *anaphora* to *psyma*, and helped by its linkage to Bevan's ethos. By repeat-edly confronting members with the question 'do we believe?'/'do we agree?', and presenting the question, each time, as essentially rhetorical as far as Labour's ideo-logical ends were concerned, Castle sought to interpellate her audience, framing her position as the strongest from the movement's perspective (see Althusser, 2008). She sought to reinforce this interpretation with the declaration, steeped in pathos and appeals to socialist ethos, that if Labour members had 'the courage and vigour of mind to do so', then they could 'come out of this defeat clearer in vision and stronger in purpose than ever before'. Returning to the rhetoric of conflict, she announced that Labour had 'won the first phase of our historical battle', telling members they must 'equip ourselves now for the second phase' by adopting her proposed policy approach, naturally – an act which would 'demand of us the highest qualities of mind and spirit' (Althusser, 2008: 28).

As shown, in these few sentences – 'her voice breaking with emotion' (Hunter, 1959: 135) – Castle called upon a rhetoric making appeals of logos, pathos and ethos to rally the Labour movement to magisterial effect. Crossman would describe it as 'the most powerful speech of the conference' which 'stole the show' and Bevan as 'the best chairman's speech I heard' (quoted in Perkins, 2003: 164–5). The *Sunday Dispatch* described it as 'an immensely powerful speech', claiming Castle carried a 'fearsome array of six-shooters' and that '[n]ot another woman in politics wields even a sharp hatpin by comparison' (quoted in Martineau, 2011: 148). She herself called it 'one of the major successes of my career' (Castle, 1993: 317).

'Making socialists'

Oddly though, for all such successes, Castle was seemingly never truly confident as a speaker at conference. Describing her speech at the 1967 conference almost a decade later, Castle (1990: 151) would thus write of how she 'got myself pretty keyed up' about it beforehand and, sitting down afterwards, 'thought it just adequate and was surprised at the applause'. Later she deemed this now half-forgotten speech on transport to have been 'a better speech than I have ever done at conference before' and her 'great breakthrough, conference-wise' at which she was 'immensely relieved'. Her audience would no doubt have been surprised to hear this. As late as 1974 Castle would write of how her speech at conference 'was received politely but tepidly', mulling that 'I am nonplussed by my continuing failure to get over in conference' and wondering if '[p]erhaps it is the blasted mikes are too high for me. Whatever the reason, I left conference feeling depressed' (Castle, 1990: 528). In 1975, again, she '[a]s usual ... tensed up in quite an absurd way' before speaking: 'No one will ever believe', she wrote, 'that all my life I have been cursed with this lack of self-confidence, which only disappears in certain circumstances and before certain audiences' (Castle, 1990: 653).

Issues of self-confidence no doubt increased with her transition from backbench rabble-rouser to First Minister of Her Majesty's Government under Wilson. Castle's personal standing was, as discussed, closely tied to her position as a left-wing firebrand and role as self-defined conscience of the party (as played to in the 1959 example). The danger in entering government was that she would find herself unable to call upon the pathos and ethos which flowed from this position as the complexities of governing and enforced conformity of collective cabinet responsibility led to political, ideological and even rhetorical compromises. Clearly aware of this Castle made sure to emphasise her left-wing pedigree when the occasion allowed. Such was the case when, speaking as a minister at the 1966 Labour conference, she opened her address with a quotation: 'Economic planning in a democratic socialist economy cannot operate successfully if wage-fixing is left either to the arbitrary decision of a wage-stop or to the accidents of uncoordinated sectional bargaining.' As she subsequently explained to her audience:

> This sentence was not written 16 days ago but sixteen years ago by a group of left-wing Members of Parliament who outlined in a pamphlet *Keep Left* their remedy for the same sort of economic crisis which plagued Britain then as plagues us now. The members of that group – Dick Crossman, Ian Mikardo and myself among others – had no doubt then that in a planned society incomes must be planned along with everything else. (Castle, 1966b)

Minister though she may be – so her message went – she had been of the left then and was of the left now, *and furthermore*, her arguments were right then and were right now also. The latter was an important part of the ethos Castle articulated, much of her rhetoric being based around a belief in her ability to convince, or rather educate, those who may, before hearing her argument, disagree with the position she advocated: 'We must start ... by getting our facts straight' she declared to one audience of public sector workers, as '[w]e shall never solve these problems by the wrong analysis' (Castle, 1974). The correct analysis, in each case, was that which she would subsequently provide the listener with.

This rhetorical attribute was there, clearly, in her 1959 Chairman's speech discussed above. Therein, Castle told her assembled comrades that Labour 'got elected in 1945 because people had learned the lessons of the 1930s', the lessons 'that it took us so long to teach ... that social crimes are also economic ones', and would 'only be elected next time when we have taught people the lessons of the new age in which we now live' (Castle, 1959: 84). Rare today are politicians who would declare the electorate need to be taught, not listened to and learned from, ascribing to themselves, rather, the ethos of the educator. Such was the case with Castle for whom, as Perkins (2003: 162) put it, '[i]f people rejected socialism, the answer was not less socialism, but more education'. Or, in Castle's own words from the 1959 speech: 'Socialism cannot be won on the second-rate! Let us begin this weekend to educate ourselves in what it will ask of us. And then let us go out and make Socialists' (Castle, 1959: 86). This is not a phrase easily imagined from a contemporary Labour leader.

The rhetoric of education was there too when, giving a rallying speech to Labour Party Officers in 1975, Castle chose to educate them on the importance of tackling inflation. 'There is no chapter in *Das Kapital* on inflation' she told her audience, 'for one reason only – because when Karl Marx was writing inflation was not an issue. Quite the reverse' (Castle, 1975). This stated, she asked them:

> do you think if Marx was alive today, sweating his brow for years in the bowels of the British Museum, he would have ignored the overwhelming evidence that on any analysis inflation is one of the single most desperate threats to the future of socialism in this country? Of course he would not. Do you think he would have deluded himself, or his followers into believing it possible for the people of this country as a whole to pay ourselves more than we earn, and still maintain employment and public expenditure at a high level? (Castle, 1975)

Her answer, again, was a clear 'no', deploying the classic rhetorical tools of *psyma* and *anthypophora*, posing multiple rhetorical questions, answered immediately, to explain why alternatives were in her words 'not possible' and 'nonsense'. She concluded with the command that – her argument made – it was 'now the duty and special responsibility of every one of us within this movement to explain to our comrades the choice which we face' (Castle, 1975). Castle having taught *them* (and corrected an oversight by Marx), their role was thus to now go forth and pass that teaching on to others.[6] Or as she put it in a speech as Secretary of State for Employment and Productivity to the Industrial Society Conference: 'My job is to tell you how and in what context we can create the political will for the change in attitudes that is so necessary' (Castle, 1968a). The emphasis here again was upon Castle's explanation and the subsequent creation and change which should follow – whether speaking to party members or communicating with electors Castle's rhetorical style remained the same.

'No feminist'

Such examples exhibit a desire on Castle's part to demonstrate to her audience her own learning and, in so doing, to demonstrate also that hers were opinions worthy of being taken seriously and not to be dismissed. As one of the few high profile female Members of Parliament (MPs) during her parliamentary career, such a need to demonstrate and assert the value of her utterances was especially important. This was particularly the case in the face of the collective House of Commons, still a bastion of institutionalised sexism today, but far worse during Castle's time as an MP (see Lovenduski, 2005). The emphasis upon her own ability was, in this sense, undoubtedly an appeal to ethos (linked to logos) as a worthy parliamentarian.

Unsurprisingly, however, such displays were themselves turned against Castle by critics (even ostensibly friendly ones) through the invocation of the old misogynistic trope of the 'nanny' often wielded against female politicians (see Childs, 2008). This trope was easily married with that of the 'fiery redhead', already discussed, to portray her speaking style as that of the finger-wagging, hectoring 'schoolmistress' telling off the 'boys'. A perfect example of such a portrayal is found in Crossman's description of Castle's winding-up speech in the debate, on 3 July 1969, over the settlement with the Trades Union Congress (TUC) regarding the *In Place of Strife* white paper:

> I arrived just as Barbara was getting up to boos and cheers and for the first seven minutes she was on her feet, she only got out half a dozen sentences. I was sitting right at the end below the Speaker's chair and I saw her trembling as she got up, nervous, tense and tiny and somehow pathetic. If you are little and can only just see over the top of the dispatch box, if you have a high-pitched woman's voice and if you are trying to still the post-prandial, alcoholic clouds of noise you are at a terrible disadvantage, especially if you are a bit schoolmistressy and try to hector and lecture them at the same time. (Quoted in Perkins, 2003: 326)

Castle's own view of the speech was itself lacking in confidence, writing in her diary: 'I can't make up my mind whether my winding-up speech … was a triumph or disaster … Certainly it was the roughest ride anyone could have' (Castle, 1990: 350). Ultimately, despite Castle's belief in her justness and own self-ability to convince, when faced with insurmountable obstacles such as the opposition, in this case, to *In Place of Strife*, even she recognised that her powers of oratory could only get her so far (which was not to say, of course, any admission that she was not absolutely in the right).

Speaking in the House of Commons was generally 'a nerve-racking ordeal' for Castle (Marquand, 2008: 212) and the aforementioned sexist atmosphere within the chamber was one issue which had to be dealt with. As she herself described: 'I think the men still think of us as women [when we speak] and you'll hear uncomplimentary remarks under their breath from both sides of the house which are because one is a woman' (BBC, 1972). Faced with comments from a Conservative politician, for example, which asked how her arguments matched those of her husband (at this point a Labour peer) she was withering in her response, denouncing his character:

My husband knows my view, and only the most major male chauvinist would try to involve me, in my arguments about the Common Market, with my husband's attitude ... the hon. Gentleman is living in the Victorian age when he tries to drag that one into this argument. (HC Deb, 16 February 1978, *Hansard*, vol. 944, cols. 683–761: 703)

Castle herself had, from early on in her political career, declared that she did not want to be seen as a *female* politician: in the 1945 general election, as one of only eighty-seven women candidates out of almost 1,700, speaking to 'a packed, smoke-filled, almost entirely male hall' in Blackburn she had called upon the crowd not to judge her by her gender – 'I'm no feminist. Judge me as a socialist' (Kynaston, 2007: 66) – and from the very moment she started in public life, she consciously avoided the 'traditional' women's fields for fear of being so defined (BBC, 1972). Clearly this was an issue of ethos for her and the notion that she would use her sexuality to her advantage was one which she would explicitly deny:

I have never consciously exploited the fact that I am a woman. I wouldn't dare try that even if I knew how to. I have too much respect for my male colleagues to think they would be particularly impressed. (Quoted in Phillips, 1980: 27)

Reports disagree, however. Martineau (2011: 101) describes how, as Minister for Transport in 1965, Castle, 'with her genius for self-presentation and her ability to manipulate an audience', would do 'what had worked so well for her in the past with a predominately male and potentially hostile crowd' by 'appl[ying] her femininity with a trowel'. Christopher Turgendhat of the *Financial Times* described this process, thus:

She is a flirt but it wasn't just that she flirted, it was that she liked being the important woman still attractive to younger men who were subordinate. She used her sexuality and rather enjoyed the fact that she was the one with the power. (Quoted in Martineau, 2011: 162)

It was not just in terms of sexuality that Castle – who was fastidious in her personal presentation – would allegedly use her gender to her advantage when speaking. Brian Walden describes how, '[w]hen Labour was in opposition, Barbara had a legendary ability to persuade the Speaker that she was a frail, friendless woman who simply had to be called to speak in the debate to make up for the cruel blows of an unheeding world' – where in reality 'she has more guts and vision than any six ordinary men put together ... knows exactly what she wants, and has a carefully thought out plan for getting it' (quoted in Perkins, 2003: 232).

But the manner in which gender relations may structure oratorical styles has another side to it. Discussing institutionalised sexism in British politics, Joni Lovenduski (2005: 54) describes, as an example:

the declamatory, adversarial style of Westminster debate that favours rhetoric, speechifying, posturing and arcane practice in the House of Commons rather than cooperation, consensus seeking and real discussion of alternatives. Political practices involving demagoguery, ruthlessness and aggression require qualities that are culturally accepted in men but not women. (Lovenduski, 2005: 54)

Whatever the truthfulness of Lovenduski's gendered attitudinal distinction, Castle's answer to the adversarial (misogynistic) culture of British politics was to embrace it. In fact, Castle determined that she must, if anything, be *more* adversarial than her male opponents. As she remarked to the BBC (1972):

> you have got to be totally indifferent to jibes, or laughter, or criticism. It's no good going along saying, well now don't be unkind to me you're hurting my feelings, you be chivalrous. One of the most flattering things ever said about me by a lobby correspondent writing about the House of Commons was 'she asks no quarter and she gives none'. Now if you see that quality in a woman politician you will find the House respects them even when it disagrees with them.

If the image of the 'terrifying termagant' – or in Castle's case, as reported, the 'scarlet termagant' – is, as Childs (2008) says, a trope used to symbolically represent female politicians in a gendered fashion (see above), then nevertheless, both for reasons of personality and political strategy Castle embraced the portrayal of herself as a battling warrior of fiery passion. This was not least the case in the Commons, an arena she evidently viewed in terms of a battleground; as she quipped to the previously mentioned audience at the Industrial Society Conference:

> It is appropriate – if rather ironical – that I should be addressing the lunch-time meeting of your one-day conference on Productivity and the Incomes Policy just a couple of hours before *I go into battle* in Standing Committee of the House of Commons on the Prices and Incomes Bill. The prospect of days and nights of *bitter political war* concentrates the mind wonderfully about issues which could otherwise become rather theoretical. (Castle, 1968a; italics added)

So it was that papers such as the then *Manchester Guardian* would describe how: 'In attack she provides one of the most awesome sights the House of Commons has to offer' (quoted in Martineau, 2011: 124) – and excoriating attacks by Castle are not hard to find, especially ones upon the ethos of her opponents. In a debate in 1971, for instance, she utilised rhetorical *alliteration* to savage the ethos of the government minister:

> I regret that the Solicitor-General, who is a man of considerable intelligence, should so debase the level of political dishonesty and debate as to distort the facts, as he has attempted to do and will continue to do so as long as he can get away with it. (*Hansard* C Deb, 19 January 1971, vol. 809, col. 951)[7]

In another debate she attacked the opposition for persisting 'in their rôle as latterday Bourbons, who have forgotten nothing and learned nothing' (HC Deb, 11 June 1975, col. 893), latching on to the words of one MP as a whip against his entire party:

> There was a revealing Freudian lapse in the hon. Member's remarks when he talked about '3 million votes'. Oh yes, how the Conservative Party loves to capitalise on the more obscurantist elements in our national thinking! That is their one hope of survival. Here they are again appealing to the least far-sighted and forward-looking attitudes.

Such displays of wit and vim were always easier, however, from opposition or the back benches. As a minister Castle felt constrained as '[s]he disliked writing out speeches, which she thought should be more spontaneous and responsive to the mood of her audience than her officials were prepared to tolerate ... she overprepared, even recording sections of the speech and then listening back to them' (Perkins, 2003: 296). Regarding her first speech as Minister of Labour to the House in May 1968 she wrote in her diary that she did not think she had 'ever been more petrified' and feeling that she had 'never in my whole life been worse prepared', regretting that she had not 'the time or the energy needed really to refine [her speech] and put it across' (Castle, 1990: 220).

Castle's guiding motto was that 'guts is all' and, ultimately, she herself was at her best as an orator when speaking from the gut. She was, by her own description, happiest when 'free of the responsibilities of leadership', as during her election speeches in 1992, when she 'could make daring, mocking sallies against the government' (Castle, 1993: 584). At the root of her oratorical style was a personal love of argument, of conflict – from which an inherent rhetorical appeal to pathos was born – and a belief in its ability to convince and bring change. The embodiment of the political battler for whom argument was all in the fight to achieve her socialist aims, Castle was an insurgent in her speaking pattern – a rebel against the existing order – and as such constrained and at times less effective when speaking from within the restricted position of a government post.

Conclusion: 'guts is all'

Trained, in speaking, to win and hold the street corners and town halls of the north of England, Castle developed a particular flair for rabble-rousing rhetoric and could dazzle on the public and party platform. Speeches such as her Chairman's address at the 1959 Labour conference confirmed her position as a great orator and darling of the grassroots, providing rhetorical master classes. Castle's rhetoric, though seeped in the pathos of the partisan, was also structured round an inherent self-belief in not just her own arguments but also her argumentative ability. However, despite appearances, she herself never felt truly confident as a speaker at conference or indeed in the chamber of the House of Commons.

Like the classical rhetoricians, Castle believed in argument as a social good – as the medium through which political ends should and must be won. Her speeches were arguments in the clearest sense of the term – not mere displays of her ability as a wordsmith, but deliberate interventions aimed at convincing others of her own position. They were, as such, frequently grounded in appeals to logos (the logic of her argument) and ethos (her position as the one arguing the case).

In this, the widely traded-in image of Castle as a 'fiery redhead' – as 'Red Barbara', the 'scarlet termagant' and 'bellicose Amazonian' – is a double articulation. It denotes both her genuine passion and her socialist politics but also marks her out for her rareness (and for the majority of contemporary commentators and comrades, her 'Otherness') as a female politician and minister within the context of British politics in the post-war period. Regardless of any consideration of gender, however, judged on her merits alone, Castle was one of Labour's preeminent orators whose maxim that 'guts is all' found embodiment in her oratorical style. Clearly spoken and with an unapologetic belief in the justness and correctness of her own argument – hers was the very antithesis of the 'new oratory' so derided by Hoggart. It is a style all but extinct at the top of contemporary Labour politics.

Notes

1 See: www.youtube.com/watch?v=UJWni94vAAU.
2 See: http://tvtropes.org/pmwiki/pmwiki.php/Main/FieryRedhead.
3 Rather fittingly, Miranda Richardson, who played Castle in *Made in Dagenham*, also portrayed the tempestuous Queen Elizabeth in *Blackadder II*.
4 On the masculine side, Neil Kinnock was another redheaded orator whose hair colour was often noted and arguably linked to a 'fiery' redheaded temperament (see Chapter 8 in this volume) – though in his case such references were normally of the negative 'ginger taff' variety. As he himself put it: 'Yep, ginger's not good' (Kinnock, quoted in Hattenstone, 2001).
5 It is a demonstrable oversight that all but one of the entries for Barbara Castle in this dictionary are from her diaries, not speeches.
6 This notion was even there in her reliance upon the phrase 'so, you see', to conclude her line of thought: 'So, you see, we aren't just industrial peacemakers and economists down at D.E.P' (Castle, 1968b: 1) and 'So, you see, I have a close and abiding interest in Remploy' (Castle, 1970: 2), etc. Rhetorically, 'so, you see' conveys the simple, logical message that the audience has been shown (by Castle) and thus now sees (that she is correct): they once were blind but now they see …
7 In response, Michael Fidler (Con, Bury and Radcliffe) asked: 'On a point of order. I rather thought that the Solicitor-General was being accused of political dishonesty. Is that in order?' The Deputy Chairman (Miss Harvie Anderson) responded, however: 'That was not the hearing of the Chair.'

5

The oratory of James Callaghan

Stephen Meredith

Introduction

Somewhere between Edward Heath's flirtation with, and Margaret Thatcher's zealous commitment to, monetarist economic doctrine, Jim Callaghan famously declared at Labour's 1976 Blackpool conference that '[w]e used to think that you could spend your way out of a recession … I tell you in all candour that that option no longer exists' (Callaghan, 1976a: 188). The speech was fashioned by Callaghan's son-in-law, Peter Jay, and although Callaghan stopped shy of using the second half of Jay's preferred elegy indicating the need to adopt a more entrepreneurial 'market socialist' approach, his words were taken to signal a turning point in modern British politics away from the traditional economic policies and instruments of the post-war consensus, and for some the death throes of Keynesian social democracy in an emerging era of so-called 'New Realism'. Although of course not without significant opposition, a sustained period of economic decline and the perceived failures of British economic policy from the mid-1960s provided the context for the logic of Callaghan's argument, which was enhanced through his increasing authority and credibility as prime minister after a relatively slow start in economic affairs as Chancellor of the Exchequer (Beckett, 2009a; Callaghan, 1988; Healey, 1989). Moreover, Callaghan's biographer, Kenneth Morgan, has suggested that his stewardship of the period of transition reflected in the speech represented a critical juncture and pioneering step in the long 'modernising' trajectory of the Labour Party itself in 'pursuing the Yellow Brick Road … from Attlee's Little Way to Blair's Third Way' (Morgan, 2007a). Principal themes of Callaghan's rhetoric from 1976 in economic policy, education and more latterly defence policy signified an, albeit interrupted, departure point and framework for successive stages of social democratic and Labour revisionism and modernisation (Bogdanor, 2007; Morgan, 1998; 1999; 2007a). Certainly, the cherished belief that social goals could be achieved by fiscal means was now under intense scrutiny as Callaghan announced to his party that this 'cosy world we were told would go on forever, where full employment would be guaranteed by the stroke of the Chancellor's pen … no longer exists' (Callaghan, 1976a: 188).

Callaghan's speech concerning Britain's macroeconomic future remains his most recognisable rhetorical flourish and is often held to denote the so-called crisis and turn of British social democracy in the mid-1970s, but represents only one of a number of oratorical interventions in party and national policy. Callaghan famously held all four major offices of state as Chancellor, Home Secretary, Foreign Secretary and Prime Minister in a long political career that saw him first enter Parliament in the Labour landslide victory of 1945, which helped to generate something of the trust in his experience and character that he was to appeal to in his political oratory. Consequently, his political and public profile involved experience across a range of recurrent themes of Labour and Britain's post-war trajectory, including national economic management, education policy, industrial relations strategy and labour movement relations, home affairs, Britain's relationship with Europe and the wider world and latterly Labour's international and defence policy.

This chapter assesses Callaghan's oratory across the spectrum of his political and public roles and experience, and evaluates his relative success in advancing his position or that of the Labour Party as evidenced by his party and wider public impact. It suggests that, with obvious notable exceptions, Callaghan demonstrated undoubted party and public communication skills, often in difficult circumstances during his prime ministerial tenure, and held it to be one of his core political strengths. His identification with the 'touch-stone of public opinion', expression of the 'personal touch' and ability to communicate a message of calm and reassurance were regarded as the essence of his political method and appeal, even in the darkest days of his Labour government (Morgan, 1997a: 308–9, 515–16; 1997b; 2007b).[1] Building on his affinity with public opinion and personal popularity, Callaghan's oratorical interventions and presentational nous were perhaps more developed, innovative and forward-looking than one might expect.

Political oratory, Callaghan and the Labour Party

Broadly defined, oratory refers to the art of public speaking and the means and style of delivery and rhetoric denotes the language and content of the speech. The concept of political rhetoric has increasingly developed negative connotations as 'just empty words' and is viewed in unfavourable contrast to 'substance' or action (Fairclough, 2000: vii; Jamieson, 1988: ix; Toye, 2010: 2–3). Equally, the art of political oratory has been transformed or even supplanted by the immediacy and abbreviation of new electronic media. Fortunately, the majority of Labour orators here are those who traverse more recent developments of the electronic media, retaining at least one foot in the pre-Twitter age and belong to the 'last generation of British practitioners' whose careers were enhanced by their 'skills as performers'. Nevertheless, developments of electronic and public media have diversified traditional channels and skills of political oratory. If we have not quite reached the point at which 'an interview on the *Today* programme' always matters more than a set-piece parliamentary speech, or alighted at an emaciated political culture in which critical political communication is conveyed exclusively through Twitter and similar blogs, we have arrived at the stage at which the long trajectory of technological change has invited, in the words of one analyst reflecting on the momentous effects of previous 'new media', a cosy 'fireside chat' as much as the prototype 'fiery oratory' (Jamieson, 1988: 42; Richards, 2011).

Collectivist developments and interpretations have dominated analysis of Labour's character and progress, yet the role of individuals can have a significant impact on perspectives of a party's disposition and performance. The role of oratory and use of rhetoric remains an important dimension and weapon of a politician's armoury as a tool to shape persuasive argument and to advance (or otherwise) their cause and appeal. 'Speech is a powerful master', evinced Gorgias, and Aristotle emphasised both aesthetic and practical elements and virtues of the use of language as rhetoric as 'the available means of persuasion' and their proper combination as effective presentation and witness of precision and clarity of thought (Aristotle, 2004: vii). Modern political analysts suggest that the study of speech and rhetoric 'as a form of and mode of political action in its own right' offers a potentially fertile means to analyse and explain core themes of political enquiry in the study of 'political institutions, ideologies and strategies'. Recognition of the 'rhetorical tradition' and the addition of 'argument' to the realm of ideas as the basis of 'political persuasion and preference transformation' allows for a more coherent understanding of the 'strategic and collective nature of political decision-making' (Finlayson, 2007: 545–6; Finlayson and Martin, 2008: 445–6; Thomas Symonds, 2006: 65).

Building on the insights of the 'classical authorities', Dennis Glover identifies 'three forms of proof of a speaker's case', as the distinction between (or combination of) logos or 'logic' supported by evidence; pathos or 'emotion' as the appeal to the particular emotions of the audience; and ethos or 'character' as the appeal to trust through the speaker's character and experience (Glover, 2011: 56; Aristotle, 2004). Callaghan's oratory as we shall see is firmly set within the latter category. Each represents an outward appeal to a particular audience, and the classical authorities agreed that a further component of successful oratory involved the adjustment of the orator to the differential contexts, perceptions and expectations of their audience. Effective oratory is dependent on the production of a speech 'apt for the occasion' (Glover, 2011: 56) and the ideal orator is one who can present 'commonplace matters simply, lofty subjects impressively, and topics ranging between in a tempered style' (Cicero, quoted in Glover, 2011: 57). Drawing on Cicero, Glover (2011: 60) suggests that the first task of successful speechwriting and delivery is 'to find out who will be in the forum', to '[k]now your audience'. In Labour's case, this includes the parliamentary arena, as the focal point of British political discourse and debate; wider party, movement and conference audiences, traditionally central to questions of Labour's distribution of power and intra-party governance and indicative of the prevailing mood of the wider party (Minkin, 1978); and wider public and electorate through public meetings and the mass media. As was the case with other Labour figures in the volume, Callaghan's notable oratory occurred largely outside the parliamentary arena, to wider Labour movement and conference audiences and through public appearances and the national media. As Labour leader and prime minister, he contributed to party and national debates on developments and future direction of economic and education policy and although it has arguably declined as the key forum of political communication, also contributed several noteworthy parliamentary interventions across a range of core themes of domestic and international policy. Largely departing from the predominantly logos and/or pathos led rhetorical traditions of leaders of the Gaitskellite revisionist right and 'hard' left, there was more of a sense of collegial and negotiated ethos to Callaghan's oratory.

Callaghan occupied a relatively fluid and non-ideological location of 'pragmatic labourism' at the juncture of Labour's centre and traditional right and, as such, was unencumbered by 'hard' association with any political grouping or ideological affiliation (Heppell *et al.*, 2010: 69; Meredith, 2008: 114–15; Morgan, 1997a: 384–5; Plant *et al.*, 2004: 1–3, 120–4). As party leader, he was unsympathetic to minority groups and unwilling to endorse even factions of the centre-right leadership-loyalist variety, such as the Manifesto Group (Callaghan, 1980; *The Times*, 1976). He was also intent to retain a wider platform of support in the party, to appeal to the 'soft centre' as well as the party right (Manifesto Group, 1979; Morgan, 1997b).

While it may have appeared to Labour's more impassioned, ideologically-grounded orators that his rhetoric lacked some of their rousing emotional intensity, Callaghan's lack of a distinctive ideological position allowed him to appeal to a wider party platform than for instance colleagues of the 'new' or post-revisionist Labour right, such as Roy Jenkins, with clear benefits for his pragmatic and 'incremental social democratic' approach (Williams, 2002). There was a sense in which he 'always positioned himself in such a way that he could strike out in a number of different directions' politically and rhetorically, which delivered 'some rather unexpected alliances notably when in the period of opposition when he does … tactically appear to move to the left both on trade union matters and on Europe in 1971–2' (Callaghan, 1971; Morgan, 1997a: 383–4; 1997b). In the corrosive atmosphere of Labour politics of the early 1970s, Callaghan's more collegial, less polarising and alliance-shaping style and language were less divisive than those such as Jenkins. His successful challenge for the party leadership in 1976, in a contest crowded with candidates of the centre-right, is testament to his ability to cast his net beyond the parameters of the party's defined ideological groupings to elicit support from a wider cross-section of the party (Heppell *et al.*, 2010). In his appeal to centrist left and right opinion and twin focus on loyalty and party unity and moderation and 'common sense', he adopted an approach that proved successful and popular with those apprehensive of the divisive tendencies of factional figureheads of left and right (Callaghan, 1976d; Radice, 2002). In 1976 he was successfully able to garner support from the 'labourist' centre, centre and social democratic right and centre-left of Labour's ideological spectrum (Heppell *et al.*, 2010), largely through his ethos and its appeal to trust in his ability to maintain party unity as the least divisive of the respective candidates, and the value of his experience, relationships and rapport with the wider party and movement.

Conference, movement and nation

Recurrent problems of recession, limited growth, inflation and unemployment set Callaghan at the forefront of debates regarding Britain's macroeconomic future, and his most notable oratorical intervention occurred at Labour's 1976 Blackpool party conference in which he undertook the perilous mission to convince his party and labour movement allies of the need to accept a fundamental review of traditional tools of economic management in challenging and shifting circumstances:

> We used to think that you could spend your way out of a recession, and increase employment by cutting taxes and boosting Government spending. I tell you in all candour that that option no longer exists, and in so far as it ever did exist, it only worked on each occasion since the war by injecting a bigger dose of inflation into the economy, followed by a higher level of employment as the next step. Higher inflation followed by higher unemployment. That is the history of the last twenty years. (Callaghan, 1976a: 188)

Callaghan's evolving rhetoric in this respect attempted to subvert core assumptions of traditional social democratic political economy. The cherished belief that social democratic values and goals could be achieved by fiscal means was now under intense scrutiny.

Preceding his transformative set-piece speech, Callaghan delivered preparatory 'warm-up' speeches to various labour movement and national audiences on the recurrent theme of economic 'realism' (Callaghan, 1976e). Largely adopting ethos-driven rhetoric to create trust in his message and leadership, he set out his stall directly in his first prime ministerial broadcast in April 1976. Addressing the nation, he conveyed his intention to take them into his confidence, 'to give you, the people of Britain, and to share with you, my thoughts about our country and what we should be doing'. Unsurprisingly, the substantive political theme involved national 'economic prospects' and the priority of tackling twin evils of inflation and unemployment (Callaghan, 1976e). In the deliberative style and language of his delivery, Callaghan attempted to draw his audience in to his vision and to make responsibility for the task as inclusive as possible, both congratulating the labour movement for its co-operation and reminding it of the need for even greater effort. His rhetoric combined a strong sense of ethos with a feel for pathos, playing to the emotions and conscience of his audience, and emphasised issues of experience, co-operation and partnership and trust. Clearly leading with a sense of ethos, '[s]peaking as one who has served in all of the five Labour Governments since the end of [the] war', he identified a 'combination of purpose and experience' as the basis of success. In the form of the 'social contract', it was clear that the Labour government's aim was to pursue a persuasive conciliatory partnership with the trade unions (in contrast to 'Mr Heath's ruinous policy of confrontation') to combat the pressure points of an ailing economy and tense industrial relations (Callaghan, 1976e). Again, the logos or logical coherency of his case was enhanced by his primary appeal to ethos and auxiliary pathos of his presentation.

The watchwords of Callaghan's rhetoric, and illustrative of the fusion of ethos and pathos to underpin the logic of his argument, were those of candour and transparency in the presentation of 'no soft options', a sense of common and shared purpose, a focus on progress and positive advances, combined with a cautionary tale of a job only half done. He routinely pursued the link and fusion of national and sectional interests, and declared that it was a national problem that could only be improved with a 'national effort' of 'everyone in it together'. He evoked the Lincoln-esque idiom of '[g]overnment ... by consent', when he declared '[t]ell the people, consult the people, trust the people, and we can win the people to whatever measures are required', and attempted to convey a positive message that his was not just a defensive government but one that retained a desire to demonstrate Labour's progressive principles and reforming edge in improved conditions (Callaghan, 1974; 1976e). Again demonstrating evidence of strong rhetorical ethos, speaking as someone 'with a lifetime understanding of the strength of the Trade Union Movement and the stresses that are placed upon it', allowed him to identify common interests and objectives. He was not asking them to be 'soft-hearted' just because they supported a Labour government, but to be 'hard-headed' in acknowledging that their 'real interests' lay with wider national interests. He employed this intimacy and a sense of shared and aspirational pathos to both express common ground and purpose and to challenge the trade unions to persist with 'the same understanding and co-operation' to defeat inflation and to 'begin to improve our real standard of life based on increased efficiency and productivity' to build a 'brighter future in which the positive purpose and shared principles and values of the Labour government and trade union movement can flourish' (Callaghan, 1976f; 1976g).

A further common refrain of Callaghan's pre-Blackpool speeches to both the labour movement and wider public audiences was to identify the need for and record the progress of the 'new air of realism' in economic expectations, exhorting audiences to respect the link between spiralling wage claims and price rises and high rates of inflation and unemployment. He claimed that a 'new air of realism' had permeated the national consciousness of mid-1970s Britain, and attempted to link the role and responsibilities of the trade unions with this wider shift 'throughout the country', while acknowledging their unique position and influence in this respect (Callaghan, 1976e). Increasingly, Callaghan's rhetoric evolved around and linked three consistent themes. The first appeal to economic 'realism' was framed within the second claim that the adverse economic circumstances were not just a Labour or British problem, but rather the 'effect of the economic blizzard that has struck the world since 1973', which, third, served as a means of managing the expectations of his audiences of Labour activists and trade unionists and as a reminder of the need to subscribe to wider national interests, priorities and developments. Rhetorically, Callaghan framed his delivery by utilising and linking his appeal to ethos and pathos to advance the logos of his argument and case, which broadly reflected his moderate centrist position and perspective:

> The most important happening in Britain in 1975 was the new air of realism which swept the country about our economic prospects. People realised and then openly said that wage increases could not continue at last year's fantastic rate without sending prices through the roof ... One final word to you, the Labour activists. Twice in the last thirty years Labour Governments have been called to office at times when the nation has faced massive economic problems. Twice we have been able to call on the British people for self-sacrifice and discipline. Each time they have responded only for we, the movement, to falter, lose our way and lose their confidence. (Callaghan, 1976c)

1976 annual conference speech

Callaghan's 1976 conference speech represented a further set-piece attempt to alert those of his own party and Labour alliance of the new realities and possibilities of economic policy (Conroy, 2006). The subsequent logos of Callaghan's appeal, or at least the parts which 'made the fur fly' (Callaghan, 1988: 425–7), provoked a mixed response and ambiguous meanings. It would have been something akin to music to the ears to the more liberal instincts of embattled revisionist social democrats and organisations in the party such as the Manifesto Group of centre-right Labour MPs pressing for some revision of Labour's economic thinking, and offered hope of a reappraisal of the strained precepts of Labour's traditional social democratic political economy to circumvent a potential economic and electoral void (Manifesto Group, 1977; 1979; *The Times*, 1977). The directness and admission of the key evolutionary passage, '[w]e used to think that you could spend your way out of a recession, and increase unemployment by cutting taxes and boosting Government spending. I tell you in all candour that that option no longer exists, and in so far as it ever did exist, it only worked by injecting a bigger dose of inflation into the economy, followed by a higher level of unemployment at the next step' (Callaghan, 1976a: 188), was explicit indictment of both prior Conservative profligacy and traditional social democratic Labour policies in challenging and fluid economic circumstances. In this respect, Callaghan added some sense of logos to his rhetorical armoury through more of an evidential analysis to complement the overarching ethos of his delivery. It represented repudiation of the unproductive first months of the Labour government, when public expenditure and rising inflation ran unchecked and, tied to acceptance of International Monetary Fund (IMF) terms, anticipated the onset of a change of economic template routinely pursued by successive governments. Whether anything of the package of reforms associated with 'Thatcherism' would have been enacted if Labour had won in 1979 remains a moot point, but arguably there is a sense in which the 'winds of change' were already airborne in Callaghan's address.

Others in the party and wider movement believed that Callaghan's speech suggested that Labour's leader had perhaps too readily accepted resurgent governing economic orthodoxies and monetarist principles, but negative responses to Callaghan's ambiguous rhetoric again implied that something significant had changed. It appeared to represent a 'renunciation of the full-employment policy all governments since the ...War had pursued' and rejection of the key role of public expenditure. Callaghan himself was no 'theologian of monetary doctrines', but rather 'remained prudent in economic affairs' and believed that 'certain monetary disciplines were essential to good economic management ... and ... sustained economic growth' (Callaghan, 1988: 427; Conroy, 2006: 95–6). He later claimed that the speech was not intended to argue that governments should 'never increase public expenditure or reduce taxation as methods of boosting employment', but 'in the circumstances of 1976 these measures were not appropriate'. Based on his particular and relatively successful appeal to ethos, it may have been only Callaghan among Labour's leadership who could have even hinted at taking his party beyond its economic comfort zone at this point. His ethos allowed him to adopt a clear forward-looking strand to his rhetoric that was not reliant on traditional tools as alternatives 'to facing up to the long-term changes that were required in our economy and in our society' – interpreted in sections of his audience as the 'first flickering of monetarism in post-war Britain putting the fight against inflation ahead of the aim of maintain full employment' (Callaghan, 1988: 427; Conroy, 2006: 95–6).

Morgan (1999: 149; 2007b) suggests of the longer-term meaning and implications of Callaghan's 'momentous' and, for good or bad, transformative 1976 conference oratory that, if nothing else, it demonstrated his 'capacity to move on' in economic policy and more broadly, and questions lazy views of him as a 'limited machine' politician and 'standpat symbol of Old Labour'. Although it remained unsurprisingly ambiguous, Morgan identifies the tiniest seeds of Labour's subsequent, admittedly lengthy, modernising trajectory, and even something of the 'new economics of New Labour' in Callaghan's rhetoric. Some later evangelists of 'New' Labour, who perceived Callaghan's leadership to represent the death throes of the old corporatist order, needed to acknowledge that 'it was then that many of their party's social and economic policies were modernized and redefined' (Morgan, 1997a: 557–8; 1998). Callaghan's rhetorical ethos based on moderate pragmatic social democracy underpinned the logos of 'moving on' and offered the first footprint of second-stage social democratic modernisation, whether inside or outside the party.

'Education, education, education': 1976 Ruskin speech and the 'Great Education Debate'

In the period of relative calm before the storm, between successful navigation of the IMF crisis and upturn in economic fortunes and the disquiet of the first rumblings of the 'winter of discontent', Callaghan was able to pursue themes of particular interest in his public oratory (Jay, 1980; Morgan, 2007b). His landmark speech at Ruskin College, Oxford, in October 1976 'heralded the Great Debate' on national education policy and raised issues of the 'quality of educational instruction ... in a way that was prophetic' (Callaghan, 1976b; Kogan, 1985; Morgan, 1999: 149; 2007b). Echoing Tony Crosland's recent warning to local authorities that 'the party's over' and some of the principal notices of his 1976 conference address, Callaghan's Ruskin speech was intended as an intervention in the debate over national education policy and standards in state schools, provoked in part by his frustration with views that the quality of provision was merely a monetary issue. He asserted that 'there is a challenge to us all in these days and a challenge in education is to examine its priorities and to secure as high efficiency as possible by the skilful use of existing resources' (Callaghan, 1976b; Morgan, 2004: 46).

Callaghan's speech represented a courageous intervention in the closeted world of education policy. At the time, it was considered unusual for generalists and prime ministers to 'interfere openly' in this private sphere, and the speech caused 'some surprise' and the sense that he 'must have ulterior motives', particularly from within the educational establishment and among the Labour left who interpreted it as an assault on 'progressive' education (Callaghan, 1996). Relatively 'mild in language but firm in intent', the understated pathos and logos of Callaghan's rhetoric 'transformed and continues to define public debate about education' (Woodward, 2001). If expressed by Tony Blair at the peak of New Labour, it might have been considered familiar and unexceptional, but in the context of the time it was 'revolutionary', opening up a 'great debate in public' on education and lighting 'a flare that has illuminated education reform ever since' (Adonis, 2006). The speech erected 'a bridge between one era and the next', passing from an 'era of consensus' to an 'era of accountability', as a landmark of post-war educational history (Barber, 1996). It raised issues that have dominated the discourse of education ever since: accountability, quality and effectiveness, the (core) curriculum and, perhaps most profoundly, the relationship between teachers, parents, government and industry.

Callaghan's rhetoric again attempted to inclusively link national issues of access and improvement in education with the values of the labour movement, and the ethical socialist influence of R.H. Tawney provided a benchmark. Successfully combining pathos and logos, he posed the typically intimate question of 'what do we want from the education of our children and our young people?', (Callaghan, 1976b) for which he drew on Tawney for an answer: '[w]hat a wise parent would wish for their children, so the State must wish for all its children', and challenged vested interests to recognise both the moral and practical dimensions and value of educational provision as a national and labour and working-class priority (Adonis, 2006). Responding to the concerns of parents and industry that the balance had shifted too far in a non-vocational direction in some of the 'new informal teaching methods' and lack of a core curriculum, Callaghan chose to intervene in the rarefied world of education in the national and labour interest:

> The goals of our education ... are to equip children to the best of their ability for a lively, constructive place in society and also to fit them to do a job of work. Not one or the other; but both. For many years the accent was simply on fitting a so-called inferior group of children with just enough learning to earn their living in the factory. There is no virtue in producing socially well-adjusted members of society who are unemployed because they do not have the skills ... In today's world, higher standards are demanded than were required yesterday and there are simply fewer jobs for those without skill. Therefore we demand more from our schools than did our grandparents. (Callaghan, 1976b)

Utilising the logos dimension of his delivery, Callaghan identified core themes he wanted for further discussion. These included review of the 'methods and aims of informal instruction', the 'strong case' for a 'core curriculum of basic knowledge', the 'proper way of monitoring the use of resources in order to maintain a proper national standard of performance', the 'role of the inspectorate in relation to national standards', problems of the examination system, particularly in relation to 'less academic students staying at school beyond the age of 16' and the 'need to improve relations between industry and education' (Callaghan, 1976b) all at 'a time before the national curriculum, before Ofsted, before league tables' (Woodward, 2001). Through the relative intimacy and candour of the linked pathos and logos of his delivery, Callaghan's intention was to stimulate national debate and was successful in the sense that it provoked what has been termed 'the Great Debate' that has largely continued unabated ever since. He was a politician of the broad left concerned openly about 'new informal teaching methods' and school standards, and a generalist prime minister offering a view of 'what should be taught and how it should be taught'. Callaghan's accumulated and enhanced ethos and refusal to take advice 'to watch [his] language' in public discussion of a 'core curriculum' meant his rhetoric 'at a stroke would end 100 years of non-interference in state education' (Callaghan, 1976b; Woodward, 2001).

Callaghan's Ruskin speech was representative of a broader approach in his oratory to articulate his party and government's philosophy through an overarching national theme, in this case 'public standards, related to social cohesion' and a socially responsible citizenry. It represented an attempt to divert educational debate away from

sectarian arguments over selection and comprehensive education to a more fundamental concern over national educational standards (Morgan, 1997a: 503, 540–1).
The tone of the speech also reflected a further point of departure between Callaghan
and the Labour left, who regarded his emphasis on national standards and 'quality
control' as 'traditionalist' and 'reactionary'. Tony Benn was appalled by what he perceived to be a 'right-wing' attack on comprehensive schools. Benn's wife, Caroline,
expressed her belief that it represented a direct assault on the '"lefties" who are teaching the social sciences', but with a typical appeal to ethos through his 'homely' and
'common sense' rhetoric, embodying personal commitment and practical knowledge, never far away, the speech 'struck a powerful chord' (Barber, 1996; Benn, 1989:
626–7; Callaghan, 1996; Morgan, 1997a: 541). In the economic context, the 'Great
Debate' failed to gather momentum, but Callaghan's Ruskin speech is regarded as a
landmark of British educational thinking. Core themes of a national curriculum, system of assessment and new emphasis on professional skills and training of teachers
were subsequently adopted in more confrontational circumstances than Callaghan
envisaged. Its starting point and central concerns became almost conventional as
the basis of political and public debate on education, both within 'New' Labour and
beyond (Adonis, 2006; Barber, 1996; Blair, 1996; Morgan, 1997a).

1978 TUC conference speech

Callaghan's 1976 conference speech may have been ambiguous in the extent to
which it marked a decisive turning point in the political economy of social democracy, but it was his address to another labour movement forum at the 1978 conference of the Trade Union Congress (TUC) that generated no little confusion and
potentially damaging consequences for Labour's immediate electoral prospects. He
(in)famously adopted the lyrics of a music hall song to 'entertain' delegates about his
decision *not* to call a general election for the autumn, a decision, speech and mode
of delivery that was seen to test the patience of trade union 'allies' and damage fragile morale. For once, he appeared to desert his tried and tested ethos in favour of an
unsuccessful attempt to incorporate an element of pathos in his rhetoric, given that
he intended to beguile his audience with humorous cultural references but generated only confusion and irritation. Economic fortunes had to some extent revived
in the aftermath of Callaghan's 1976 'bombshell' and subsequent IMF settlement.
Callaghan's profile and popularity were considered to be significantly higher than
those of his Conservative opponent (Jay, 1980; Morgan, 1997a: 558; 2007; Shore,
1993: 116). Although not a fact universally acknowledged (Shore, 1993), the decision not to call an election for the autumn may have been a strategic mistake that
undermined Labour's electoral chances, but it was the context and manner of the
announcement that bemused and alienated his trade union audience and reflected
clear oratorical misjudgement. Although he had not been previously averse to using
a degree of 'praise-and-blame' rhetoric with trade union audiences in relation to

economic circumstances and priorities, there is a sense in which he reverted to mis-judged epideictic rather than deliberative oratory, which was perhaps ill-fitted to the gravity of the situation and to some extent left Callaghan outside his rhetorical comfort zone. At a critical juncture for the Labour government and, given the concerns of an increasingly testing relationship with his anxious audience, engagement in deliberative discourse and his more conventional and appropriate ethos-led delivery may have produced a different reaction and responses from a core audience. The speech certainly did not serve to highlight the co-ordination and harmony of the Labour alliance. Delegates had expected Callaghan to use his speech to announce the date of an October general election, but instead he treated them to his own (misattributed) version of Vesta Victoria's old music hall favourite, 'Waiting at the Church', to convey the message that he had not promised and nor would there be a general election that year:

> There was I waiting at the Church, waiting at the Church, waiting at the Church, when I found he'd left me in the lurch, Lor' how it did upset me. All at once he sent me round a note, here's the very note, this is what he wrote, 'can't get away to marry you today, my wife won't let me!' (Callaghan, 1978a)

On completion of the ditty, he reiterated that 'I have promised nobody that I shall be at the altar in October nobody at all' (Callaghan, 1978a; 1978b; Trade Union Congress, 1978: 522). Delegates were perplexed to hear the Prime Minister burst into song, which many observers misinterpreted to mean that he would call an election for the autumn and it would be the Conservatives who would be 'left … in the lurch', 'waiting at the Church' (McKie, 2005; Morgan, 1997a: 642–3; 2007a; *The Times*, 1978). Core economic messages of Callaghan's speech around a 'strong defence' of the 5 per cent pay norm were lost or unheeded in the confusion of the non-election announcement. The communication of the decision to hang on until the spring of 1979 represented a public relations disaster and the first of a series of political and communication errors that plagued Callaghan and his government in its denouement (Conroy, 2006; Morgan, 1997a; 1999; 2007a). Callaghan's mis-placed reliance on pathos and seemingly flippant treatment of labour movement allies was carried over in a speech to open the new Transport and General Workers (TGWU) building in Cardiff, when he joked to general secretary, Moss Evans, 'I tell you what Moss if you promise not to make another speech about pay policy, I'll promise not to sing' (Callaghan, 1978c).

Although Callaghan's generally relaxed and genial manner and communication were considered core strengths of his broadly effective public image, there is a sense in which his public pronouncements from late September 1978 lacked the appropriate degree of gravitas and appreciation of circumstances, culminating in the very public gaffe of (the misquoted) 'Crisis, what crisis?' on his sun-tanned return from a conference in Guadeloupe. Morgan concludes of the misguided 'showbiz turn' that set in motion the train of strategic and public communication errors that hindered the latter stages of his government, '[i]f politicians decide to borrow from popular culture' in political rhetoric, then 'ambiguity is a dangerous thing' (Morgan, 1997a: 497, 643; 2004: 47; 2007a). Callaghan's increasingly misplaced attempts to adopt pathos in his delivery conflicted with his image of ethos-driven logos and, combined with increasing use of epideictic oratory incompatible with a core audience expecting and accustomed to his deliberative style, served to undermine his ethos at a critical point of his government's labour movement and public dialogue and negotiations.

Callaghan, Parliament and policy

Callaghan's 'era-shaping' oratory, often expressed with 'characteristic understatement' (Woodward, 2001) was largely confined to wider public and labour movement arenas, but he also made notable contributions from within Parliament in other areas in which he might be seen as a reformer, or at least in a manner that helped to revise or 'attain a better balance' to Labour attitudes and perspectives on issues such as law and order, Europe and defence (Morgan, 2004: 46; 2007). One such example late in his parliamentary career, at a point when Labour was attempting to revise its ideological and policy platform away from recently dominant left-wing themes, was his rhetorical assault on the party's left-led defence policy in 1987, reflecting something of Callaghan's old animosity towards the Labour left. His language was far less 'collegiate' and 'conciliatory' on this occasion and was intended as a direct attack on Labour's 'confused' stance of unilateral nuclear disarmament and to ridicule and undermine the notion of a 'fixed' ideological position on the issue in rapidly changing circumstances. With 'realist' echoes of Bevan's 'naked into the conference chamber' speech to Labour's 1957 Brighton conference, and allowing a little logos to creep into his case, he argued:

> The question whether we go ahead with Trident is a moot point ... I would not take a fixed view on Trident for ever [but] I would not abandon it now. The situation may change ... Certainly we should not give Trident up for nothing. We must negotiate our way out of this ... I hope that all hon. Members, wherever we may sit, will continue to review the changing circumstances in defence as events occur. The position today is certainly not the position of four years ago and it is even less the position when I left office. No one should adopt a fixed position for ever and allow considerations on defence weapons to be turned into ideology. That would be absurd. (Callaghan, 1987a)

The impact of Callaghan's speech in the twilight of his parliamentary career should not be underestimated. Again, utilising his accumulated ethos in a modernising party environment, he maintained his rare capacity to enrage and downgrade the concerns of the far left of his party, but more widely was perceived to represent the reassuring voice of 'common sense' Labour. In addition to John Prescott's tea-room opprobrium, there was an immediate outcry from the Labour left attacked in their inner sanctum, and huge correspondence from members of constituency Labour parties and the wider public in reaction to the views and language of Callaghan's speech. While some decried his 'public criticism of Labour's defence policy' (Morgan, 1997a: 728–9) and the potential damage to Labour's election chances by showcasing internal divisions, others congratulated him on his 'courage' and 'stand' against the continuing 'extremism' of Labour's official policy and for placing the 'country's welfare before party politics'. The views expressed in the speech were considered to reflect those of the majority of Labour voters rather than a minority of hard core activists and left-wing ideologues of Labour's policy-making apparatus. Although Callaghan's intervention failed to help Labour in the 1987 general election, the party delivered a stronger performance than in 1983 and Callaghan's contribution supported Labour's rolling process of renewal and grail-like search for credibility and electability (Callaghan, 1987b; Morgan, 1997a). He was prepared to court unpopularity to voice opposition to left-wing policies he considered damaging to Labour's wider profile and prospects. Again utilising his re-emerging ethos in a changing party environment, and with an echo of another, more recent, Tredegar-born leader, he told sceptical delegates to Labour's 1987 party conference:

> What the movement has failed to understand is that it reversed the traditional policy of the Labour Party on which we had fought eleven successive elections without any real attempt to convince the British people what we were doing was right. I happen to believe it is wrong. But you make a fundamental mistake by believing that by going on marches and passing resolutions without any attempt to try to tell the British people what the consequences were, you could carry their vote. And you lost millions of votes. (Callaghan, 1987c)

Callaghan also spoke with authority and no little effect in a series of major set-piece parliamentary debates on issues of foreign affairs during this period, which had the effect of both again demonstrating Labour's capacity for statesmanship in this sphere and upstaging the Conservative leadership. He was considered to have performed more effectively than his party leader during the Westland affair in January 1986. Clearly adopting linked ethos and logos to privilege his status and experience as a former prime minister, he contrasted his own defence of British aerospace interests in developing the joint European airbus in 1978 in the face of a challenge from Boeing with the current government's appeasement of the US Sikorski option at the expense of Europe. Morgan concludes that it was a 'highly effective performance', which added to Thatcher's discomfiture in a crisis that witnessed the resignation of Michael Heseltine and her own close call (Callaghan, 1986a; Morgan, 1997a: 728). Again, Callaghan spoke authoritatively in debates on the US attack on Libya in April 1986. He roused the House with his admission that, if he was still prime minister, he would not have allowed the United States to launch its bombing raids from Britain, and endorsed Heath's statement on how he had refused use of British bases in Cyprus during the 1973 Yom Kippur War. On this occasion, Thatcher was enclosed by enemies from without and within (Callaghan, 1986b; Morgan, 1997a).

In aspects of domestic policy, Callaghan's parliamentary work and presentation provided initiatives and developments of lasting party impact. These included as Home Secretary, developments of law and order and race and immigration policy, which had the effect of reworking Labour discourses and attitudes on these themes. On law and order, he is considered to have struck a balance for Labour between support for the police and 'championing free speech' and toleration of 'popular protest', for example in the case of the anti-Vietnam War protests in Grosvenor Square in March 1968 (Morgan, 2007a). As a former Police Federation representative and utilising the tried and trusted ethos associated with his politics of moderation and balance, his careful and measured rhetoric in this respect helped to rebut some of the more lurid anti-police attitudes of constituency activists and helped establish Labour as 'truly [a] party of law and order' (Callaghan, 1968b; Morgan, 1998, 2007a). In terms of his difficult stewardship of the thorny immigration context of the late 1960s, a stronger sense of pathos and logos filtered through Callaghan's oratory as he negotiated the well-trodden pragmatic-populist dimension of political rhetoric, in which he articulated some of the socially conservative tendencies associated with the wider labour movement and working-class electorate. In the wake of the perceived liberalism of his predecessor, Roy Jenkins, Callaghan expressed more of the conservative instincts of his own non-conformist and 'labourist' background and appealed to a position he felt would be 'popular amongst Labour voters in industrial parts of the country'. Although his response was shaped by the immediacy and pressure of events, it represented a departure from the liberal Jenkins and conveyed a changing discourse and legacy for Labour on immigration, reflected perhaps in the 'pragmatic-populist' outlook of future Labour home secretaries such as David Blunkett and John Reid. We are reminded that it was Callaghan and the Labour government of the late 1960s, not the Conservative government of the 1990s in its anti-refugee policies, which identified intrinsic dangers of the 'right of uncontrolled entry at any time in any numbers' for race relations (Callaghan, 1968a; Karvounis *et al.*, 2003: 312). Callaghan's rhetorical and oratorical impact on the longer-term development and trajectory of his party went beyond the later (in) famous set-piece occasions for which he is best remembered. Again, his rhetorical contributions across a variety of issues of home affairs were largely founded on his moderate, pragmatic and centrist and consensual political character and associated ethos, but he was not averse to the use of pathos and/or logos as the issue or situation and his audience demanded.

Conclusion

Callaghan was comfortable with his personal style and public communication. As strategic discussions of Labour's National Executive Committee (NEC) for the

1979 general election campaign reveal, he was the first prime minister to indicate his willingness to take part in a televised debate, but it was Thatcher's refusal to take him on in this arena that denied the public their first opportunity to see the party leaders battle it out 'face-to-face' (Callaghan, 1979). Yet Callaghan was not a performer of the fire and brimstone variety, and his oratory lacked some of the emotional zeal of Aneurin Bevan. He adopted a largely 'realist' rather than 'romantic' style of oratory, but not necessarily one that relied on the highly rational presentation of factual evidence and reasoned argument of Hugh Gaitskell. Neither did the non-university educated Callaghan attempt to appeal to and construct an ethos of particular or specialist competence in the mode of Gordon Brown's (sometimes confusing and inaccessible) emphasis on economic expertise. Callaghan's was an appeal to ethos mediated through a message of experience, familiarity, candour and mutual respect and responsibility in an atmosphere of collegiate and consensual leadership, peppered with a relatively loose sense of logos on the grander set-piece occasions of his 1976 conference and Ruskin speeches. He wanted to take his audience with him, but only 'steady as she goes' as a 'calm pilot in the storm', with occasional recognition that the times, they are a-changin'. He made no claim to charismatic leadership, and as prime minister lacked some of the 'presidentialism' of a number of his successors. He preferred to operate collectively at party and movement, government and national levels, and his rhetoric was intended to inspire a sense of trust and broad consensus (Morgan, 1997b; 2007a).

This approach had strengths and weaknesses, successes and failures. We know that he could be overly informal, relaxed and casual in his communication on occasion. In spite of the amusement displayed by some of the more senior members of the audience who recognised his music hall reference and refrain, Callaghan's misguided and obscure non-election announcement to the TUC in 1978 served only to both confuse and demoralise key allies in the trade unions and undermine Labour's fragile election prospects. It was interpreted as indecisiveness on Callaghan's part, and thereafter his government found itself 'on the defensive' and 'at the mercy' of minor nationalist parties in Parliament. Misconceived communication of wage claims policy from the leader who best 'understood the … unions' (Morgan, 2007) also helped to undermine the fragile 'social contract' and precipitate the 'winter of discontent'. He announced the government's decision of a 5 per cent pay limit unexpectedly in a television interview and, while the level of increase outraged many of Labour's natural constituency, the forum and manner of its delivery was equally unanticipated and disconcerting. Sun-tanned from a visit to the Caribbean island of Guadeloupe, he is also eternally associated with a misguided (and misreported) response of 'Crisis, what crisis?' to questions about Britain's ailing condition, which was taken to show how disconnected or nonchalant he had become about the situation (Morgan, 2007a).

However, key set-piece rhetorical interventions, to some extent forced upon him and only in prototype, were ahead of their time (and his party), anticipating some of the principal themes of later 'New' Labour (Morgan, 1998; 2007a), and providing a clear, if interrupted, link in Labour's revisionist modernising trajectory. In economic policy, in education, in justice, he at least attempted to be a party and national reformer and, as prime minister, demonstrated a pragmatic, if largely thwarted, capacity to move forward. Arguably, Callaghan's greatest single oratorical achievement was to commit 'old-style' socialism as a serious proposition to the political ashes. The principal turning point in British political economic management and priorities was not in 1979 and with the election of Thatcher, but in 1976 as Callaghan opined to the Labour Party conference 'I tell you in all candour that that option no longer exists'. Unfortunately, he was unable to cajole and take his party and movement with him on the 'gentler, consensual, non-confrontational' path he expressed and represented. It was left to the full-frontal assault of Thatcherism to oversee the transformation in full, a fact which the public (and Callaghan) recognised (Donoughue, 2009: 483–4, 492–3; Morgan, 1997a: 697; Sandbrook, 2008):

> There are times, perhaps once every thirty years, when there is a sea-change in politics. It then does not matter what you say or what you do. There is a shift in what the public wants and what it approves of. I suspect there is now such a sea-change, and it is for Mrs Thatcher.

Notes

1 Callaghan's allegedly casual response to questions about 'mounting chaos' in the country on his return from an international conference in January 1979 did little to promote a mood of calm and reassurance in the heat of the 'winter of discontent'. His attempts to present a reassuring public manner were increasingly viewed as inappropriately relaxed to the point of complacency in critical circumstances. Neither could his earlier, seemingly dismissive and brusque, treatment of political allies in the trade unions in announcing his decision not to hold a general election in September 1978 (itself considered to be a fatal strategic error) be considered a public relations success (Morgan, 1997a, 1999).

6

The oratory of Michael Foot

David Stewart

Michael Foot is renowned as one of the outstanding British political orators of the twentieth century. An aptitude for public speaking was an invaluable asset for Foot's generation of politicians, who were expected to adapt to a diverse range of political settings ranging from Parliament, party conferences and broadcast studios to open-air demonstrations and workplace meetings. Foot was one of the few Labour Party politicians who could lay claim to mastering all of these settings. His political career has been the subject of detailed biographical work by Kenneth Morgan, Mervyn Jones and Simon Hoggart and David Leigh. Morgan describes Foot's oratory as 'a fusion of the Cornish chapels, the Oxford Union and the soapboxes of the Socialist League', while Hoggart and Leigh highlight the 'often savage power of his oratory' and his 'evangelical' delivery style (Hoggart and Leigh, 1981: 3; Morgan, 2007b: 484). Jones concludes that Foot was 'one of the few politicians who [has] been equally effective on the platform and in the House of Commons' (Jones, 1995: 40). However, the existing historiography tends to confine its coverage of Foot's oratory to his parliamentary speeches and offers limited analysis of his wider oratorical style.

In order to redress the balance, this chapter examines Foot's oratory in several settings and contexts: Parliament; Labour Party conference; Constituency Labour Party (CLP) meetings; public demonstrations; and the media. The chapter charts Foot's oratory through three chronological phases: 1945–70; 1970–80; 1980–83, and is underpinned by the oratorical constructs of ethos, logos and pathos. It examines the role of Foot's oratory in constructing and popularising the concepts of the 'Guilty Men' and the 'politics of persuasion'. The chapter also considers the ways in which Foot's speeches drew on parliamentary sovereignty and collective memories of the 1930s and 1940s to heighten their salience. This in turn raises the question of Foot's patriotism, which is scrutinised through his speeches on British membership of the European Economic Community (EEC) and devolution for Wales and Scotland. His espousal of unilateral nuclear disarmament and liberal internationalism is interwoven throughout the chapter. The chapter begins by focusing on the evolution of Foot's oratory during the early stages of his political career as MP for Plymouth Devonport.

The flame of liberty, 1945–70

Foot's style of oratory was shaped by his close friend and leading Labour left MP, Aneurin Bevan's mantra 'to always address yourself to the strength of your opponent's case, not the weakness' (Foot, 1962: 261). Foot's speeches tended to be delivered 'across a range of intonations in a series of barks' and punctuated by dramatic pauses caused by his asthma (*Independent*, 2010). He rarely spoke from notes when addressing public meetings, 'leaving much to chance and spontaneous combustion' (Morgan, 2007b: 484). Due to his involvement with Keep Left and the Bevanites, Foot was excluded from the rostrum at Labour Party conference until 1959 by the moderate party leadership and trade unions. However, from 1949 Foot became a regular contributor to the current affairs television programme, *In the News* (Jones, 1995). Hoggart and Leigh attribute his effectiveness in this arena to the formal debating structure of the programme, while Jones highlights BBC viewers' perceptions of Foot as 'intolerant, humourless and fanatical' (Hoggart and Leigh, 1981: 104; Jones, 1995: 178).

Yet Foot was most anxious to prove himself as a parliamentary orator. Foot was steeped in the history of Parliament and believed that the oratory of individual MPs could make a difference through upholding democracy and pursuing progressive reform. His maiden speech asserted his irreverent, anti-establishment ethos by promising to 'sink from that high level of pure affability which we are supposed to attain in our maiden speeches' (*House of Commons Debates*, 20 August 1945). The speech, which concentrated on the pursuit of liberty and democracy in foreign affairs, balanced logos and pathos. Foot's appeals to logos drew on a class-based analysis of 1930s international relations, reminding MPs that 'when the war came, when Hitler made his attack, there were very few friends of Hitler to be found in the workers' homes in Europe, and there were very few friends of democracy to be found in the precincts of the palaces and the offices of big business' (Foot, 1945). Thereafter, the diplomatic and moral failings of appeasement were dissected, as Foot urged the Labour Party not to 'submit to instruction on the principles of democracy' from the Conservative Party, which had taken the 'mass journey to Damascus a little late'. The speech concluded with a patriotic appeal to pathos, which sought to infuse Britain's post-war international role with the spirit of national independence and democracy generated during 1940:

> At the end of this great war and after this great Election, the British people can play as conspicuous a part before the gaze of all mankind as they played in 1940 … Surely it is the duty of our great country not to be content with some secondary role … As we look out across this stricken Continent and as we see a new hope in the struggle to be born across this wilderness of shattered faiths, may it not be our destiny as the freest and most democratic and a Socialist Power to stand between the living and the dead and stay the flames?

Future speeches built upon these themes by evolving a narrative in which the Conservative Party represented an unpatriotic, privileged 'vested interest' associated with private monopoly and international capitalists who were intent on sparking an economic crisis in the UK to prevent further socialist reform (*House of Commons Debates*, 28 October 1947). This also reflected Foot's concern that anti-socialist vested interests were using their influence within the Establishment and civil society to undermine the Labour government. He delivered several speeches attacking the Kemsley press empire, which he alleged undermined freedom of speech and democracy by enforcing proprietorial control over the editors of Lord Kemsley's nationwide network of newspapers. During these debates Foot's ethos as a leading opponent of wartime press censorship came to the fore. Foot asserted that 'Lord Kemsley's newspapers do distort the news, they do suppress the evidence, they are used as vehicles for the expression of the political opinions of Lord Kemsley. And the word "gutter" is a good old English word which makes its meaning tolerably plain' (*House of Commons Debates*, 29 October 1946).

Foreign affairs continued to form a central focus of Foot's oratory throughout his time as MP for Plymouth Devonport. Although Foot's speeches supported collective security, he defied the Labour Party leadership by opposing membership of the North Atlantic Treaty Organization (NATO) and promoting British neutrality in the developing Cold War. Foot envisaged Britain and its Commonwealth working alongside the United Nations (UN) instead to promote peace and humanitarianism. When not speaking on these issues Foot concentrated on constituency interests in Plymouth. Foot became one of the leading back-bench spokespeople for the Blitzed areas and naval dockyards, demanding that investment in new housing and jobs should be given special priority in these areas as a reward for the people's sacrifices during the war (*House of Commons Debates*, 18 March 1947; *House of Commons Debates*, 8 March 1948; *House of Commons Debates*, 21 March 1949; *House of Commons Debates*, 5 December 1951; *House of Commons Debates*, 25 February 1952).

Foot's defeat at Devonport in 1955 was followed by the revisionist Hugh Gaitskell's election as Labour Party leader in 1955. With Foot's democratic socialism marginalised within the party, he further developed his media profile through participation in ITV's *Free Speech* current affairs programme, cultivating a reputation for incisive debate and a lack of deference, which were at odds with consensual contemporary broadcast media practices. Simultaneously, Foot broadened his interests through involvement with the Campaign for Nuclear Disarmament (CND) (Jones, 1995: 225–31). When he was allowed to address the Labour Party conference for the first time in 1959 Foot spoke on this matter. Foot also used the platform to aggressively challenge Gaitskell's efforts to revise Clause IV of the party constitution: 'we are never going to convert or win an election if we ourselves do not believe in our own principles of public ownership ... it is a fallacy to try to separate the ends and the means because socialism, in my view, is a doctrine which reveals how only by mobilising the resources of the community can you achieve the ends' (LHASC, 1959: 122). This rhetoric and activism further alienated Foot from the

Labour Party leadership, and enabled him to popularise his ethos as a democratic socialist tribune.

Meanwhile, the death of Bevan and Foot's election as his successor in Ebbw Vale in 1960 signalled the beginning of a new phase in Foot's oratory. Ebbw Vale intensified Foot's socialist passion through its association with Bevan, added to his national profile, broadened his industrial interests to include the key staple industries of coal and steel, and brought him into contact with the influential National Union of Mineworkers and Iron and Steel Trades Confederation. Foot used his first major parliamentary speech as MP for Ebbw Vale to pursue the cause of unilateral nuclear disarmament. The speech utilised ethos, logos and pathos in equal measure. Foot's ethos as heir to Bevan was interwoven throughout his oratory, 'No one could be more conscious than I am of my unfitness to represent the constituency which he made famous' (*House of Commons Debates*, 13 December 1960). Attacking the lack of parliamentary control over Britain's nuclear arsenal and its deployment with American-led NATO forces, his appeal to logic was once again built around notions of liberty, democracy and national independence:

> [O]ne of the most sinister features of our society induced by the invention of these weapons is that political control, and, even more, anything which can properly be described as Parliamentary or democratic control, is corroded almost to the point of extinction. It is the essence of the nuclear strategy that the decisions which govern all our lives shall be taken by a very few people, possibly even by one man. That is the very opposite of liberal or democratic debate. Therefore, on the supreme question of all supreme questions, we have accepted the notion of dictatorship, and even dictatorship by a foreign power. (*House of Commons Debates*, 13 December 1960)

Thereafter, Foot's oratory reached a passionate crescendo as he aligned CND with the national interest, 'fortunately for the honour of this country there is a great and growing number of people throughout the land who are protesting against the policies pursued by the Government ... who are protesting against the suffocation of democratic responsibilities which goes on in this matter, and they have every right to do so' (*House of Commons Debates*, 13 December 1960). Through this oratory Foot became the figurehead of a large vocal unilateralist minority within the labour movement.

Foot's concern for parliamentary sovereignty also led him to oppose membership of the EEC. His oratory forcefully contrasted the EEC's 'bastard form of Cobdenism' with the 'primary concern of this House and of the country ... to develop the economic relations between the developed and under-developed areas of the world' (*House of Commons Debates*, 28 June 1961). Labour and Liberal Party advocates of entry, who contended that Britain should pursue progressive policies from within the EEC, were mocked with humorous invective which presented the EEC as an elitist rich man's club: 'it is like a man saying that he wants to become a member of the Carlton Club, but in order to avoid difficulties and the opprobrium which this might arouse among his friends, he intends later to turn it into a Left-wing coffee house.'

Although less fractious, Foot's relationship with Gaitskell's successor as Labour Party leader, Harold Wilson, was complicated. The Labour left, now organised through the newly established Tribune Group, placed high expectations on Wilson who was a former Bevanite. At the Labour Party conference Foot urged Wilson to implement in full Labour's 1964 general election winning manifesto, while simultaneously using his influence in the Tribune Group to discourage back-bench rebellions (LHASC, 1965; Morgan, 2007b). The economic crisis of 1966–67 proved a turning point. Despite the delivery of steel nationalisation, Foot became increasingly alienated over the implementation of a statutory incomes policy, public spending reductions and proposed industrial relations legislation. Addressing the 1966 and 1968 party conferences Foot launched scathing critiques of the government which were shaped by pathos and Foot's democratic socialist ethos. Foot skilfully presented himself as the socialist conscience of the Labour Party, using phrases such as 'I say, as a socialist' and 'I say we can break out of it if we have faith in our own principles'. Both speeches passionately linked the loss of national economic independence with the pursuit of conservative economic policies, 'We shall not beat this economic crisis with the rusty weapons of our opponents. We will not solve this problem by dressing ourselves in the deflationary clothes of the Tories'.

Given the limited time allotted to Foot at the rostrum he deployed emotive language to spark a reaction from conference, 'We are not our own masters. So great is the crushing burden of our overseas expenditure, so perilous is the position which our attempt to maintain ourselves as a world banker imposes upon us … I say: any Government worth its salt, particularly a Labour Government, would do anything in its power to escape from that position of humiliating dependence'. Foot's rhetoric also sought to empower conference delegates by highlighting their ability to change policy, 'What we have to do is to use this Conference as one of the great instruments for persuading our movement to readopt the socialist policies on which we were elected, the socialist policies which can most quickly make this country independent, the socialist policies which can reinvigorate our movement' (LHASC, 1966: 237; LHASC, 1968: 146). These speeches were of profound significance as they enabled Foot to elevate his standing in the labour movement by aligning with the trade unions, which were becoming more militant in response to rising inflation and deindustrialisation.

In the period 1945–70 Foot's oratory on the core issues of public ownership, unilateral nuclear disarmament, industrial relations and the party manifesto broadened his personal appeal within the labour movement and established a middle-class support-base in CND. His appearances at party conference proved particularly influential in shifting his oratory from the left-wing margins of the Labour Party towards the centre of debate. Foot established a reputation as the most eagerly anticipated speaker at party conference and a powerful parliamentary orator sought after by media broadcasters. Although much of his oratory appealed to pathos and logos it was underpinned by Foot's democratic socialist ethos, as he urged the party leadership to have greater faith in the labour movement and its democratic socialist convictions.

The 'politics of persuasion', 1970–80

Foot's election to the Shadow Cabinet in 1970 was recognition of his extended appeal within the labour movement and would transform his political career in the period 1970–80. Foot's front-bench position allowed him greater time at the rostrum at party conference and enabled him to lead parliamentary debates with much greater regularity. Although there were continuities in Foot's oratory, his speeches reflected the transition from back-bench rebel to government minister by incorporating greater pragmatism. Addressing public meetings and CLPs during the 1973–74 mining crisis, Foot's oratory drew on a combination of pathos and logos. Pathos was to the fore in Foot's speech to Nelson and Colne CLP, which was intended to convey Labour's narrative regarding the mining dispute and reassure activists that the party would deliver its radical *1973 Programme*. Foot deployed a series of combative rhetorical questions intended to ignite his audience's indignation, 'Doesn't he [Heath] know that the pits have been short of miners for years? Doesn't he realise that a defeat for the miners could have disastrous consequences throughout the coalfield? Doesn't he realise that you can only recruit miners in mining communities?' (Foot, 1973b). This was accompanied by apocalyptic language regarding the future of the mining industry: 'This indeed may be our last chance to keep a coal industry in this country at all … We cannot allow the most essential industry in the country to be crucified on the cross of an unfair and unworkable incomes policy' (Foot, 1973b).

Although Foot's January 1974 speech to a public meeting in Taunton utilised logos to a greater extent, his language was more aggressive and contained strong class overtones, 'We must have miners. They will only come from mining communities. People in Bexley or Broadstairs who may imagine that the coal drops like manna from heaven may not be able to understand that, but somebody should have drilled it into Heath's thick skull by now' (Foot, 1974b). With a national miners' strike imminent, much of the speech sought to justify the miners' position and condemn Edward Heath for pursuing an intentionally destructive and confrontational strategy akin to 1926, 'It cannot be repeated too often that the trade union movement went to extreme lengths to offer Heath a way out … but instead of seizing this obvious chance of a settlement, Heath and his colleagues are apparently to spend the next few weeks and months pouring still more millions of the national wealth down the drain in the attempt to mobilise the electorate against the miners' (Foot 1973b). Both of these speeches contained in microcosm the appeals to logos and pathos that Labour would deploy during the 1974 general elections.

As Employment Secretary between 1974 and 1976 Foot negotiated the 'Social Contract' with the trade unions, a voluntary wages agreement which formed the centrepiece of the government's economic strategy. Foot's address to the 1975 party conference utilised a combination of ethos, logos and pathos in an attempt to generate solidarity and win delegates' approval of the policy. Foot astutely drew on his reputation for rebellion to appeal for the trust of conference:

> I have heard it many times before; I dare say I may have said it myself at some time; who knows? People sometimes say: we will agree to some arrangement between the Government and the trade unions about wages, but only when you have the full panoply of socialist measures actually put into full operation. I understand the argument but I say it is unworkable. (LHASC, 1975: 163–6)

Logos also came to the fore as Foot highlighted the Social Contract's compatibility with democratic socialist values:

> you can do it by not so many methods. You can do it by the brutal capitalist methods of the nineteenth century, or you can do it by the equally brutal, or maybe even more outrageous methods of twentieth century Stalinism, or you can do it by the politics of persuasion, by the Social Contract. You can do it that way. You can do it the democratic way, which is the heart and soul of our Labour Movement. (LHASC, 1975: 163–6)

Thereafter, the speech fused pathos with Foot's literary ethos, exhorting the movement to display the 'red flame of socialist courage' and avoid the divisive errors of 1931:

> We face an economic typhoon of unparalleled ferocity, the worst the world has seen since the 1930s. Joseph Conrad wrote a book called 'Typhoon', and at the end he told people how to deal with it. He said, 'Always facing it Captain McWhirr: that's the way to get through'. Always facing it that is the way we have got to solve this problem. We do not want a Labour Movement that tries to dodge it; we do not want people in a Labour Cabinet to try to dodge it. We want people who are prepared to show how they are going to face it, and we need the unified support of the Labour Movement to achieve it. (LHASC, 1975: 163–6)

Foot's newfound emphasis on party unity reflected his concern over the emergence of aggressive neo-liberal Conservatism under Heath and Margaret Thatcher, which Foot described as the 'politics of force' due to its advocacy of anti-union legislation and hostility towards the public sector (Foot, 1974c). According to Foot the overwhelmingly pro-Conservative media was complicit in the promotion of the 'politics of force'. Speaking in Thatcher's Finchley constituency in 1978 he accused the Conservative supporting media of being 'neo-fascist' in its manipulation of opinion poll evidence and coverage of industrial relations (Foot, 1978). He also extended this critique to Thatcher, and her neo-liberal ally, Keith Joseph, whom he accused of using the Saatchi & Saatchi advertising agency to disseminate 'Tory propaganda' intended to mislead the British people into accepting 'the pernicious doctrine that inhuman market forces must be allowed to dictate to human beings how they should behave and how they should live in communities together' (Foot, 1978).

Foot's oratory was shaped by memories of the 1930s and 1940s. Speaking to Barrow-in-Furness CLP in 1976 he presented the Social Contract as the only democratic means to prevent a return to the economic depression of the 1930s and stem the drift towards 'near-fascist conditions' (Foot, 1976). Parallels were drawn between the economic crisis facing the Labour government and the wartime crisis of 1940, directly implying that British democracy was under threat. This concern underpinned Foot's public speeches and media interviews attacking the idea of peacetime coalition government (Foot, 1979). Addressing the Society of Labour Lawyers during a period of minority Labour government in 1974 Foot used logos to dismiss coalition government as an 'evil and impractical' notion associated with the 'Guilty Men' of the 1930s:

> Let us recall the year 1931 when the call for a Government of National Unity became overpowering. The clamour from Fleet Street and Threadneedle Street and Westminster and Whitehall succeeded, and on a note of triumph and self-congratulation, the worst British government of the century took office, and led us inexorably to 1940 and the most perilous moment in our history. (Foot, 1974b)

However, after the loss of the government's majority in 1977 Foot further embellished the ethos underpinning the 'politics of persuasion' by negotiating an agreement with the Liberal Party in order to sustain Labour in office. Foot was at pains to emphasise that 'there is no question of any coalition ... Nor is there any question of any Lib-Lab pact as has been discussed in previous years. It is an agreement between us, made in good faith on both sides, to try to make this Session of Parliament workable in the interests of the nation and the people' (*House of Commons Debates*, 23 March 1977).

Meanwhile, rising support for the Scottish Nationalists and Plaid Cymru at the 1974 general elections added to the sense of crisis by bringing the future of the UK into question. The Labour government responded by proposing the establishment of devolved Scottish and Welsh assemblies, for which Foot assumed responsibility following his appointment as Leader of the House in 1976. Logos dominated Foot's oratory on this issue. During the parliamentary debates Foot drew parallels between devolution and the nineteenth-century reform acts, arguing that it would strengthen democracy while maintaining parliamentary sovereignty (*House of Commons Debates*, 3 August 1976; *House of Commons Debates*, 30 November 1976; *House of Commons Debates*, 16 December 1976; *House of Commons Debates*, 15 February 1978). With the Labour Party divided on devolution the debate at the 1976 party conference became fractious, leading Foot to expand upon the 'politics of persuasion' by describing Labour as 'persuaded devolutionists' while highlighting long-held Labour support for the policy: 'Keir Hardie was a strong supporter of something similar for Scotland and when he stood for Merthyr Tydfil and when elected he was in favour of such a proposition for Wales as well … if Keir Hardie was here … he would have asked why we had not got on with it before' (LHASC, 1976: 201–2). Furthermore, Foot urged conference to support devolution on the pragmatic grounds that it was sustaining the minority Labour government in office through conditional support from the Nationalist parties and the Liberal Party while helping to deliver manifesto commitments, such as nationalisation of the shipyards.

Foot's advocacy of devolution was interlinked with his concern for the interests of Britain's industrial communities. Anxiety over accelerating deindustrialisation led Foot to broaden his critique of British membership of the EEC to include its detrimental effect on the steel industry. He explained that:

> if there is a proposal for building a great new steel works in this country, there will be arguments about whether it should be built in Wales, Scotland or elsewhere. But one of the by-products or associated facts of entry into the Community may be that the building of such a big new plant, a major new investment of the Steel Corporation, will take place in Europe instead. (*House of Commons Debates*, 3 November 1971)

Foot's rhetoric reflected the interests of his own constituents in Ebbw Vale, but by seeking to defend industrial Britain he also added to his standing in the Parliamentary Labour Party (PLP), which contained a disproportionately large number of Labour MPs who represented industrial communities grappling with the twin problems of deindustrialisation and unemployment. Therefore, Foot performed strongly in the 1976 Labour Party leadership contest and was elected deputy leader later that year (Crines, 2011). When the Labour government fell in March 1979 Foot was widely recognised as the leading Labour left MP.

Indeed, Foot delivered one of his finest parliamentary performances during the Confidence Debate which brought the government down. The speech was underpinned by logos as Foot restrained his passion to provide a contrast with the 'almost hysterical tension' of the preceding debate. Foot's newfound ethos as a 'parliamentary fixer' was evident as he humorously warned the Speaker of the House that 'they are trying to stop me from getting your vote as well' (*House of Commons Debates*, 28 March 1979). Portraying the Scottish Nationalists and Liberals as pawns of Thatcher, the speech primarily sought to discredit the minority parties intent on voting against the government by highlighting their connivance with the Conservative Party, 'what the right hon. Lady has done today is to lead her troops into battle snugly concealed behind a Scottish nationalist shield, with the boy David holding her hand'. Foot's reference to 'the boy, David' skilfully presented the young Liberal Party leader, David Steel, as immature in siding with the Conservatives, and was reinforced by the damning assessment that '[Steel] has passed from rising hope to elder statesman without any intervening period'.

This intelligent use of logos, which presciently predicted that Steel's error of judgment would result in the deterioration of the Liberals' electoral prospects, was also directed against the Scottish Nationalists. Foot's oratory highlighted the contradictions underlying their parliamentary leader Donald Stewart's alignment with 'those who are most bitterly opposed to the establishment of a Scottish Assembly' and commented on the 'remarkable allegiance that the right hon. Gentleman commands from his followers' in an attempt to encourage left-leaning Nationalists to defy Stewart (Wilson, 2009: 192–7). The speech concluded with a powerful patriotic attack on the Conservatives, which once again drew on memories of 1940 and 1945:

> What will once again be the choice at the next election? It will not be so dissimilar from the choice that the country had to make in 1945, or even in 1940 when the Labour Party had to come to the rescue of the country. It was on a motion of the Labour Party that the House of Commons threw out the Chamberlain Government in 1940. It was thanks to the Labour Party that Churchill had the chance to serve the country in the war years. Two-thirds of the Conservative Party at that time voted for the same reactionary policies as they will vote for tonight. It is sometimes in the most difficult and painful moments of our history that the country has turned to the Labour Party for salvation, and it has never turned in vain. (Wilson, 2009)

Although the balance of Foot's oratory shifted towards logos during the period 1970–80 through his articulation of the 'politics of persuasion', Foot's democratic socialist ethos was integral to the credibility of this rhetoric. Foot was at the height of his oratorical powers and his speeches at party conference and in Parliament were central to sustaining the Labour government in office. Despite the collapse of the Social Contract during the 'winter of discontent' and the triumph of Thatcher's 'politics of force' at the 1979 general election, he left office with enhanced esteem within the labour movement. This was primarily due to Foot's efforts to sustain Labour Party unity and preserve relations with the trade unions while delivering manifesto commitments. These factors would result in his surprise election as leader of an increasingly divided Labour Party in November 1980 at the age of sixty-seven, ushering in a new phase in his oratory.

The politics of emasculation, 1980–83

The internal divisions that Foot inherited profoundly influenced his oratory as Labour Party leader. Under his leadership Labour was confronted with the tripartite problems of the Social Democratic Party (SDP) split, Militant Tendency entryism and the Bennite left (Shaw, 1996). Foot's speeches on these issues displayed pathos and ethos and were underpinned by his commitment to parliamentary sovereignty, Labour Party democracy and liberal party management. Tony Benn, who led a hard left grouping on the National Executive Committee (NEC) intent on transforming

Labour's constitution through conference and NEC control of the election mani-
festos and mandatory reselection of MPs, was the main target of Foot's oratory
(Panitch and Leys, 2001). Foot's speech to the 1981 party conference, which took
place in the immediate aftermath of Benn's narrow defeat by Denis Healey in a deputy leadership contest, sought to achieve the difficult balancing act of restoring party
unity while discrediting the key demands of the Bennite left. His oratory blended
ethos and pathos, quoting Benn before drawing on his own personal reputation for
rebellion to challenge Benn's position:

> Tony said – and I quote his words, and I listened, as they were addressed especially,
> I think in a sense to me – He said about the Parliamentary Party that he wanted to
> have: 'a better internal democracy so that he is never again told he is there being "a dog
> licence issued by a prime minister"' ... I give Tony and everybody else concerned this
> absolute undertaking here and now that no such dog licenses will be issued by me.
> Indeed, I can recall the first occasion when that was said, because I was in the party
> meeting when it happened ... I protested against that statement then. I have protested
> against the idea behind it ever since. (LHASC, 1981: 121)

Foot's democratic socialism was at the heart of the speech, as he sought to contrast Benn's criticisms of party democracy with the undemocratic implications
of his constitutional demands: 'I accept partners – that is what it has got to be.
The partnership has got to be one in which the Parliamentary Party does not
presume the right to dictate to the Party Conference, and the Party Conference
does not presume the right to dictate to the Parliamentary Party'. Foot also used
deprecating humour to highlight the hypocrisy of Benn in questioning previous
Labour governments' integrity by reminding conference that he had 'not been
in quite as many Labour Cabinets as Tony has'. Thereafter, pathos came to the
fore as Foot returned to the theme of 'the politics of force' in an attempt to focus
the party's attention on the genuine threat posed to democracy by Thatcherism,
'almost week by week, the collapse of the Government's economic policies causes
them to attack our free institutions. They must find scapegoats. So with every
economic failure they turn more viciously on the local authorities or the trade
unions or the nationalised industries or on the obligation of Parliament itself to
provide full employment'. Although the speech helped to stem the rise of the
Bennite left, the scale of Labour's internal divisions resulted in Foot's oratory
remaining inward-looking.

Due to these divisions Foot's leadership became increasingly reliant on the
support of moderates intent on marginalising the Bennite left (Crewe and King,
1997; Golding, 2003). This reliance was accentuated by the formation of the SDP
in March 1981 by 'liberal revisionist' defectors from the Labour Party (Meredith,
2008: 14–19). Foot presented the SDP/Liberal Party Alliance as a 'disparate group
of disillusioned people thirsting for power and willing to coalesce with anyone
who will help them on their way', and accused the Labour defectors of 'bringing

aid and comfort to the most reactionary government we have had in this country in this century' (Foot, 1981a; 1982). Meanwhile, Foot relented to moderate pressure and compromised his liberal party management through the establishment of a register of proscribed organisations intended to facilitate the expulsion of the Trotskyite entryist group, the Militant Tendency (Thomas Symonds, 2005). This decision exposed Foot to accusations of hypocrisy given his previous involvement with the Socialist League, Bevanites and Tribune Group, accusations which he responded to with a highly emotional speech at the 1982 party conference: 'I will be opposed to witch hunts in the party until the day I die ... when people say to me that Militant Tendency are just like Stafford Cripps or Aneurin Bevan ... it is not like that at all ... There was no secret conspiracy with Stafford Cripps or Aneurin Bevan ... They were accused of trying to form a party within a party, but it was not true ... but in this case it is true, and that is the big difference' (LHASC, 1982: 51–2). However, this appeal to pathos and ethos failed to conceal Foot's diminishing authority amongst the Labour left and the growing emasculation of his leadership.

These trends were accentuated by the media's near singular focus on Labour's problems. Foot's televised interviews with the former Labour MP, Brian Walden, on *Weekend World* proved particularly difficult as Walden's combative questioning style unsettled Foot, who in turn resisted the 'sound bite' interview technique (Foot, 1981b; 1981c; 1983). This interview technique partly stemmed from the tabloid media and the growing involvement of advertising agencies in British politics. However, Foot argued that this approach represented a threat to democracy by crudely simplifying complex ideological and policy debates within Parliament, party conference and the PLP. As a result of his refusal to adapt to modern media methods, Foot suffered from a poor media image and struggled to generate popular appeal (Shaw, 1996). Foot's advisors sought to overcome these difficulties by encouraging him to make his televised speeches and interviews more factual and policy centred but this only succeeded in neutralising Foot's one remaining asset; his passion.

To compound matters Foot's style of oratory, which prioritised principle over policy detail, was ill-suited to conveying the programmatic politics of Labour's Bennite-influenced Alternative Economic Strategy. His addresses to the 1980 Liverpool and 1981 Glasgow unemployment demonstrations are illuminating in this regard. Both speeches were dominated by pathos as Foot sought to empower his audiences and enflame their political passions through the use of emotive and aggressive language. Speaking in Liverpool he urged the demonstration to 'kill the lie that there is no alternative to mass unemployment ... Banish the despair which mass unemployment brings in its train. Of course we can stop the whole wretched process of industrial ruin if we have the will. Prepare to destroy at the ballot box, which is the only place they can be finally defeated, the Party of Unemployment' (Foot, 1980). His appeal to pathos reached a crescendo in Glasgow. The speech skilfully sought to align Scottish patriotism with anti-Conservatism while presenting a united labour movement as the vehicle to rescue Britain from Thatcherism: 'Comrades, have you brought your diaries with you? Mark down this date ... This is one of the great historic days in the history of Scotland when we tell the Tory Government what we think of them ... we have had some great crises in the history of our country, 1940, 1945 and in all of them it is this Labour movement of ours that has had to come in and saved the country as a whole' (Foot, 1981d). Foot's memories of the 1930s were omnipresent in both speeches, 'No the 1930s are not to be allowed to return to plague us. The fresh martyrdom of new generations is not to be tolerated'. However, in tapping into collective memories of the 1930s and 1940s and binding Labour to the democratic socialism of 1945 Foot ran the risk of appearing backward-looking and highlighting his advancing age, which was increasingly perceived as an electoral liability.

Foreign policy speeches proved equally problematic. Foot developed a fierce critique of American foreign policy which he contended was recklessly aggressive in the nuclear arms race and responsible for an 'evil' imperialism in Latin America (Foot, 1981e). He pledged to remove American cruise missiles from UK soil and questioned the British–American special relationship. In response the Conservative Party and its media supporters portrayed him as an unpatriotic Communist 'fellow traveller'. The only occasion in which Foot caught the patriotic pulse of the nation was in the emergency parliamentary debate over the Falklands crisis in April 1982. Indeed, Morgan describes the speech as 'perhaps Foot's last great parliamentary performance' (Morgan, 2007b: 411). Although the speech made appeals to logos and pathos, it was underpinned by Foot's long-standing reputation as an opponent of appeasement. Foot deployed logos by posing a series of probing questions intended to hold Thatcher personally accountable and reveal the diplomatic failings of her government:

> What has happened to British diplomacy? The explanations given by the right hon. Lady, when she managed to rise above some of her own party arguments ... were not very full and not very clear. They will need to be a good deal more ample in the days to come ... Above all, more important than the question of what happened to British diplomacy or to British intelligence is what happened to our power to act? The right hon. Lady seemed to dismiss that question. It cannot be dismissed. (*House of Commons Debates*, 3 April 1982)

This incisive analysis was accompanied by a powerful patriotic challenge to Thatcher to take action on behalf of the Falkland Islanders:

> [T]here is no question in the Falkland Islands of any colonial dependence or anything of the sort. It is a question of people who wish to be associated with this country and who have built their whole lives on the basis of association with this country. We have a moral duty, a political duty and every other kind of duty to ensure that that is sustained ... So far they have been betrayed. The responsibility for the betrayal rests with

the Government. The Government must now prove by deeds – they will never be able to do it by words – that they are not responsible for the betrayal and cannot be faced with that charge. (*House of Commons Debates*, 3 April 1982)

Yet differing pacifist, anti-imperialist and anti-fascist interpretations of the crisis within the Labour Party subsequently led Foot to pursue a dual-track approach of supporting the despatch of the British taskforce while proposing a UN negotiated settlement, which negated Foot's patriotic rhetoric and created a sense of confusion (Frank *et al.*, 2010).

Foot's prevarication was in stark contrast to Thatcher, who cultivated the image of a conviction politician intolerant of dissent and opposed to compromise. In effect, Foot's leadership style had little appeal in the polarised political climate of the time. Between 1980 and 1983 Foot's oratory was driven by determination to preserve Labour Party unity and a sense of personal affront at the divisive effect of the SDP split and the Bennite left's constitutional manoeuvring. Ethos and pathos became his most prominent oratorical weapons in this internal labour movement conflict. Yet Foot's over-reliance on character and passion frequently inhibited his appeal to logos and conveyed an impression of confusion and indecision to the wider electorate. Foot was less assured at party conference where he faced an increasingly critical audience and during Prime Minister's Question Time Foot was frequently exposed by Thatcher's aggression, speed of response and command of her brief. Consequently, Foot's oratory was at its weakest in the period 1980–83, debilitated by a combination of internal party divisions, greater media focus on image over substance, and his inability to combat an aggressively populist Thatcher.

Conclusion: the red flame of socialist courage

To conclude an analysis of Michael Foot's oratory on the prism of his leadership would leave a distorted picture of its wider significance to the Labour Party. Foot continued to deliver notable parliamentary speeches until his retirement in 1992. In particular, his speeches on the Westland affair and Yugoslavia stand out. Logos was to the fore in both speeches as Foot assumed the ethos of elder parliamentarian. During the Westland debates in January 1986 Foot focused on Thatcher's duplicitous and undemocratic behaviour to expose her as divisive and untrustworthy:

[Michael Heseltine] said the other day that there was a constitutional crisis – a breach in the constitution ... I never thought it was a breach of the constitution. To me, it is a matter of common decency and plain speaking. It is a matter of coming to the House of Commons and telling the House the truth ... The reason why the Prime Minister is quite prepared to apply one rule of confidentiality to one lot and another rule of confidentiality to another lot is because she works on the principle, 'Is he one of us?' She operates with those who are 'one of us' and that is the way that this Government has been run and this country has been debased. (*House of Commons Debates*, 27 January 1986)

Foot's final parliamentary speech in March 1992, which focused on conflict in the Balkans, also drew on the theme of democracy. It was underpinned by Foot's anti-appeasement ethos as he urged the government to commit UK troops to a UN peacekeeping force in the region in order to curb Serbian aggression. Once again he passionately drew comparisons with the 1930s:

> What the [Serbian] federal army tried to do [in Dubrovnik] was one of the worst acts of that nature that has occurred since the bombing of Guernica ... Conflicts similar to these led people to say that we must have an international authority with the power and the capacity to send in troops speedily and the authority to settle disputes. To some of us, that was almost the first lesson to be learned from the failures between 1918 and 1945. We wanted a real United Nations with the power to act strongly. (*House of Commons Debates*, 5 March 1992)

Foot contributed to nearly all of the major political debates that shaped post-war Britain. He developed a delivery style that blended his knowledge of literature with rapier wit and disregard for deference. Foot's oratory was characterised by a sense of history, interweaving the English civil war, parliamentary reform and nineteenth-century radicalism with the evolution of the labour movement. The extent to which logos, pathos and ethos featured in Foot's oratory differed over time, as did the impact of his oratory on external and internal opponents and the wider electorate. As MP for Plymouth Devonport Foot's oratory was characterised by logos and pathos, and his oratorical pursuit of the 'Guilty Men' during these years, which emphasised the Conservatives' lack of patriotism and association with appeasement and unemployment, proved crucial to his victories in 1945, 1950 and 1951. After succeeding Bevan as MP for Ebbw Vale the force with which Foot's oratory conveyed his democratic socialist ethos proved integral to elevating his standing within the labour movement, and establishing Foot as the 'most consistently articulate and powerful speaker in the House' and at party conference (Morgan, 2007b: 484). Prior to 1970 Foot's chosen role as the democratic socialist conscience of the Labour Party brought him into regular conflict with the Labour Party leadership. In particular, his oratory helped to thwart Gaitskell's attempts to revise Clause IV and curtail Wilson's *In Place of Strife* proposals.

As Foot assumed Shadow Cabinet and ministerial responsibility during the 1970s his pursuit of the 'politics of persuasion' led to logos being combined with ethos in his oratory. The positive electoral impact of his oratory at national level was confined to this period as his exposure of Heath's inept handling of the 1972 and 1974 miners' strikes and portrayal of the Conservative Party as an incompetent and elitist vested interest was integral to the Labour Party's victory in the 1974 general elections. Ironically, Foot's success in securing more liberal party management during this period was subsequently exploited by the Bennite left and

Militant Tendency under his leadership. During his time as leader Foot's appeals to logos were overshadowed by his reliance on ethos and pathos when address-ing labour movement audiences. Although his oratory proved pivotal to preserving the foundations upon which party unity could be rebuilt after 1983 by preventing mass defections to the SDP and avoiding 'hard left' dominance of the party it also revealed some deep contradictions and ironies. Foot had been elected party leader as the unity candidate, and it was anticipated that his powers of oratory would expose the less intellectual and articulate Thatcher. Yet the main strengths of his oratory – conviction and incisive analysis – failed to shine through due to a com-bination of internal divisions and age. The pursuer of the 'Guilty Men' and trib-une of democratic socialism came to be perceived as appeasing the 'undemocratic' hard left and trade unions while prevaricating over causes that he had pursued for a generation, such as unilateral nuclear disarmament. These difficulties were accentuated by Foot's poor media image. During the 1950s his lack of deference and incisive analysis marked Foot out from contemporary politicians but by the 1980s his refusal to deliver 'sound bites' or alter his appearance undermined his ability to effectively communicate with the wider electorate. Although Foot con-tinued to perform strongly at public rallies and demonstrations, his style of oratory based upon an extended vocabulary, and a command of history and literature, had become outdated.

Nonetheless, Foot's oratory impacted on Labour policy and the party's political thought. Foot's vision of democratic socialism as the means to achieve the great-est individual freedom, advance democracy and secure national independence was translated into a progressive patriotic current of the Labour Party's wider political thought. This progressive patriotism associated the labour movement with the 'spirit of 1940', embraced the multinational diversity of the UK through advocacy of devo-lution, and promoted regional policy as a means of reducing inequality. For much of Foot's career the impact of his oratory on policy was limited due to his reputation for left-wing rebellion and passionate pursuit of causes. The policy areas over which Foot exerted most influence were the EEC, industrial relations and devolution. From the 1960s Foot was the most consistent and articulate Labour Party opponent of British membership of the EEC, combining the socialist case against member-ship of the European 'rich man's club' with parliamentary sovereignty. During the 1970s his passionate advocacy of the 'politics of persuasion' underpinning the Social Contract proved pivotal to its endorsement by trade union leaders and the Labour Party conference. Indeed, Foot's presentation of the Social Contract as both fair to workers and in the national interest shaped Labour's relationship with the unions for the following decade. Foot's speeches were equally important in delivering devolu-tion legislation whilst in government and in ensuring that the Labour Party retained the commitment to legislative devolution for Wales and Scotland under his leader-ship, despite deep internal divisions on the issue.

Throughout his life Foot's oratory was defined by its passion, humanity and con-viction. During an era when the Labour Party leadership was dominated by political economists attracted by rationalist methods of electoral communication, such as Gaitskell and Wilson, Foot's oratory humanised Labour's socialism by emphasising the need to appeal to the emotion as well as the intellect of the electorate. Foot's speeches acted as a moral compass for the Labour Party, reminding the party of its responsibility to the working class and its historic relationship with the wider labour movement. Despite variations in their appeal to pathos and ethos, Foot's speeches always exhorted his audience to kindle 'the red flame of socialist courage'. Foot made the greatest contribution of all post-war Labour orators to preserving the ideal of the Labour Party as a democratic socialist cause.

7

The oratory of Tony Benn

Mark Garnett

No serious student of Labour Party history could deny Tony Benn a prominent place in a roll-call of the party's best public speakers. At the time of his retirement from the House of Commons in 2001, he was generally hailed as not just a notable platform speaker, but a shining example of an endangered species – the great 'parliamentarians'. His 'retirement', of course, did not mean that he was going to give up speaking, writing and broadcasting; and in his own mind, the Commons had become a far less important forum over the course of his career. As he put it in perhaps his most memorable phrase, he was leaving the Commons to 'go into politics'.

However, not everyone accepts this evaluation of Benn as a speaker. One well placed observer of post-war British politics denied that he was an orator at all; this witness argued that there was no such thing as 'oratory'. On this view, if a speaker believes in what he or she is trying to express, no 'art' is involved; the words come unbidden from the heart. According to Benn – the commentator in question – substance, rather than skilful presentation, is what matters in political speeches.

Benn's argument has an excellent pedigree, stretching back at least to Socrates' complaints about the Athenian Sophists. In the terms deployed in this volume, it is a claim based on the notion that logos is the only legitimate tool of persuasion. But the obvious rejoinder to Benn (and Socrates) is that facts cannot speak for themselves. Benn's critics, indeed, thought that he was not merely an orator but an exponent of a pernicious approach to public speaking, using the usual range of rhetorical devices for mischievous purposes. On this view, he was a *demagogue* who sought easy publicity by telling untutored audiences what they wanted to hear, despite the fact that he had voiced very different opinions in the past.

The case of Tony Benn thus presents us with an unusual instance of a politician who can be denied oratorical distinction from two contradictory perspectives. On one view (his own), he could not have been an orator because he spoke honestly even when it would have been convenient to 'spin' or dissemble; on the other (that of his detractors), he belonged at best to a discredited branch of the art because he sought cheap popularity with crowd-pleasing rhetoric which conflicted sharply with his earlier pronouncements. The present analysis eschews both of these extreme positions. It argues that Benn should in fact be classed as an orator who made use of logos, pathos and ethos – albeit in a highly distinctive fashion. His approach showed obvious congruence with a long-established and much-honoured speaking style – that of the nineteenth-century dissenter. The dissenting tradition has produced numerous writers and orators who claimed to be 'Plain Speakers', while using modes of communication which were anything but 'plain'. While the tradition has usually been associated with radical liberalism, Benn regarded himself as a socialist. The following discussion thus includes a brief analysis of his ideological development, as well as a summary of the major episodes in his career within the Labour movement.

Apprenticeship

Later in his career Benn was often accused of hypocrisy, on the grounds that he had enjoyed a pampered lifestyle; he was more than happy to relinquish a peerage in order to retain his right to sit in the House of Commons, but was not prepared to give up the more solid material advantages he had inherited, or acquired through marriage. It would have been more pertinent (but probably less damaging) for Benn's enemies to point out that his family background made him an excellent example of a type whose influence has been widely decried in recent years – the 'career politician' (Oborne, 2007). Even if Benn (to borrow Edmund Burke's phrase) was not exactly 'swaddled, rocked and dandled into a legislator' – and it would be misleading to describe his origins as 'patrician' – he was born into a very prominent political family (Morgan, 1992: 301). His father, William Wedgwood Benn, was elevated to the House of Lords as Viscount Stansgate in 1942 in recognition of long and distinguished political services to both Labour and the Liberals. Viscount Stansgate had followed more successfully in the footsteps of his own father, John, a Liberal MP who had been knighted in 1906 and made a baronet in 1914. These upward steps within the honours system were far less important than Tony Benn's socialisation into the political milieu; even his uncle, Sir Ernest Benn, wrote popular (and vehemently liberal) political books and pamphlets.

Benn's religious background was another inherited ingredient. As his biographer Jad Adams has written, 'The twin pillars of religion and politics run through the Benn ancestry' (Adams, 1992: 6). Julian Critchley – a political opponent, though not an unfriendly one – wrote that in an earlier century Benn would have been 'a well loved clerical eccentric', and that he even had the attributes of a saint (Critchley, 1990: 114). Benn himself thought that his pious elder brother, Michael, would have achieved clerical eminence had he survived the Second World War (Adams, 1992: 37). Yet the Benns belonged to a tradition which rejected idolatory, or any other form of authority which lacked a democratic basis. As befitted a family with deep roots in the Liberal Party, they had long been prominent dissenters from the established Anglican Church. Tony Benn himself felt that those who understood the true message of Christianity would recognise its connection with socialist, rather than liberal, principles. Whatever the doctrinal linkages, there is no doubt that religion strongly affected Benn's speaking style. The overall impression is redolent of nineteenth-century dissent, rather than secular post-war Labour.

Benn's oratorical apprenticeship began in an auspicious nursery – the Oxford Union, which he served as president in 1947, after returning from his own war service. Reporting on his elevation to the presidency, a correspondent in *Isis* magazine wrote that 'If Mr Benn has made a bad speech in the Union, we have yet to hear it' (quoted in Adams, 1992: 42). Already meticulous in his preparation for important speeches, the young Tony Benn was at his best when he enlivened his message with well-timed flashes of humour. His first foray, indeed, had been characterised as 'satirical', even though it had dealt with the serious subject of social security. However, in other early efforts he was too much in earnest; after one speech he was advised to 'avoid treating the House as a class or a Salvation Army meeting' (Adams, 1992: 29). In short, at Oxford Benn could not hope to sustain his initial positive impact unless he stopped taking it for granted that his audience would agree with his moral message.

Reflecting on reports of an Oxford Union speech Benn delivered in March 1943, Jad Adams identifies characteristics which were easily detected in a mature style where logos and pathos were both clearly present, but difficult to disentangle:

> first there is a statement which is not supported by any evidence, but before there is time to understand and question the statement, along comes an irrefutable truth ... examples follow, both easily appreciated and clearly visualised ... An appeal to the higher emotions rounds it off. There is no marshalling of arguments, but the audience should feel – for there is enough to think about as the examples and paradoxes tumble out – that the conclusion follows logically from the previous statements. (Adams, 1992: 31–2)

In the early 1980s the parliamentary sketch-writer Simon Hoggart detected similar tendencies, though he was less reverential in praising Benn's 'debating technique, [which] like that fluid you can put in a leaky car radiator, is entirely self-sealing. Whenever a gap appears in his logic, another part of the argument is rushed forward to close it up' (Hoggart, 1983: 140).

Benn's successful stint at the Union meant that he was picked as one of three speakers for a four-month debating tour of the United States, beginning in October 1947. One of his fellow-travellers (Kenneth Harris, who became a well-known journalist) recalled that on the outward journey Benn had delivered a speech on party politics which was 'very pedestrian stuff'. However, once Benn had become accustomed to the American style of debating – more attuned to the training of lawyers than of professional politicians – he quickly found his stride. According to Harris, 'Benn got funnier and funnier as we went on'. Significantly, Harris thought that before the American tour Benn 'could bore people'. After his return to Oxford, he gave 'one of the ablest and funniest speeches I have ever heard at the Union or anywhere else' (quoted in Adams, 1992: 48).

The ability to exhibit a sense of humour amid expressions of high principle was vital in helping Benn to win the Labour nomination for the seat of Bristol South-East when it fell vacant in 1950. At the time, the seat was held by the Chancellor of the Exchequer, Sir Stafford Cripps, who was standing down due to chronic ill-health. Like Benn, Cripps believed that Christian beliefs underpinned socialism, rather than conflicting with it; but his speeches had never been noted for rib-tickling interludes. To those who attended the selection meeting after Cripps' resignation, Benn must have seemed like a heaven-sent successor. He was young and vigorous, unlike Sir Stafford whose health had been indifferent for several years; and although Benn was heir to a peerage, the fact that Cripps had been a genuine 'patrician', born into an affluent, landed family, had not prevented him from serving the constituency well and espousing radical causes. While Benn's speech to the selection meeting demonstrated his serious purpose, he also proved able to inject some (well-rehearsed) levity (Adams, 1992: 63–5).

After a comfortable victory in the ensuing by-election Benn became the youngest serving MP at the age of twenty-five. He was advised that 'about the middle of February' would be the best time to deliver his maiden speech, and another young MP, Roy Jenkins, suggested steel nationalisation as a suitable topic. Jenkins' advice might have been a mischievous attempt to entice a potential rival into making a false start, and Benn was certainly taking a risk in accepting it. Maiden speeches were supposed to be uncontroversial, rarely straying beyond effusive compliments addressed to the new member's predecessor and constituents – and the nationalisation of iron and steel was one of the hottest political topics of the time. Benn himself tried to play down the controversial nature of the subject by emphasising its lack of novelty, reflecting that 'everything that could possibly have been said on the subject had been said', so that 'the only way to tackle it was to set out the case simply and, if possible, amusingly' (Benn, 1994a: 138).

Benn might have felt equal to the task of wringing an uncontroversial speech out of a deeply contentious issue because his father had supplied him with a recipe for success in *any* Commons' performance: 'simplicity, sincerity, modesty, clarity' (Benn, 1994a: 138). It was difficult to fault him on any of these criteria, judging by the written record of his speech (*Hansard*, vol. 483, cols. 1778–83, 7 Februrary 1951). However, at one point there was an over-abundance of 'sincerity', when the newcomer implied that private iron and steel companies might profit from rearmament while the rest of the country was still suffering from the effects of 'austerity'. The *Hansard* scribes reported an 'interruption' at this point – an occurrence that was even more unusual during a maiden speech than the injection of controversial matter. Benn's meticulous biographer, Adams, does not mention this incident; but Benn himself recorded that after his awkwardly phrased remark he 'sensed a change of feeling – and a wave of hostility'. This was not surprising; the Opposition leader, Winston Churchill, had opened the debate with an uncompromising speech which had aroused partisan passions on both sides of the House. Remembering his father's advice about 'modesty', Benn quickly apologised and by the end of his speech he 'was aware of growing friendliness and laughter' (Adams, 1992: 72–3). As before, his ability to show a sense of humour, combined with his obvious ability and charm, overcame the misgivings of his listeners; and this sensitivity to changes of mood in the audience proves that, at this stage of his career at least, Benn was certainly not a speaker who eschewed pathos and ethos in his determination to bear witness to the simple truths within him.

The next speaker, the Conservative Sir Ralph Glyn, duly paid an eloquent tribute to the speaker and his father; in words which would seem highly ironic during the 1980s, he anticipated that despite the obvious ideological differences 'all of us on this side ... will look upon the Hon. Member as a colleague for whom we have great respect and whose future we shall all gladly cheer as he goes up the ladder of success in the House' (*Hansard*, vol. 483, cols. 1783–4, 7 February 1951). As Adams records, Benn's speech was warmly praised by Michael Foot in the *Daily Herald* (Adams, 1992: 74). However, Benn was given due warning that in future debates he would not be handled so tenderly if he transgressed parliamentary decorum; and it was obvious that his contentious reference to profiteering would not have been forgiven so easily if it had been made by a new MP who lacked a widely respected father.

Just three months later, Benn discovered how limited parliamentary tolerance could be once he had used up the licence his father's career had granted to him. During a debate on the appropriate compensation due to former prisoners in Japanese camps, Benn drew a comparison between the treatment of prisoners of war (POWs) and the atomic outrages against Hiroshima and Nagasaki. This can only be regarded as a distraction from the point of the debate, since the British government (let alone the POWs who had suffered in Japanese camps) could not be held responsible for the attacks which brought the war against Japan to an end. Benn was interrupted and criticised during his speech by members of his own parliamentary party as well as Conservatives; and instead of apologising and jumping out of the hole he had dug for himself, he persevered with his line of argument, claiming (with irrelevant accuracy) that the British had been equally inhumane in their treatment of prisoners during previous conflicts.

There is no contemporaneous record of Benn's feelings in his published (and skilfully edited) diary; given the comprehensive nature of his humiliation it would not be surprising if he had decided not to leave even a private record at the time. In an interview conducted in 1989 for the purposes of Adams' biography, Benn sensibly accepted that 'I was insensitive about the suffering of the Far East POWs. I know it made me unhappy because I hadn't got it right. I should have done it differently' (Adams, 1992). However, when Benn's diary for the relevant period was published five years later, his retrospective commentary was very different. While acknowledging that his remarks drew criticism from inside the chamber and from the public at large, Benn claimed to be 'still glad that I drew the comparison' between the treatment of POWs and the various crimes committed by representatives of the British empire and the assailants of Hiroshima and Nagasaki (Benn, 1994a: 154). Judging Benn by his own high standards, the excerpt from the Adams interview reads like a moment of candour, while the diary commentary sounds like the product of ethos – an attempt to perpetuate his own legend as a man who dared to utter the truth even when it was impolite to do so.

Adams suggests that 'in [Benn's] maiden speech and in this one on the British prisoners of war was represented in embryo the whole of his future parliamentary career: oratorical brilliance applauded even by his opponents followed by a stand on a matter of principle which arouses indignation in equal measure' (Adams, 1992: 75–6). There is much to be said in favour of this verdict, but it can be questioned in three respects. First, Benn's maiden speech was not 'brilliant'; although the best passages had certainly demonstrated his potential, he was interrupted because he had introduced an extra layer of controversy into what was already a contentious subject. Second, it was customary for the political opponent who (inevitably) followed the maiden speech of a new member to say something nice about it – and the remarks about Benn's speech had been unusually warm at least in part because of affection for his father. Although Cripps provides an unfair comparison – Cripps was already a renowned barrister before being persuaded by Labour to enter Parliament – after his own maiden effort no less a judge than David Lloyd George had hailed him as 'one of the most distinguished Parliamentarians of this generation' (Estorick, 1949: 85). Finally, the 'insensitive' remarks about British POWs can hardly be counted as a matter of principle, unless the 'principle' in question really was a belief that the sufferings of British prisoners had been exaggerated. Benn, of course, was right to draw attention to the brutal treatment of innocent Japanese civilians, and it is unquestionable that at various times members of the British armed forces have tortured, starved or humiliated captive individuals. None of this, though, had much bearing on the point at issue during the specific context of the debate, and in the House of Commons of 1951 it could only be judged as a calamitous misuse of pathos.

Since he could no longer expect his colleagues to forgive him out of fondness for his father – and parliamentary performances could still make or mar a political career – the speech might have been a devastating setback for Benn, just a few months after he had entered Parliament. Fortunately for him, he had a new weapon at his disposal. The BBC radio programme *Any Questions?* was recorded in Bristol, and even before the parliamentary setback of May 1951 the young and personable local MP had been asked to join the panel. In this format Benn could show his true potential; thanks to careful preparation he was usually ready with a plausible reply even when the questions had not been divulged in advance, and a sprinkling of humour was sure to make a positive impact on the radio audience. Benn's progress through the Labour ranks over the following decade undoubtedly owed much to his ability to master the electronic media which was alien to so many of his colleagues.

The making of a 'demagogue'

In 1957, Anthony Wedgwood Benn was appointed a frontbench spokesman on the RAF – not an exalted position, since Labour was in opposition and the party had two spokespeople for each branch of the military service. Within a year he had resigned from this position over Britain's development of a hydrogen bomb. It was an undemonstrative departure, despite the contemporary clamour concerning nuclear weapons which had already led to the formation of the Campaign for Nuclear Disarmament (CND). Benn remained on the fast track to meaningful promotion, and after the 1959 election he was recalled as shadow transport minister. However, in November 1960 his father died, and he was faced with the prospect of an unwanted 'elevation' to the House of Lords. Benn could still hope to serve as a senior minister, though Number 10 Downing Street would be ruled out by his ineligibility for the Commons. However, his main impetus in resisting his removal clearly arose from a sincere belief that his democratic rights had been infringed.

The details of Benn's successful campaign to renounce his father's peerage need not be followed closely here. For our purpose, the main points are that the prolonged episode enhanced his confidence in the good sense of the British people – his constituents in Bristol gave him a resounding endorsement at the ballot box in 1961, despite the likelihood that he would be barred from taking his seat – and sharpened an antipathy towards 'the establishment' which was a crucial component of his dissenting heritage. Since high principle was at stake and Benn's plight was hardly a laughing matter, there were limited opportunities for him to utilise his favoured formula in speeches during this period. However, the struggle which resulted in the 1963 Peerage Act was almost guaranteed to win widespread sympathy for Benn and his cause. In this struggle Benn was obviously swimming with the 'meritocratic' tide of the era, in which 'the establishment' was coming under unprecedented scrutiny. With hindsight, the passage of the 1958 Life Peerages Act had made Benn's case for him; had that measure been introduced before 1941, William Wedgwood Benn would surely have been given a life peerage rather than the hereditary one he was given in that year. The resistance of the 'establishment' to the idea of renunciation – such an obvious counterpart to the introduction of life peerages – was bound to give Benn the potent public image of a plucky underdog who also happened to be right.

Before the matter was resolved, 'Rab' Butler had shown the true value of Glyn's prediction that Conservative MPs would gladly cheer Benn's progress when he confided that 'there was a strong feeling in the Party against you personally' (Benn, 1994a: 394). In light of such provocative comments – and the less than unanimous support of his own side – the successful passage of the Peerage Act could easily have made a less substantial character than Benn into a rabble-rouser. However, once he had won another by-election and resumed his seat in the Commons he settled back into the routine of an orthodox ministerial aspirant, writing speeches for his new party leader Harold Wilson.

After Labour's narrow victory in the 1964 general election, Benn became Postmaster-General – an office outside the Cabinet, from which he still managed to attract publicity through his modernising ideas. When the government was re-elected more comfortably in 1966 Benn was promoted to the Cabinet as Minister for Technology. He remained on the front bench until deciding not to stand for re-election to the Shadow Cabinet after the 1979 general election.

Years later, Benn wrote that he was a very rare example of Cabinet minister who had been 'radicalised while in office'. His experience as Minister for Technology certainly increased his awareness of 'thousands of skilled and unskilled workers whose legal status in relation to their employer was little better than high-grade serfdom' (Benn, 1979: 16). In a justly-celebrated polemic published many years later, Foot praised the Benn of 1971 for delivering a measured speech to the Fabian Society. At this time, Foot argued, Benn was careful to include himself in criticisms of the Wilson government after its defeat in the 1970 general election. Foot commented that 'The whole tone was tentative and reflective; no one from any section of the Party could object' (Foot, 1986: 111). Probably for good reasons of his own, Foot played down the most important feature of Benn's speech – his acceptance that on several key questions the party leadership had blundered, and had acted on its mistaken conclusions despite the well-founded objections of the Labour movement as a whole. Thus, even in 1971 Benn believed that the party leadership should be much more accountable to ordinary members in future.

At the time of the Fabian speech, Benn was serving as chairman of the party – not the most powerful of positions on paper, but nevertheless one which could create a slightly exaggerated sense of personal responsibility in the mind of a sensitive ex-minister. Benn clearly believed that the parliamentary party had to re-connect with the wider movement (which, in his own mind, had proved itself to be so astute between 1964 and 1970). However, a senior figure is sure to arouse the suspicions of colleagues when he or she tells the party faithful that their wisdom deserves a more respectful hearing from leaders. At this time, Benn also threw himself into an exhausting speaking campaign, and was more than happy to identify himself with causes which few of his senior colleagues were prepared to touch. In particular, he supported various efforts by workers to take control of mismanaged industrial plants. As a result, trade union activists began to shed their initial misgivings about this middle-class ex-minister – and Benn's equally middle-class colleagues became increasingly convinced that his protestations of principle were brazen attempts to curry favour among Labour's key supporters in the unions and constituency parties (Hatfield, 1978).

In November 1971 Benn stood for the Labour Deputy Leadership, and finished third of three contestants, trailing badly behind Jenkins and Foot. Since Benn had made well-publicised attacks on the Conservative government's industrial strategy, he had some reason for feeling qualified to join the contest; but he had no realistic hope of winning against two rivals who enjoyed a devoted following within the parliamentary party. Adams, whose biography is generally very sympathetic, notes that

Benn 'had no emotional mechanism for dealing with failure' (Adams, 1992: 315). The defeat seems to have triggered off a profound reassessment, which took Benn beyond the relatively measured Fabian Society speech. In 1972 he made a decision which, on the face of it, was rather trivial. However, dropping his middle name of 'Wedgwood', so soon after his defeat in the deputy leadership election, was a maladroit move which could only inspire the suspicion that he was trying to conceal his relatively privileged upbringing. Although friendly colleagues like Barbara Castle continued to call him by the affectionate nickname of 'Wedgie', from this time even they tended to interpret all of his major moves as attempts to bolster his personal position within the party. He compounded the error by expunging his privileged educational background (public school as well as Oxford) from his *Who's Who* entry (Castle, 1980). Jenkins, having resigned as Deputy Leader after Benn's successful campaign to commit Labour to a referendum on European Economic Community (EEC) entry, launched a thinly-coded counter-attack, warning a fringe meeting at the 1972 conference that 'populism … cannot possibly be equated with democracy' (Hatfield, 1978: 70).

By this time Benn had been identified by the right-wing press as Labour's 'bogey man' in the glaring absence of other radical candidates. Far from rallying around a victimised colleague, even members of the Labour 'left' acted as if there was some substance behind the media witch-hunt. In a cabinet meeting of July 1974, Castle noted that Foot, for one, gave every sign of thinking that Benn was 'obsessed with ambition'. Others, who sympathised with Benn's views, were 'getting a bit sick of his clear determination to strike attitudes publicly wherever he can'. In September 1975, Castle referred to Benn's love of 'demagogic politics' as if that were now an established fact about him (Castle, 1980: 312).

In short, Benn's honourable desire to lead and rejuvenate his party had been con-strued even by senior sympathisers as a symptom of unhealthy egotism, thanks to a mixture of circumstances, tactical errors, and inability (or unwillingness) to com-municate his true intentions even to his friends. Another self-inflicted wound was Benn's frequently rehearsed argument that politics should be about *principle*, rather than *personality*. This was a perfectly respectable aspiration in the abstract, akin to the footballing precept of playing the ball and not the man. However, it was increas-ingly implausible in an era of televised politics – a development which, as we have seen, raised Benn's own profile more than most. Benn's ebullient personality had served him well during his career, particularly when he was campaigning for the right to renounce his peerage; it meant, for example, that some people like Castle continued to find him endearing even though some of his actions had aroused their instinctive disapproval. Equally, when he criticised the policies of his own party, it would have taken a super-human degree of self-abnegation for the leaders who had formulated those policies to regard his attacks in anything other than a personal light. It could also, in a convoluted way, be seen by opponents as a means by which Benn could preserve his *amour propre* despite all the clamour against him; when elements of the press portrayed him as an unhinged fanatic, in his own mind they were not expressing any *personal* dislike, but rather concentrating their fire on him as a champion of unpopular truths. This strategy of self-preservation must have been unusually important during and after the 1975 referendum campaign, when his speeches attracted enormous and adulatory audiences, but his argument for leaving the EEC was heavily defeated in the ballot and opinion polls found him to be among the most unpopular politicians who had spoken on either side.

The final brush-strokes to the picture of a self-appointed 'tribune of the people' were provided by Benn's public oratory after his defeat in the deputy leadership contest. The 'Salvation Army style' had returned, inspired by a redoubled sense of moral purpose which he displayed both in and out of the Commons. Thus, in February 1975 Castle recorded a debate in which Benn had been subjected to 'a sustained barracking' by Tory MPs, and showed considerable courage in repelling the attacks. Nevertheless, Castle wished that 'he could manage to sound less like a lay preacher helping everyone else to find the right road to God' (Castle, 1980: 312). After such a protracted series of personal setbacks, compounded by his demotion from Industry to Energy as soon as the referendum was over, it was not surprising that Benn continued to develop a more robust critique of the system which had prevailed in Britain since the war. When, after Labour's defeat in the 1979 general election, he took to criticising the record of the Wilson–Callaghan governments, colleagues like Foot could not conceal their disgust. In their eyes, Benn had forgotten his even-handed approach of 1971, and was now levelling an indictment of *collective* personal guilt against his colleagues, while tacitly absolving himself.

Benn refused to serve in the Shadow Cabinet formed by James Callaghan after the 1979 election. Annoyingly for his critics, though, his first speech from the back benches in 22 years was described by Hoggart as 'well reasoned, witty and logical even if it was enlivened by the occasional flashes of lunacy' (Hoggart, 1981: 11–12). It seemed that Benn had finally decided to treat the House of Commons like the Oxford Union; self-deprecating humour was essential if he was to retain anything like a respectful hearing amongst the unconverted.

When speaking 'out of doors', however, Benn knew that his audience would be happy if he reverted to 'Salvation Army' mode; indeed, at this stage of his career his followers expected nothing less than moral lessons. Max Atkinson has presented a detailed and fascinating analysis of a speech which Benn delivered at the Labour Party conference of 1980, when his popularity within the movement was at its highest. Characterising Benn as a 'spellbinding' orator, Atkinson remarks on his effective use of gestures, his ability to speak without referring to a written text, and even his refusal to wear glasses which would have obscured his large and luminous eyes – emblems of burning sincerity among his supporters, and hallmarks of incipient lunacy to his opponents. According to Atkinson's analysis, a final touch of oratorical genius was Benn's ability to continue speaking even after delivering lines which were guaranteed to win applause. This gave the impression that the speaker was too impatient to deliver himself of the truth to pause until the acclaim had died down – in other words, that anyone who supposed that he had used pathos (or even ethos) simply to please the crowd was mistaken, and that his sole purpose was to unburden himself of the plain truth without undue delay (Atkinson, 1984).

In the semi-privacy of his diary, Benn rated his speech to the 1980 conference, where he denounced the party leadership for betraying its promises, as 'the best speech I have ever made at conference, probably the best speech I have ever made in my life at a public meeting' (Benn, 1994b: 32). Given Benn's insistence that he was never an orator, this is an instructive verdict. He implies that he might have delivered better speeches at meetings which were not 'public' – presumably in places like the Oxford Union, the Commons, or indeed the Cabinet, Shadow Cabinet or Labour's National Executive Committee (NEC). Even so, Benn's account does leave the impression that this speech meant so much to him because of its reception, which in the context of the time could have depended on factors other than its content. In his diary Benn noted that he received a standing ovation from the people who mattered most to him – namely, the activists within Constituency Labour Parties; amid the euphoria, he was observant enough to notice that some trade union leaders were 'looking very uncomfortable', but that only added to his sense of triumph on what was 'a most thrilling day' (Benn, 1994b: 32). Taken as a whole, Benn's judgement on his speech – which was too focused on the internal party controversies of the time to make much impression thirty years later – is characteristic of a master craftsman reflecting on a superlative performance, rather than the purveyor of truth which, at the time and for many years later, Benn claimed to be.

However, Benn's opponents outside the hall were less impressed by hyperbole which compared Margaret Thatcher and Sir Keith Joseph to Adolf Hitler; and even well-wishers were disconcerted by his willingness to join forces with activists who could be accused of fomenting a civil war within the Labour Party and hoping to do something similar to Britain as a whole if (as seemed likely in 1980) the Conservative government fell apart (Atkinson, 1984). Benn's attack on his former colleagues might have been the high point of his career as an orator, but it triggered the chain of decisions which thwarted him in 1981 when, for the second time, he stood for the deputy leadership of his party. In the feverish circumstances of 1980, it had proved possible for a master-orator like Benn to furnish a combination of logos, pathos and ethos which could prove 'spellbinding' to a party audience in which his followers were numerous and highly vocal. But an experienced politician should never have mistaken this for a formula which could carry Labour to victory in the near future; and this consideration persuaded even party members who agreed with Benn's message to withhold their support in the knife-edge contest against Denis Healey.

Benn's beliefs

Despite all the unfair comment on Benn's family background, it is tempting to explain his strange political odyssey in terms of his unusual heritage. His father was a progressive liberal on principle, although he was raised to the peerage by the Labour Party he had adopted. Benn absorbed his father's principles; but while Viscount Stansgate had felt compelled by personal circumstances to work within the Labour Party, the dilemma was much more acute for his conscientious son, who naturally wanted to feel that he really *belonged* within the impressive movement which his father had joined for tactical reasons. Until the second half of the 1960s it was possible for Benn to act as if the dilemma didn't matter to him; his role as a promising and prominent 'technocratic' moderniser, with vaguely iconoclastic attitudes towards the monarchy and a rooted dislike of racist attitudes at home and abroad, seemed to identify him with the modestly radical wing of a party which, thanks to its substantial social base, represented the governing party of the future. Labour's unexpected defeat in the 1970 general election put paid to these complacent visions; and in any case, as Minister for Technology Benn had become intimately acquainted with the extent of injustice within Britain. It was not surprising that, in the aftermath of defeat, he should explore the founding principles of the Labour Party and concentrate on the socialist elements of the 1918 constitution – which, it seems, he had not previously regarded as sacrosanct.

Instead of deflecting him, the attacks of opponents in the right-wing press merely assured Benn that the numerous historical accidents which had given him a prominent role within the Labour Party constituted a kind of destiny. Unlike Cripps, whose initial radicalism had been arrested by the experience of the Second World War, the mature Benn was able to conclude that his ministerial colleagues lacked both insight and courage in their attempts to address the problems of the 1960s and 1970s; like most new converts, he tended to regard them as cynical traitors to the cause which he had only just adopted.

In the late 1970s and early 1980s, while the right-wing press curdled the public blood with predictions that the Labour Party was on the verge of adopting fully-fledged 'Bennery', the new hero of the left was widely accused of 'totalitarian' instincts. Even after Benn's influence within the Labour movement had started to wane, Kenneth Morgan commented that 'His approach has been presented in a tone of illiberal dogma which recalls the puritanical excesses of the Fifth Monarchy men' (Morgan, 1992: 312). The association of Benn with seventeenth-century British radicals is suggestive; but the 'illiberal' label, as applied to Benn personally, is highly misleading. His popular book, *Arguments for Socialism* (1979), was criticised by Morgan himself on the grounds that 'what the book conspicuously does not argue for is socialism' (Morgan, 1992: 311). Bearing on almost every page its author's detestation of control from the centre and his desire for free, popular participation, *Arguments for Socialism* is in fact a testament to Benn's continued ideological allegiance to a humane form of *liberalism*. Far from idolising the millenarian Fifth Monarchists, Benn preferred to lavish his nostalgic affection on their contemporaries the Levellers, who can plausibly be regarded as proto-Thatcherites rather than harbingers of Marxism. The same remarks, of course, can be applied to Benn's eighteenth-century hero, Thomas Paine. It was ironic that, by the early 1980s, almost the only thing that seemed to unite Benn and Foot was their shared admiration for noted liberal rebels of the distant past; but when one considers that Foot, like Benn, was a liberal by inheritance whose allegiance to Labour arose from historical happenstance rather than logic, the odd choice of heroes is more explicable.

Having convinced himself that one *had* to be a socialist if one was to be an honourable member of the Labour Party – and, perhaps, having realised that, prior to 1970 at least, his ideological credentials in this respect were highly dubious – Benn threw himself into the task of making up for lost time. He even studied Karl Marx's writings, and (predictably) found that they offered plenty of precepts which could be squared with Christianity. Being a true socialist within the Labour movement entailed, in Benn's view, that one should always regard trade unionists as underdogs – even when a more objective observer would acknowledge that post-war governments tended to be accorded more respect than their employers. When the trade unions seemed to accept Benn as a dependable advocate of workers' rights, he believed that his socialist credentials were now established beyond contradiction, and after 1970 he showed his gratitude by trying to contort his own (characteristically liberal) views into a defence of their growing power within the Labour Party and Britain itself. For Benn the orator, the big pay-off in this new alliance was that activists within the trade unions and the constituency parties showed every sign of enjoying his own preferred manner of speaking; instead of the rebukes he received in Parliament (or the Oxford Union) when he forgot to inject humour into his political sermons, these audiences were deeply appreciative of a humourless preacher.

Conclusion

On the most charitable view of Tony Benn's career after 1970, he failed in his attempt to remind the Labour Party of the purpose for which, in his view, it had been formed. The reminder was badly timed – the 1970 defeat, after all, showed that Labour had no hope of winning elections if it merely preached to the converted, however eloquent the preacher. Leaving aside the unfounded charge that Benn was born a 'patrician', a more relevant criticism was that as he became more convinced by the case for radical change, the less discriminating was his choice of associates. In the years between Labour's electoral defeat of 1979 and his own dismissal by the voters of Bristol South East in 1983, he seemed to have made himself the unfailing champion of every cause which was calculated to undermine his party's chances of returning to power.

In taking this approach, though, Benn was reverting to the intellectual heritage which always informed his oratory, except on those occasions when he remembered that he was addressing an unconverted audience. In the Oxford Union, he learned that he would lose his listeners unless he sprinkled his speeches with humour. He was reminded of those lessons when he entered the Commons, and although he occasionally strayed from the successful formula, by the end of the parliamentary phase of his career he had adapted his style of oratory (and his knowledge of procedure in the House) to such a pitch that even his ideological opponents regarded him with respectful affection. However, in the years between 1970 and 1983 – the pivotal period of Benn's career – he tended to speak on party platforms as if command of the Labour movement would be sufficient to change the course of British politics. As it turned out, the undoubted force of his oratory was not even enough to win him the deputy leadership of his party; and in 1980, when he came within a whisker of winning that post, the Labour Party was in the process of proving that it could only rely on the unquestioning support of a shrinking segment of the British population.

The idea that someone could 'go into politics' after leaving the Commons contrasts with John Stuart Mill's view of the elected chamber as 'an elevated Tribune or Chair from which to preach larger ideas than can at present be realised' (quoted in Reeves, 2007: 355). In 1974, Benn told the journalist Hugo Young that 'It takes ten years for an idea to come to fruit', suggesting that even if a speech lacked immediate impact its effects would be felt one day (Young, 2008: 45). Clearly by 2001 – forty years after his impassioned campaign for the right to stay in the place – Benn had decided that the House of Commons was not a suitable place to plant the seeds of radicalism. Given that the effect of public speaking depended almost entirely on the media, it would not be unreasonable to suggest that Benn's decision to leave Parliament, and the reasons which lay behind his retirement, mark the end of radical oratory in Britain, at least in any of the forms which became familiar in the post-war period.

Despite his repeated disclaimers, in practice Benn was as ready as Socrates himself to use pathos to advantage. Characteristically, in his heyday of the early 1980s, this would occur when he sensed that his audience shared his feeling of outrage at some iniquitous decision or practice of the Labour leadership, although as we have seen he was also capable of comparing Conservatives to Hitler. In his lengthy analysis of Benn's speech at the 1980 Labour Party conference, Atkinson shows that he used gestures as well as finely-honed vocal techniques to add weight to his proposals for reform of the party's constitution (Atkinson, 1984: 94–104).

In terms of ethos, Benn's career as an orator is even less consistent with his self-evaluation. He is an example of a politician who habitually argued that principle is far more important than personality, but who nevertheless became the focus of a personality cult on the left of the Labour Party. An unkind critic would characterise this as a calculated move by Benn to promote his own career, as a one-man antidote to the personalised politics pioneered by Wilson. On a less hostile assessment, Benn's role of charismatic leader of the left was largely foisted on him by his enemies within the media. Whether antagonistic or friendly in intent, judgements of Benn's oratory must accept that the impact of his speeches depended not just on what was said and the manner of its delivery, but also on the public image of the person who was speaking; and the notion that the speaker was not interested in his own advancement was a major component of the image that Benn sought to project.

For most of Benn's career his style was one which has generally won the widest approval in hindsight – that is, when the orator's political career is either finished or in its twilight phase. This is not to say that Benn was a demagogue, either, unless one adopts an unusably elastic definition of the term. His ambition was no greater than that of most other able British politicians; and if, like them, he hoped to attract devotees in significant numbers, he believed that the admiration should be earned, rather than won at the cost of his conscience. In fact, if Benn is judged against the usual standards of careerism, the well-developed conscience which he had absorbed from his liberal (and Liberal) ancestors could be counted as one of his misfortunes. Circumstances, inevitably, played a crucial part in the development of his 'demagogic' image; his enemies, in Parliament and the media, did most of the additional work. Nonetheless, Benn was also impulsive and he made more avoidable mistakes than the majority of his counterparts. Indeed, while many observers at the peak of his influence compared him to his friend Enoch Powell because they were held to represent rival 'extremes', it can be argued that their most piquant parallels arose from their shared tendency to commit career-marring gaffes at the most unseasonable times.

However, while Powell believed that all political careers end either in premature death or failure, a partial exception can be made in Benn's case. On the public platform, the winning charm and self-deprecation returned to his speeches when there was no longer any chance that he could satisfy his ambition of leading his party and country. In the early 1980s he had hoped to secure decisive influence over domestic policy; in later years his most effective orations were delivered in foreign affairs, particularly when denouncing Britain and its allies for engaging in armed conflict. Here, as elsewhere, biographical details were important; judged solely on the basis of his most notable speeches Benn might be mistaken for a pacifist, since he consistently advocated the peaceful resolution of disputes even when war seemed inevitable. Nevertheless, having played a role in the war which claimed the life of his brother, when he spoke out on such issues Benn could adopt the guise of a warrior who only chose to fight when the justice of the cause was established beyond dispute. His stance on conflicts like the 1991 Gulf War, and the 2003 invasion of Iraq, gained him the respect of many people who had regarded him as a public menace in the 1980s. But although Benn was a much more popular figure by the time that he relinquished his seat in the Commons, he had only secured the consolation prize customarily awarded to unsuccessful radical orators, even by their erstwhile enemies: the title of 'national treasure'.

8

The oratory of Neil Kinnock

David S. Moon

Introduction: on *hwyl*

> Mr. Speaker, ladies and gentleman, can I begin by dismissing one rumour that is in the process of being born; I have *never* orated, at the breakfast table. (Kinnock, 2011)

Whether or not Neil Kinnock the family man orated at the breakfast table, his biographers agree that oratory was at the heart of Neil Kinnock the politician. Kinnock, according to Robert Harris (1984: 12), is a man who 'built his career on his talents as a speaker', public speaking being his 'greatest skill' and his 'voice' his 'greatest political asset' (1984: 52, 73). For G.M.F. Dower (1984), Kinnock is 'the finest Labour orator since Bevan' (1984: 67), a man whose oratory was 'his great strength' (1984: 136) having the 'gift' of 'being a great communicator with the common people' who 'admire his oratory' even if not his views (1984: 14, 63). Michael Leapman (1987), meanwhile, describes Kinnock's 'talent' for 'passionate oratory' and 'ability to bring an audience cheering to their feet' (1987: 37, 178); Martin Westlake (2001: 78) calls him a man who 'made almost a trade of public speaking'; and Eileen Jones (1994: 179) declares Kinnock's 'strongest point' to be his 'power as an orator who could move large audiences'. These statements find support in claims such as Dennis Glover's (2011: 101) that Kinnock won the Labour leadership by being the party's 'best orator' and the British Political Speech website's declaration that it has 'no hesitation in considering Kinnock to be one of the great orators of British politics'.

This chapter does not depart from this accepted consensus: Kinnock, indeed, offers one of the finest examples of British political oratory. Similarly in line with consensus, it argues that few individuals' oratory has had as significant and important an effect upon the fortunes and future of the British Labour Party as Kinnock's. In his aim as leader of fundamentally changing the culture and politics of the Labour movement, Kinnock can claim success. Yet, where a note of caution *is* sounded regards the impact of his oratory outside of the party. As an orator, Kinnock was perfectly placed to stir-up a particular mixture of ethos, pathos and logos targeted at the party which made it possible to drag Labour from its unusual sojourn on the hard left towards a softer-left, electable position once more. The very same characteristics which made Kinnock perfect to re-position the party, however, were also part of the reason he was unable to reach his ultimate goal of winning electoral power for his party.

In making this case the Welsh concept of *hwyl* is introduced as an explanatory tool and incorporation into the wider terminology of oratorical and rhetorical literatures. *Hwyl*, as here outlined, is valuable as a means to understand Kinnock's oratory as a particular form of *Labour oratory* and his successes and arguable failures which thereby resulted. Stylistically, although Lord Kinnock remains a thriving and vital figure in Labour politics, he is herein referred to in the past tense since the period focused upon specifically covers his time as (and in parts before being) Party leader. Having 'always [been] more of a Party man than a House of Commons man' for whom 'the conference platform, not the Despatch box, remained the scene of his triumphs' (Jenkins, 1989: 220–1), whilst reference is made here to the three oratorical arenas of Parliament, conference and communication with the electorate, the emphasis of the piece is predominantly upon the second arena as the key venue within which Kinnock the orator performed and had his greatest effects.

On oratory and oratorical techniques

Kinnock clearly understood the importance of political oratory. How could he not? It was, after all, key to his political success well before becoming Labour leader – from his victory winning speech at the Bedwellty nomination meeting in 1969, to his steadily won climb up the National Executive Committee (NEC) votes (see Harris, 1984). But he also recognised the importance of oratory for Labour more generally, as part of 'a talking movement' 'constantly engaged in reporting to each other, debating with each other and trying to get our message over to everyone else' (Coyte and Kinnock, 1980: 4). For Kinnock, oratory's significance here stemmed from Labour's position as a movement which rose *against* those with power, against the dominant forces of society, in a struggle it had not yet escaped: 'Our movement has won the right to speak' he claimed as the party's eighth decade opened, 'but still has a struggle to win the right to be heard' (Coyte and Kinnock, 1980: 4). How then did Kinnock propose this struggle be taken up? Through what techniques, to his mind, could (and should) members of the Labour movement wage their verbal war of position?

There is a degree to which Kinnock, faced with this question, professed not to know the answer. In such cases his ability as an orator – the means of the struggle – were framed as something which came not from conscious technique, but rather flowed from some indeterminable, within; bubbling up from below, with only the props of practical experience as an unquantifiable support. It is true to this end that Kinnock often spoke 'off the cuff'. Dower (1984: 65), for example, describes his penchant to simply 'arrive at a meeting and, not even bothering with a few words on a scrap of paper ... just start talking'. Indeed, according to Kinnock himself, many of his most famous passages were made up on the spot, telling Jones (1994: 99), for example, that '[t]he thing about [the speech in] Llandudno' (see below) was 'that what's remembered are the parts I didn't write – I just said them "from the soul"'.

One particularly notable, self-announced example of such off-map 'from the soul' speaking came in a passionate address made to the House of Commons in 1973 on the subject of Chile; therein an angry Kinnock declared:

> I had prepared notes for my speech, but I have been so appalled by the attitude of Conservative members that something more than a rehearsed speech is called for. If hon. Members wish to call it emotion they can do so. I call it history and a sense of decency ... we must vote with our stomachs and hearts in saying whose side we are on. (Quoted in Harris, 1984: 60)

While he would, in his time, describe the Commons rather dismissively as 'like a factory ... where I happen to work' (Jenkins, 1989: 219) such oratory was more than workman-like and the notion, raised therein, that the aforementioned organs were – and should be – valuable sources of oratorical and political inspiration, in preference to deliberate intellectually craft, was a significant insight to how Kinnock saw political speech as an act/action. This subject was reflected upon by Kinnock in 1995, telling a BBC documentary:

> I suppose that my abilities, and one of the main reasons I became elected leader of the Labour Party, lie in the field of being a mobiliser, an advocate, an articulator, an enthuser. Roy's [Hattersley] attributes are perhaps more cerebral. And I could, I guess, defend the difference on the basis that in order for a body to have life, it needs a heart and a stomach, and a backbone, as well as a brain. (BBC, 1995)

Passionate conviction, or pathos – i.e. the heart and the gut in tandem – is a key element of Kinnock's oratory (and, as described below, of the concept of Welsh *hwyl*). But beyond such claims to instinctual speechmaking, Kinnock knew the importance of oratory as a political tool. This was demonstrated in the foreword he penned to the pamphlet *How to Speak in Public* (Coyte and Kinnock, 1980), produced for Labour's membership on the titular subject. Kinnock opened with a firm refutation of oratory as a science (or art) which can be taught or learned through theory: 'This is not a booklet designed to produce orators', he wrote, as '[t]here is no such booklet, book, tome, or library in existence'. Rather, in an appeal to action over calculation, he advised that practical experience is the only education available: 'No-one learns to swim on dry land and no-one can learn to speak by reading about it. You have to get up and do it' (Coyte and Kinnock, 1980: 3).

Nevertheless, Kinnock did proffer some practical advice. First, that '[t]he key... is confidence', though '[n]ot the pomposity of the self-opinionated bore or the supercilious self-assured twanging of the public school spouter' (Coyte and Kinnock, 1980: 3–4). Second, that it 'helps, of course, if you can use wit and quotations and all of the other assets of the impressive and practiced communication' though these 'assets' were 'gravy' and '[t]he meat comes first'. But significantly, Kinnock acknowledged that Labour's 'best arguments can fail and our strongest message be lost by poor presentation' (Coyte and Kinnock, 1980: 4) and good presentation was important both in convincing *and* attracting people to the cause: 'The new members which we seek will not join us if they cannot understand us and will not remain if we bore them by being ineffectual, irresolute or inarticulate in our communication.' With this in mind, Kinnock's message to budding orators was summed up in the following example of rhetorical alliteration and tricolon (a favourite tool of his): 'If we are to "educate, agitate and organise" for the victory of democracy and socialism we must do it with conviction, with clarity and with confidence' (Coyte and Kinnock, 1980). The question remains then: through what oratorical techniques was this combination of conviction, clarity and confidence weaved by Kinnock himself? Grasping these means discussing issues of delivery, personality and articulation of content – of pathos, ethos and logos – and this requires, before all else, first grasping the concept of *hwyl*.

On *hwyl*

The Welsh word *hwyl* cannot be defined in one sentence. Conceptually valuable but notoriously difficult to translate into English,[1] it refers to something – a state, a form, a happening – recognised and felt, rather than testable and classifiable. However, in seeking to elucidate the term so as to excavate a viable concept from within its inherent complexities a number of key features should be noted. As a start, the University of Wales' *Dictionary of the Welsh Language* (2006: 3608) defines *hwyl* thus:

1. sail (of ship, windmill), also fig.; sheet, covering, pall.
2. journey, progress, revolution …; rush, assault, attack.
3. a healthy physical or mental condition, good form, one's right senses, wits; tune (of a musical instrument); temper, mood, frame of mind; nature, disposition; degree of success achieved in the execution of a particular task; fervour (esp. religious), ecstacy, unction, gusto, zest; characteristic musical intonation or sing-song cadence formerly much in vogue in the perorations of the Welsh pulpit.
4. merry-making, jollity, mirth, gaiety, amusement, fun, with humour; … derision, mockery.

Several significant points arise from this multifaceted definition of *hwyl*. Its core, such that there is one, is passion; passion both as individual temper and mood – of anger and enjoyment – but also as drive.[2]

But what is fundamental to grasp here before all else is the link between *hwyl* and the pulpit – part 3 of the dictionary definition. The description which best grasps this aspect is found in an article upon 'The Welsh Pulpit' from 1859:

What is emphatically the '*hwyl*' is a peculiarity so striking in Welsh preaching, it so immediately arrests the ear, that we are justified in giving it especial and early attention. The world *hwyl* (pronounced *hooil*), is a highly figurative one. A ship is said to be in full '*hwyl*' when it leaves port with full and spread sails, under a favourable breeze. And a preacher is said to be in full '*hwyl*' when, in happiest mood, thoughts and words come quickly and apt, and rising like a man inspired to the loftiest heights, he inevitably, and as a matter of course, *intones* or *chants* his fervid thoughts. No! English reader, let us at once confess neither of the above words adequately express this peculiarity. It is something between a chant and a song, but greatly unlike either. (*Titan*, 1858: 346)

Russell Deacon (2006: 56) notes how in Wales the 'new religion' of socialism came to displace that of the chapel in people's hearts. But if the content of that faith changed, the style of evangelising the faith remained. At its most basic *hwyl* names an 'indescribable eloquence' (Sparks, 2005: 28) which 'carries the speaker away on its wings, supplying him with burning words of eloquence, which in his calmer and normal state he could never have chosen for himself' (Raine, 1900: 94). Simply stated, oratory with *hwyl* soars. In this latter regard – as a force which offers propulsion to a speaker's speech – the notion of *hwyl* also resonates with its literal translation as the sail of a ship: with 'gusto' and 'zest' the orator demonstrating *hwyl* moves majestically forward with sails spread on the high sea of their rhetorical eloquence, *sailing* with enthusiasm into the debate and navigating towards their argument's concluding point.

This is what *hwyl* is. It is in many ways a state, rather than a form of oration. Or rather, it is four things: it is a mood (one of enthusiasm and fervour); a medium (musical cadences and magical, lilting notes); a form of oration in itself (a style of speech echoing the nonconformist Welsh preacher's); and the inexplicable drive behind this oratory itself (the sail which carries and propels the speechmaker forward). It is a style of one preaching the true faith and as such is drawn from the gut and the heart – but it is also of the navigating mind. Comprehended thus, the characteristics defining *hwyl* were evident – no doubt unwittingly – within descriptions from the *Daily Mirror* and *Financial Times* of Kinnock's 1979 speech to conference as 'silver-tongued' and 'fluent, fervent and forceful', 'in the Bevan tradition' (Harris, 1984: 127–8). Both men of Tredegar, of working-class Wales, it is telling that Kinnock and Aneurin Bevan's speechifying be tied together in this way – linked, as they are here argued to be, in the style of delivery (in their *hwyl*).

Pathos: delivery/style

Neither romantic nor realist, Kinnock's oratory performed that hardest of tasks by blending soaring, idealistic rhetoric couched within the movement's history and language (what Denis Healey (1989: 535) called 'incandescent oratory with an irresistible moral thrust') with serious, boot dirtied political realism. As Harris (1984: 35) put it with a description that tapped into *hwyl* as a lifting sail: 'On a good day

[Kinnock] can bring to a subject not only a passion but also an ability to relate it to a wider frame of historical reference or shared experience, a gift which can raise his speeches high above those of most average politicians.' This element of *hwyl*, the appeal to passion – what is known in technical terms as pathos – was the beating heart which powered Kinnock's oratory.

Silver-tongued fluency of the sort described above, underlined with a righteous anger (amounting in effect to an appeal through pathos), was clearly evident in the following extract from Kinnock's 1987 conference speech wherein he denounced the ethos of 'A government led by a Prime Minister who says that "There is no such thing as society"':

> 'No such thing as society', she says.
> No obligation to the community.
> No sense of solidarity.
> No principles of sharing or caring.
> 'No such thing as society.'
> No sisterhood, no brotherhood.
> No neighbourhood.
> No honouring other people's mothers and fathers.
> No succouring other people's little children.
> 'No such thing as society.'
> No number other than one.
> No person other than me.
> No time other than now.
> No such thing as society, just 'me' and 'now'.
> That is Margaret Thatcher's society. (Applause)
> I tell you, you cannot run a country on the basis of 'me' and 'now'. (Kinnock, 1987)

If ever proof was needed that Kinnock understood the techniques of classic oratory – whether 'book learned' or otherwise – here it is: demonstrating *parison*, whereby each clause has a similar construction and *anaphora*, repeating the same word at the beginning of successive sentences, behind the passionate enunciation, in the short sentences, the emphasised full-stops, there is a beat – almost poetic in its rhythm and flow – which grabs, holds and draws along the listener.

This same style is also evident in a campaign speech made by Kinnock to the Ogmore Constituency Labour Party Club in Bridgend, during the 1983 election battle. Speaking two days before polling opened, his voice hoarse from a punishing, self-undertaken, nation-wide campaign, Kinnock told the assembled crowd:

> If Margaret Thatcher is re-elected as prime minister on Thursday, I warn you.
> I warn you that you will have pain – when healing and relief depend upon payment.
> I warn you that you will have ignorance – when talents are untended and wits are wasted,
> when learning is a privilege and not a right.
> I warn you that you will have poverty – when pensions slip and benefits are whittled away
> by a government that won't pay in an economy that can't pay.

I warn you that you will be cold – when fuel charges are used as a tax system that the rich
don't notice and the poor can't afford.

I warn you that you must not expect work – when many cannot spend, more will not
be able to earn. When they don't earn, they don't spend. When they don't spend,
work dies.

I warn you not to go into the streets alone after dark or into the streets in large crowds of
protest in the light.

I warn you that you will be quiet – when the curfew of fear and the gibbet of unemployment make you obedient.

I warn you that you will have defence of a sort – with a risk and at a price that passes all
understanding.

I warn you that you will be home-bound – when fares and transport bills kill leisure and
lock you up.

I warn you that you will borrow less – when credit, loans, mortgages and easy payments
are refused to people on your melting income.

If Margaret Thatcher wins on Thursday –

I warn you not to be ordinary

I warn you not to be young

I warn you not to fall ill

I warn you not to grow old. (Kinnock, 1987)

These words – delivered, significantly, to an audience of Welsh party members, but broadcast subsequently around the country by the present news cameras – were apparently scribbled down on a scrap of paper in the car on the way to the club (again raising the image of Kinnock the spontaneous orator). But as in 1987, what Kinnock demonstrated was both his technical proficiency – in the masterful usage, once again, of *parison* and *anaphora* – and a style of delivery which aped, in subdued form, the cadences of the preacher and the structure of the poet.

Tied to such oratory was the oft remarked upon notion that there was a particular 'Welshness' to Kinnock's style of speechmaking. He has thus been described as shar-ing 'the Welsh love of oratory' (Leapman, 1987: 102); in *The Times* as embarking upon 'flights of Welsh rhetoric' (quoted in Jones, 1994: 41); in the *Times Education Supplement* as having a 'musical Welsh voice'; and, while decried as one who 'ped-dles left-wing rubbish', was nevertheless given the accolade of doing so 'with consid-erable charm in mellifluous Welsh tones' by a 1978 *Yorkshire Post* editorial (quoted in Harris, 1984: 127, 113).

In each of these cases what was again being tapped into were characteristics ('mel-lifluous' and 'musical') denoting *hwyl*. As such, when Kinnock spoke to the party, this *hwyl* provided more than an aesthetically pleasing rhythm to his oratorical flow. It reminded the membership also of *who he*, Kinnock, *was*: where he had come from and what – as such – he could be counted on in their mind to stand for. Technically, whether consciously or otherwise, this provided him with an indirect appeal to ethos, drawing upon his own character to buttress his arguments. For Kinnock, who faced the stark task as leader of attempting to move the party away from some of its most dearly held beliefs, this was vital as his prior reputation vouched for him in a way that, when faced with a party audience, was hugely helpful.

Ethos within the movement

Without even needing to open his mouth, Kinnock's past spoke for him within the Labour movement he had been born, brought up, and married into (Jenkins, 1989: 218). Indeed, it would be hard to find an individual more quintessentially Labour as Kinnock (or, at least, Labour in the party's romantic image of itself). He came from a working-class South Wales background – raised in the Tredegar constituency of Bevan – from a family of miners, the aristocracy of the Labour movement. It was such totems Kinnock was referring to when he stated, in the 1992 party political broadcast, that he had 'always felt Welsh ... particularly in the sense of the kind of community from which I came that gave you a confidence and identity and I think it's important to have roots' (Jenkins, 1989: 218). With the resonance of this background in mind it is unsurprising, therefore, that Kinnock *did* choose to open his mouth, and to do so frequently.

An appeal to ethos was absolutely key to Kinnock's oratory, who made much of his upbringing and family history in his speeches, taking evident pride referencing this background; in his first speech to the Commons, for example, he announced to the assembled MPs: 'I am the first male member of my family for about three generations who can have reasonable confidence in expecting that I will leave this earth with more or less the same number of fingers, hands, legs, toes and eyes as I had when I was born' (quoted in Harris, 1984: 23).

Such roots provided Kinnock not only with a socially-learned confidence to speak,[3] but an authority to do so also within the movement. Unlike that of the middle-class 'revolutionaries' whom he so disparaged, his was a socialism based upon direct experience (one born into and raised in it, it might be said). It was this experience which was at the core of some of his most well-known speechmaking, such as the passionate passage from his Llandudno speech, filmed and later incorporated into the party's 1987 election broadcast, 'Kinnock the Movie' by Hugh Hudson:

> Why am I the first Kinnock in a *thousand* generations to be able to get to university? Why is Glenys the first woman in her family in a *thousand* generations to be able to get to university? Was it because all our predecessors were '*thick*'? Did they lack talent, those people who could sing and play, and recite and write poetry, those people who could make wonderful, beautiful things with their hands; those people who could dream dreams, see visions ... But why didn't they get it? Was it because they were weak? *Weak?* Those people who could work eight hours underground, and then come up and play football – *weak?* Those women who could survive eleven child bearings – were *they* weak? ... Does anybody really think that they didn't get what we had because they didn't have the talent, or the strength, or the endurance, or the commitment?

Of course not. It was because there was no platform upon which they could stand.
(Glover, 2011: 101–2 added by author)

Quoting this speech Glover (2011: 101–2) makes much of Kinnock's technical use of *erotema*, i.e. the rhetorical question (actually, of *psyma*, asking multiple rhetorical questions and *anthypophora*, immediately answering the question) – further evidence if needed that Kinnock was *au fait*, whether he knew it or not (he says not), with the technical 'tools' of oratory. But what meant this question could *be* rhetorical, at least as Kinnock framed it, was the fact that he grounded it within his own lived experience. He was able to present himself as one who spoke having come from the communities described, but having been blessed with the platform and arrangements denied to those others – family – before him. The Welsh nonconformist preacher, it is important to note, came from within the congregation to take the pulpit; he thus spoke to his audience, from *within* his audience. Kinnock similarly took the pulpit to argue the case for those yet to do so.

One of the most striking examples of ethos in Kinnock's oratory, wherein his personal background was used to provide support for his arguments, came at the end of his 1985 conference speech where – having previously launched his famous attack upon the Militant Tendency (see below) – he concluded his speech in the second from last paragraph, with what the evening's ITN news report described as 'an impassioned Welsh hymn of what the Labour Party meant to him':[4]

> I say to you in complete honesty, because this is the Movement that I belong to, that I owe this party everything I have got – not the job, not being leader of the Labour Party, but every life chance that I have had since the time I was a child: (Applause) the life chance of a comfortable home, with working parents, people who had jobs; the life chance of moving out of a pest and damp-infested set of rooms into a decent home, built by a *Labour* council under a *Labour* Government; the life chance of an education that went *on* for as long as I wanted to take it. Me and millions of others of my generation got all their chances from this Movement. (Applause) That is why I say that this Movement, its values, its policies, applied in power, gave me everything that I have got – me and millions like me of my generation and succeeding generations. That is why it is my duty to be honest and that is why it is our function, our mission, our duty – all of us – to see that those life chances exist and are enriched and extended to millions more, who without us will never get the chance of fulfilling themselves. (Applause) That is why we have got to win, that is what I have always believed and that is what I put to you at the very moment that I was elected. (Kinnock, 1985; emphasis added by author)

These were speeches which a leftist figure such as Tony Benn – an Anglican rather than a nonconformist, to continue the ecumenical metaphor – born as he was of a different class, would never have been able to make; and in 1985 they were explicitly made to the Party/movement: 'I speak to you, to this Conference … I come here to this Conference primarily, above all, to speak to this Movement at its Conference.' In doing so, by clearly linking his working-class background ('… this is why …') to his 'duty to be honest', to talk hard truths to the movement to whom he declared himself to speak, Kinnock gave himself – and was given by this audience – the *right* to be heard out, regardless of the boos of a vocal minority. And in linking himself, his *whole life*, to the Labour movement, he did the same thing, demonstrating to his audience he was 'one of them' ('our Neil') and thus afforded the right to be listened to (Kinnock, 1985).

This was in turn helped by Kinnock's knowledge of the language of the movement and subsequent ability to speak in it. For a party as divided and traumatised as Labour was in the 1980s, the words used to address it were hugely important. As Kinnock himself later described:

> In a serious political party that was unanimously intent upon appealing to the nation and winning the election, putting a speech together would have been easy. But in the Labour Party, where that intensity of political purpose is not always evident, there was a hell of a lot that I had to do that I shouldn't have had to do. There had to be particular constructions of phrases and sentences and arguments that would maximise support for what I was trying to do, without giving the other side, as it were, ammunition. So there was a balance, a delicacy about the operation that was very trying. (Quoted in Jones, 1994: 108)

Thus, in the most famous passage from his 1985 speech, the use of the phrase 'public-school boys' and the reference to 'taxis'[5] to attack the Militant Tendency and the hard left in the party were clear attempts to place them on the wrong side of the political argument:

> I'll tell you what happens with impossible promises. You start with far-fetched resolutions. They are then pickled into a rigid dogma, a code, and you go through the years sticking to that, *out*-dated, *mis*-placed, irrelevant to the real needs, and you end up in the grotesque *chaos* of a Labour council – a *Labour council* – hiring *taxis* to scuttle round a city handing out redundancy notices to its own workers!

The further, expert turn of the knife in this magisterial attack came when, with the same breath, Kinnock tied his own position, to those of *the people* ('the masses' as opposed to 'the classes' as fellow Welshman James Dean Bradfield might put it) who Labour was *meant* to represent:

> the voice of the people – not the people here; the voice of the real people with real needs – is louder than all the boos that can be assembled. Understand that, please, comrades. In your socialism, in your commitment to those people, understand it. The people will not, cannot, abide posturing. They cannot respect the gesture-generals or the tendency-tacticians.

Of the people and for the people: the effect was a devastating combination. One reason Kinnock was able to get away with such blatant, if effective, rhetorical articulations was the fact that – prior to becoming leader – he was also known as a man of the left, or one who had come from the left, with a historical willingness to stand up for what he felt was right, even when it went against personal advancement. This was most evidently the case with regards to devolution when Kinnock spoke out not simply against the government, but against his close friend and mentor Michael Foot also. This stance was far from 'the easy option' and the decision to oppose and subsequently play a key role in defeating devolution in 1979 was to lose Kinnock some of his closest friends for life (although not Foot, with whom his disagreements were always fraternally conducted on both sides). He was also someone who had put his time and effort into the movement, travelling the country to speak to members and unions, and campaigning hard during elections – a man of the public hall meeting. It was this which had gained him the status as a darling of the grassroots (and their votes, over the years, onto the NEC).

Replete with a stabbing finger matched to his annunciation, embodying appeals, indirectly, both to ethos and pathos, what Kinnock's personal style of delivery (his *hwyl*) thus did was to reinforce and remind the party faithful of this background: Welsh, working-class, radical. When making appeals to/within the British Labour movement at all levels, the passionate pronouncements of the preacher are always likely to be embraced, gladly, by the membership of a body once described as 'a moral crusade, or nothing'. His delivery emphasised his character and as such provided reassurance to Labour members and supporters as it clothed him with an aura of trustworthiness – he was, to repeat again, *one of them* and as such a figure who could be trusted with the movement, to do it right, even as his actions might hurt. An individual such as Roy Hattersley – avuncular and literate as he was and is – could not have performed this task, not without engendering the real prospect of the party irreconcilably splitting.

Discussing the 1985 speech ten years later, Chris Mullins, a critic of Kinnock and supporter of Benn, attacked him for 'shooting at [his] own side', complaining that, because 'Neil spent all that time speaking to the Labour Party … it wasn't surprising we didn't have much luck convincing the nation' (BBC, 1995). What Mullins handily discounted is that without taking on the image of extremism within the movement there was no chance of the electorate even listening to Labour, let alone paying consideration to its arguments. In this regard 'speaking to the Labour Party' was a necessary task and one Kinnock accomplished with great success. It was not Kinnock's decision to attack the far left which led to his ultimate failure to convince a majority to vote for him as party leader. It was not the attack. But might it have been the style of his attack?

Ethos outside the movement

It was his *hwyl*, as orator, that meant Kinnock was able to persuade a distressed and fractured party to accept his reformist programme and move back towards electability. Yet, ironically, it may to some degree have also been what damaged him as a potential prime minister – at least within the audience outside the Labour movement. The reason for this, it is here argued, has to do with two key aspects of

Kinnock's *hwyl* – its remarkable passion (the form of pathos to which it appealed) and its unmistakable 'Welshness' (the form of ethos to which it appealed) – which together raised concerns *and* prejudices within some sections of the voting population who subsequently withheld their votes. Why was this?

Much of Kinnock's communication with the electorate involved the broadcast of sections of his conference speeches: 1987's 'Kinnock the Movie', for example, included the sections from both the Llandudno and 1985 conference speeches quoted above – speeches directed inwardly to Labour, re-projected at the general public outside also.

Where directing his speeches most clearly to the general public, not party, Kinnock's key message was a call to overcome the divisions being foisted on society by the Conservative government: in the course of attempting to drive out the damaging schism fostered by left-wing extremism in his own party, he appealed to the nation to conterminously drive out the division fostered by the right-wing extremism of Margaret Thatcher. Thus, during his 1984 conference speech, Kinnock presented the Conservatives not as the natural party of national government as they themselves sought to do. Instead, he described them as the party of 'conflict and chaos'; 'devoid of consensus values'; 'all spite, bile and arrogance'; and 'tearing the society apart' through their creation of 'the climate of confrontation, the conditions of conflict'; speaking 'only the language of conquest' with an 'assault on the essentials of civilised life'. They were 'a government that bases its whole policy on intimidation' (Kinnock, 1984). The same message carried through to the following year's speech where – in between the aforementioned denouncing of leftist extremists within Labour – he again lambasted the extremists running the country: they were 'the party and the government of destruction'; of 'devastation'; a party which was reducing the nation's services 'to a rubble'; bringing 'divisions'; 'dangers'; 'insecurity' and utilising a 'strategy of fear' – 'which is the only Tory policy' (Kinnock, 1985).

The flip side of this was an attempt to persuade the electorate that Labour could provide the opposite to overcome these divisions. This Kinnock attempted to do through appeals to logos, basing his argument around reason, rationalism and consensus, in opposition to Tory extremism. Thus, time and time again – to take again his 1984 speech – he repeatedly pointed to political 'reality', to 'the facts as they exist', to 'the evidence of ... injustice' and the 'rationality' of Labour's position. This he counterposed to the 'violence' of Conservative policies such as those regarding coal, for which there were 'no *rational* financial, technical, economic or market reason', 'no rational economic case', 'no rational case' at all, but only 'an irrational purpose' – that of 'political vanity' and sustaining 'uproar'. Through such declarations Kinnock aimed to reinforce the message that, unlike Thatcher, Labour offered a 'one nation' politics; yes, this politics was planted firmly and proudly on socialist ground, but while accepting the latter was 'a great cause' it was also 'a careful and cool-headed cause' (Kinnock, 1984).

To many voters – particularly, one can imagine, middle-class and southern voters – what they saw in Kinnock's rhetoric and delivery was not, however, careful, cool-headedness. Rather, it was reckless hot-headedness. The point has already been noted by Jones (1994: 31): 'the language of his oratory, which sometimes spilled over into anger, and the physical power of his delivery while speaking, were the features which brought him to prominence, almost as much as the substance of what he was saying.' However, in some cases: 'There was said to be a recklessness about his manner if he was defending a matter of principle, and it was soon apparent that few who heard him were indifferent to Neil Kinnock: either they strongly admired him or they hated him.' The same was noted by Glenys Kinnock when she remarked that: 'People either really like him or they hate him … It's the way he speaks, the language he uses. He shouts at hecklers. He gets very angry.' (Jones, 1994: 31).

Harris (1984: 67–8) agrees but goes further. Kinnock's passion, he writes, could 'so easily bubble over into anger' and this was a serious matter:

> Kinnock is normally a good-humoured and approachable man. But for all his charm there is about him on occasions a hint of suppressed violence, of anger waiting for an outlet. It is there in the way he delivers his speeches, rocking like a boxer on the balls of his feet, his head tilted back, his chin jutting forward. It is there in his language. It is to be seen repeatedly throughout his career, most commonly in spontaneously savage responses to heckling or interruptions.

This is a portrait – indelibly marked by the style of his speechmaking – of a politician who 'stands squarely in the pugilistic tradition of politics', who describes politics as a 'blood sport', and whose political motto is less careful cool-headedness more 'attack, attack, attack' (Harris, 1984: 67–8). Attack and fight – as the previously given dictionary definition includes – is another mark of *hwyl* and Kinnock, in Harris' description, 'operates close to that border where political passion can sometimes turn to physical violence' (1984: 163). For the man who left an attacker bleeding in the toilets of the Grand Hotel at the 1981 conference and once scuffled outside a London curry house (regardless that such events were provoked by the physical assaults of others), the danger that some voters perceived him as a man who lacked emotional control was a real one.[6] If Harris is to be believed, it may have been an image sustained, even promoted, by his oratory.

The fact that Kinnock made a clear and conscious decision to tone down his speeches and to show greater rhetorical restraint over his years of leadership likely points to a similar fear amongst both himself and his advisors (see Jones, 1994). That it was a latter breach of this restraint – with the infamous, emotional cries of 'We're alright!' at the week-before-poll Sheffield rally of Labour activists – which many would later over-claim to have been a cause of the 1992 election loss, is further telling in this regard. There is also, likely, another, identified by Leapman (1987: 184), that being the 'the danger of being regarded as a maker of fine phrases and little else – the "Welsh windbag" syndrome'. In recognition of this, Leapman claims

Kinnock was already by 1987 'on occasion', 'deliberately strip[ping] his speeches of vivid imagery and pyrotechnics, giving them the arid texture of academic lectures'. But this moniker – the 'Welsh windbag' – still trotted out today, demonstrates the extent to which Kinnock's gift for oratory was linked in the political consciousness to his 'Welshness' too (and the link was not a complimentary one).

This is where having/showing *hwyl* becomes a double-edged sword: just as some might negatively interpret passionate speech as hot-headedness, so too 'Welshness' could be seen, in the prejudices of some, as a character defect of another sort (Jones, 1994). While Dower (1984: 64) believed Kinnock had 'the advantage of a flat provincial Welsh accent that offended no one', more disagree. Following the 1992 election defeat, Baroness Castle, for example, told the *Guardian* she had 'detect[ed] some racist undertones emerging during the campaign' whereby 'Neil's "unfitness to govern", it appeared, had something to do with his being Welsh'. This she tied to a belief that 'Tories don't respect the Welsh whom they regard as a nation of mere plebs and poets' (quoted in Jones, 1994: 14). John Humphrys saw it as a problem that went wider than just Tories, claiming '[t]here is a kind of latent anti-Welshness among the English and that is his bad luck' (quoted in Jones, 1994: 17) and Robin Oakley also claimed that Kinnock 'suffered from what one can only call an anti-Welsh prejudice from people who for some reason decided that it would be inappropriate to have a Welsh Prime Minister' (quoted in Westlake, 2001: 714). As Castle (1993: 583) would again summarise it: 'The attacks became positively ethnic in tone implying that, because he was Welsh, Neil was not fit to be Prime Minister. They did not go down well in the Welsh valleys, but they were directed at a wider Anglo-Saxon audience.'

Whether this alleged ingrained prejudice against the Welsh existed/exists within the electorate of Middle England – and canvassers for all parties produced claims to have encountered something of the kind (Castle, 1993: 715) – it is certainly the case that, as James Thomas (1997) has described, the London-based tabloid press ran with it as the 1992 general election approached. Kinnock was thus labelled as not only the 'Welsh windbag', but the 'bumbling boyo', 'Taff the Lad', 'Teflon Taff' and the 'Wild Man of the Valleys'. In this way:

> The Labour leader's nationality was clearly and consistently used in a derogatory way which would have been inconceivable had he been born black or Jewish ... The obvious intention of these attacks was to draw upon alleged anti-Welsh prejudices in the crucial marginal constituencies of South-East England. (Thomas, 1997: 95–107)

As the latter 'Wild Man' title demonstrates, such representations inverted the positives of Kinnock's pathos and ethos, making further not-so-subliminal links between Welsh identity and an intemperate personality – to the image of a 'fiery' (red-headed) temperament which basically amounted to on-the-edge aggressiveness as described above. In this, they also linked anti-Welsh prejudice with class prejudices; specifically, to the notion that someone of such an obviously working-class pedigree (here lazily articulated as one of working-men's clubs, beer, rugby and macho-ism) was not fit to be prime minister. It was not a prime minister from Wales such people did not want (Callaghan, at least nominally, could have claimed that title). Rather, it was a prime minister from a *particular* type of Wales. As Jon Snow would subsequently remark:

> Neither Kinnock nor his advisers were able to alter what he symbolised: a traditional Welsh working-class *Cwmardy* ethos of community and care for the less fortunate very much out of place in the Thatcherite eighties ... This was an ethos very much linked in with a Welsh culture of solidarity and community which Kinnock, like his political hero Aneurin Bevan, very clearly represented. (Quoted in Westlake, 2001: 716)

It was precisely this symbolisation, emphasised and backed up by the style –incandescent, passionately Welsh, *hwyl* – and content of his oratory – drawing strength, with pride, from his origins in working-class Wales – which made it possible for Kinnock to lead Labour away from the excesses of extremism. Kinnock was perfectly positioned to pull Labour back from the brink; there is an extent to which only *he* could have achieved that job. But oratory has different effects on different audiences. It is, as such, at the very core of his greatest success, yet, if the above is true, while it would be pure folly to claim that it was Kinnock's style of oratory which lost Labour the 1987 and 1992 elections, there remains the depressing likelihood that it may have been a contributing factor.

Conclusion: wither *hwyl?*

In summary, what can be said of Kinnock the orator? Kinnock was admittedly never a 'Commons man' who has described his dislike of Prime Minister's Questions (PMQs) and the ilk. Similarly it was not in his much remarked upon abilities as a communicator with the general public that he was at his most effective. Rather, this was in his speeches to the Labour movement itself, most notably to party conference. For a divided Labour in the mid to late 1980s, these were the key arenas within which the internal party wars over the soul of the movement were waged and it has been upon this arena that this chapter has subsequently placed much of its emphasis.

Focusing therein on the three key concepts of pathos, ethos and logos, a clear narrative presents itself, tied inexorably into the notion of Kinnock as a purveyor of *hwyl*. There is the lifting, rousing passion of the preacher (pathos) tied to the social history of a radical, Welsh nonconformist working-class culture (ethos) which combined provided Kinnock with an oratorical appeal to the party faithful few could match. It was this mixture (this *hwyl*) which meant Kinnock was perfectly placed to guide Labour away towards an eventual electability.

Yet, in an inversion of these positive attributes, these very same characteristics of Kinnock's oratory – of pathos, ethos and logos – were also, likely, part of the reason he was unable to reach his ultimate goal of achieving a Labour government with himself as leader. Thus, what was seen as a righteous passion within Labour was framed and interpreted as a hot-headed 'wildness' for many outside. Similarly, his background, echoed in his speech, became an inexplicable mark against his suitability for office, rather than the asset it was within the movement. Indeed, within this negative media-supported narrative, wildness, working-class and Welsh were basically articulated as the same thing – an ugly, patronising and even racist caricature captured in the previous descriptions of Kinnock as the 'bumbling boyo' and 'Wildman of the Valleys', in the face of which appeals to logos in attempts to portray Labour as rational and reasonable in opposition to the divisive extremism of Thatcherism fell on ground resolutely stony for many. The end result was a perfect catch-22 for Labour and Kinnock.

Wither, then, *hwyl*? Arguably none have had as strong an ability to lift the spirits of the Labour faithful, to rouse the movement since Kinnock. Tony Blair's oratory had much of the pulpit about it stylistically also (though if socialism was Kinnock's religion, *religion* was Blair's religion). But Blair's background meant he could *never* be a vessel for *hwyl*, since he had not come from amongst the working people, from amongst the 'plebs'. Blair's was a socialism, such that it ever was, which was learned rather than lived. Kinnock's *hwyl* made him a specific kind of *Labour* orator – one bred within the movement – and like the passionate moralism of his fellow 'Bevanites' Castle, Foot (and of course Bevan himself), it is an oratory which has been rarely glimpsed since the 'New Labour' era.

Notes

The author would like to give a special thank you to Lord Kinnock for his extremely helpful personal comments on the first draft of this chapter. Thanks also go to the editors and several individuals who offered advice following the presentation of this chapter at the special conference out of which this collection arose.

1 This is not a singular example. Alan Sandry (2011: 39) has discussed the Welsh expression *hiraeth* which 'has no unambiguous meaning in translation'. Offering attachment to those who associate themselves with or have love for Wales, *hiraeth* 'can mean longing or desire, but ... also express passion and emotion'.
2 Passion *qua jouissance*, perhaps? (See Vighi, 2010.)
3 Harris (1984: 29) makes the flattering but over-romantic claim that 'Politics is discussed in South Wales with the enthusiasm and spontaneity which in England is devoted to sport and the weather'.
4 See report here: www.youtube.com/watch?v=bWLN7rIby9s&feature=related.
5 A symbol of anti-socialist decadence – as Leapman (1987: 103) notes, the word was almost 'spat'.
6 The flip side of this point, as put by Kinnock himself, is that, as the alternative to hitting back was to get battered – 'not really an acceptable possibility' – that ironically the events were in reality evidence of a 'clinical coolness' on his behalf rather than the uncontrolled heat many in the public evinced (personal correspondence).

9

The oratory of John Smith

Robin T. Pettitt

Introduction

When exploring almost any aspect of John Smith's political life there is a palpable sense of viewing a never to be completed work in progress. This makes him a difficult subject to deal with. Because his life was cut short just as he was about to reach the pinnacle of his career, very likely becoming Labour's first prime minister in more than a decade and a half, his legacy as a politician is one of incompleteness.

This sense of work in progress and incompleteness has an effect on how one approaches Smith's oratory. Oratory is shaped partly by the personality of a political leader (either genuine or manufactured), what Aristotle calls ethos, which in turn is shaped by events and context (Pettitt, 2012). Most leading politicians will go through a process of rise, 'greatness' and decline, each stage of which is likely to affect their oratory. In 1994 Smith was on the cusp of the highpoint of his career. His far too early death meant he never had to face the consequences of the inevitable decline and fall that is the lot of all party leaders. In short, the conclusion to Smith's oratory is missing.

Hence, this chapter will focus on what was at the core of Smith's oratory and deal less with how it evolved, since that process of evolution was cut short. After having considered Smith's background and some general trends in his oratory, the rest of the chapter will be based around three case studies associated with Parliament, the party conference and the public arenas. First there will be two of his contributions to parliamentary debate, namely those which twice won him the title of Parliamentarian of the Year; second there will be his speeches surrounding his most significant contribution to the Labour Party's organisational development: the introduction of One Member, One Vote (OMOV); and finally there will be his very last speech in which he asked, on behalf of the Labour Party, for the opportunity to serve. Smith's parliamentary speeches will be given the greatest attention since it was here that he was widely regarded as being at his strongest. The chapter will conclude with an evaluation of Smith's oratory, his use of ethos, pathos and logos, and the impact his oratory had on the party.

John Smith as orator

Politically Smith was very much a centrist and is said to have been wedded to the 'politics of pragmatism' (Stuart, 2005: 387) which certainly characterised his leadership of the Labour Party. He is described as 'a conciliator, ruling from the centre of the party' (Stuart, 2005: 386). Unlike his political hero Hugh Gaitskell 'he had the capacity to unite the Labour Party whereas Gaitskell, to succeed, had to defeat a section of it' (MacPherson, 1994: 7–8). In this respect, Smith also differs from both his predecessor and his successor. Neil Kinnock had to defeat Militant Tendency and their fellow travellers on the hard left in order to bring the party back from the brink after the 1983 general election. In turn Blair felt the need to almost constantly place himself in opposition to the 'Old Labour' elements of the party, which essentially meant anyone who disagreed with his modernising agenda. Smith's conciliatory style of leadership can therefore partly be put down to the fact that there were no dragons, real or imagined, to slay within the party. It is doubtful whether Smith would have been able to take such a moderate approach to leading the party if he had been faced with the same challenges that Kinnock faced after 1983. If he had, he would either not have been able to cope, or would have to have been a very different type of leader. In short, his conciliatory leadership may have been partly down to his personality, but it was also to a large extent down to the fact that Kinnock had laid the groundwork which made Smith's conciliatory style possible.

There are four key issues to keep in mind when considering Smith's oratory: first his personality and especially his self-confidence; second his conciliatory style of leadership; third his background as a lawyer; and fourth the fact that he was known more as a parliamentarian than an organisationally focused party man. These four issues had a considerable impact on his style of oratory and will be considered in turn.

Clare Short wrote after Smith's death that 'Because he knew himself and was at ease with himself he treated everyone with respect' (Short, 1994). This is echoed by Mark Stuart who writes that 'Smith was utterly secure about the person he was' (2005: 394). This no doubt goes part of the way towards explaining his conciliatory style of leadership. Because of his self-confidence he did not feel threatened and under siege the way some Labour leaders, rightly or wrongly, have in the past.

Perhaps because of this strong foundation of self-confidence Smith was a distinctly 'unflashy' speaker: 'For all politicians public speaking is part of the job. For some a dramatic setting, the flashing phrase, the right gestures liberated by auto-cue shape the end product. John was not of that school. He actively distrusted and disapproved of anything that he saw as "flash"' (Dewar, 2000: vii). According to Donald Dewar, Smith 'had no ambition to be an orator in the grandiose sense of the word' (Dewar, 2000: viii). Hence, his approach to oratory can probably be classified as falling in the 'middle style' of oratory: 'characterised by urbanity and incisiveness [and] associated with satire and epigram and especially with rhetorical proof and disproof'

(Cockcroft and Cockcroft, 2005: 162; see also Glover, 2011: 51). This description of rhetorical style chimes with Dewar's claim that for Smith 'a speech was an exercise in persuasion and logic' (Dewar, 2000: vii).

The fact that Smith was a conciliator rather than an in-fighter and 'good hater' made a difference to his oratory. Because of the absence of dragons Smith did not need to use his party speeches to attack internal enemies. Gaitskell had to 'fight, fight and fight again to save this party we love' (Kinnock, 1985); Kinnock attacked 'impossible promises' (Gaitskell, 1959); and Blair felt the need to deal with 'the forces of conservatism' not only on the opposition benches, but also, and perhaps especially, within the Labour Party. There are no similar lines associated with Smith. Not because he was adverse to a cutting phrase or two, but because when speaking to the party he did not have the need for such phrases. The closest Smith came to speeches like the ones cited above was his OMOV speech. However, even here he is focused on persuasion and inclusiveness rather than preaching and browbeating.

The last two elements of Smith's style as an orator, being a lawyer and a parliamentarian, are so closely interlinked that they will be dealt with together. Smith's oratorical home was very much in the Commons, rather than on the party platform – something which several writers have commented on. Stuart argues that '[Kinnock's] style was highly successful in the country. He developed a real flair as a party organiser, and became a great platform orator. In contrast John spent most of his time in the House of Commons' (2005: 147) and refers to the House of Commons as Smith's 'natural home' (2005: 157). Dewar writes that Smith's 'trade was debate and there he reigned supreme' and therefore he was at his best in the Commons (2000: viii). By contrast he was a lot less comfortable with speaking at the party conference (Dewar, 2000). In the cut and thrust of House of Commons debate he found a natural outlet for his 'sharp wit' and 'funny and acidic ad-libbing' (Brivati, 2000: xiii). Smith had plenty of what Cicero called *ingenium* (creativity), something which served him well in the House of Commons, but was less useful in set-piece and scripted situations. Stuart (2005) also writes that Smith never developed an intimate knowledge of the party rule book, a document having the status of gospel to many party activists, and never made it onto the National Executive Commitee (NEC), the site for many of the party's battles in the 1980s, until becoming leader. He was in short, a 'dedicated parliamentarian' (Brivati, 2000: xiii).

However, it is important to consider what it means to be a 'dedicated parliamentarian'. The situation in Westminster has been described as one where:

> the opposition is reduced to making speeches against the government's proposals not in hope of bringing about a change in its plans but as part of an attempt to persuade the electorate that the opposition has alternative and better policies. For opposition MPs, speaking in the chamber through ostensibly a contribution to the policy making-process, is no more fruitful than 'heckling a steamroller'. (Gallagher *et al.*, 2006: 63)

This naturally has an effect on the style of oratory used in Westminster. The opposition is not expected to engage with the government's suggestions with a view to extract concessions. The above quote suggests that the purpose of debate in Westminster is often simply to make the other side look bad. This is reflected in how Smith's work in the House of Commons has been described. Dewar (2000: viii) referred to Smith's use of 'destructive logic'. Stuart writes that as a leading opposition spokesperson Smith's 'primary responsibility was to harry the government of the day' (2005: 137, see also 131) and that he was referred to as 'the leading discomfiter of the government' (Stuart, 2005: 161). This very aptly exemplifies the role of the opposition in Westminster: to harry and discomfit – not to engage or improve. This will obviously have a major impact on the style of oratory employed by a 'dedicated parliamentarian' such as Smith.

This is where Smith's background as a lawyer was useful. A lawyer in a courtroom is there to hold a particular position regardless of the actual merits of that position. So it is in the British Parliament – whatever the merits of the proposals being put forward the role of the opposition is often to demolish it, something Smith proved very skilled at. Smith described one part of the Westland affair as being a 'bit like a courtroom' (Stuart, 2005: 135). Early on in the Westland affair the situation was seen as one where 'poor rap-taking Leon Brittan was to look then, like the prisoner in the dock' (Pearce, 1992: 4–5). Again during the Westland affair Smith said in a speech in the Commons that the situation 'takes me back to my days in the criminal courts' (*Hansard*, 1986, vol. 90, col. 683). In short, the point of oratory in the House of Commons is less about participating in a deliberative process, and more about scoring points against the other side. Smith's experience as a lawyer prepared him well for that environment.

The parliamentary arena

The two House of Commons speeches that led to Smith being named Parliamentarian of the Year were both, as could be expected, fine examples of Westminster rhetoric where the main, indeed only, purpose was to attack the government. However, they also exemplify very different approaches to doing so. Classical rhetoric operates with three types of speeches:

1) Deliberative speeches designed to get someone to 'do or not do something, to accept or to reject a particular view of things' (Corbett and Connors, 1999: 121). These speeches are what one would expect to find in assemblies gathered to make decisions on some course of action.
2) Judicial speeches designed to 'defend our actions or views, to impugn the actions of others, or to dispute the wording, interpretation, and application of texts of all kinds' (Corbett and Connors, 1999: 124). Such speeches are obviously most often associated with a court of law.

3) Ceremonial speeches with the main purpose of either praising or censuring someone (Corbett and Connors, 1999: 127).

The first speech made on 27 January 1986 is the culmination of Smith's attack on the government in connection with the Westland affair. This speech is best understood as a judicial speech since the main purpose was to expose the alleged wrongdoings of the government. The second speech, made on 7 June 1989, can be seen as a ceremonial speech. Its main purpose was to expose the divisions between the prime minister and the Chancellor of the Exchequer, and thus put the government in a bad light. It is worth noting that neither is a deliberative speech. Deliberative speeches have very little role to play in the House of Commons since there is little chance of the government being persuaded to change its mind based on a debate in the legislature. Hence the main purpose of oratory in this context is to accuse the other side of wrongdoing or incompetence.

The judicial character of the Westland speech was underlined by the fact that Smith specifically levelled 'charges' against the government (*Hansard*, 1986, vol. 90, cols. 681–2). Indeed he commented that the situation reminded him of 'my days in the criminal courts' (*Hansard*, 1986, vol. 90, col. 683). Corbett and Connors (1999) argue that there are three stages or elements to a judicial speech – whether a thing is (*an sit*); what it is (*quid sit*); and of what kind it is (*quale sit*). First it is necessary to establish what happened, that is presenting and evaluating the evidence; second it is necessary to establish what the evidence means: that is, what is the exact charge being made, what laws have been broken, who was harmed and how badly; third and finally, it is necessary to explore the motives and causes of the action that was taken.

Smith's Westland speech had all these three elements and in that order. At the beginning of the speech he said 'Let us examine what the Prime Minister told us today' (*Hansard*, 1986, vol. 90, col. 680). Having underlined the meagreness of the prime minister's contribution he quoted from a letter written by the Solicitor General which concluded that a 'flagrant' violation of certain rules had taken place. Having established that rules had been broken, he then examined in great detail what the prime minister did once it had been found that rules had been broken. Thus he has established *an sit*. On the basis of that evidence he outlined two specific 'charges', using that exact word, against the prime minister (*Hansard*, 1986, vol. 90, cols. 681–2) thus establishing *quid sit*.

Having done that he moved onto the final phase of establishing *quale sit*, why the breaking of rules happened. Here the speech began to slip into a more ceremonial style, as he started to censure the government. The problem, argued Smith, was not that a mistake had been made. Rather, the problem was that 'the standards of good government have been deteriorating under the Prime Minister and her Ministers' (*Hansard*, 1986, vol. 90, col. 683). Hence Smith used the need to establish *quale sit* as an opportunity to censure the government and present its alleged lack of integrity.

Obviously, whilst the situation may have reminded Smith of his 'days in the criminal court' the Commons is not a court, there is no jury or judge and no verdict will be cast: hence why the speech had to end on a ceremonial note. The ultimate point of the speech was to show the government in a bad light which required a ceremonial rather than a judicial approach. However, by starting the speech in a judicial style, Smith had a good basis on which to use the more ceremonial style at the end of the speech to censure the government.

The speech as a whole was heavily based on an appeal to reason (*logos*). It was a careful and detailed presentation and analysis of the evidence, obviously done in such a way as to show the government in the worst possible light, what Alfred Lee and Elizabeth Lee (1939: 95–104) refer to as 'card stacking'. There was no attempt at humour, which would have undermined the sense of the seriousness of the charges being levelled. To the extent that any appeal to emotions (or *pathos*) was used it was at the end of the speech where the ceremonial elements were clearly designed to evoke a sense of distrust of the government. There was an underlying sense that Smith was also relying on *ethos*, that is, his own character. His reference to 'charges' being made and 'my days in the criminal courts' seemed designed to draw attention to Smith's background as a lawyer. Part of the reason for this was certainly the desire to make the government look suspect, and even criminal. However, a separate purpose was to encourage the impression that Smith's role in this affair was not that of a point-scoring sophistic politician. Rather, by hinting at his lawyer's background and casting the Commons as a court of law, Smith was painting himself as a serious professional carrying out the important task of bringing wrongdoers to justice.

The second speech, made in the Commons on 7 June 1989, was another example of a superb Westminster speech – that is devoid of deliberative content, and designed to 'heckle the steamroller' (Gallagher *et al.*, 2006: 63). This is a feature it had in common with the Westland speech. However, that was also the extent of their similarities. The second speech was clearly designed to make the government look bad, but where the Westland speech used a judicial style, the second speech employed a ceremonial style.

There were two main points to the speech. One was to expose divisions between Margaret Thatcher and Nigel Lawson. The second was to present the government as economically incompetent. A ceremonial speech is concerned with praise and censure, and to that end draws out the virtues and vices of a subject (Aristotle, 1991; Corbett and Connors, 1999). There are probably no more severe vices in politics than being divided and economically incompetent, and Smith, in his careful and measured manner, presented the evidence for both the dividedness and the incompetence of the government. As with the Westland speech there is very little in the way of rhetorical frills, but rather a reliance on cutting wit, combined with the detailed marshalling of evidence. This speech is notable for three key elements: the use of pathos (that is emotion, in this case humour); the use of what was referred to above as his 'sharp wit'; and finally the devastating use of the opponents' own words against them.

The use of pathos was primarily exemplified by Smith citing the *Neighbours* theme tune. This was a good example of what Aristotle called *topoi*, the use of a well recognised piece of popular culture to make a point. Smith led up to it by citing Thatcher's own words. Early on in the speech he quoted from an interview she gave in which she said that 'Nigel is a very good neighbour of mine and a very good chancellor' (*Hansard*, 1989, vol. 157, col. 248). This allowed Smith to use the *Neighbours* theme tune, including the line 'That's when neighbours become good friends' to highlight the fact that whilst the prime minister and the Chancellor may have been neighbours, they were most certainly not good friends. The contrast between the sickly-sweet nature of the theme tune and the reality of the relationship between Thatcher and Lawson served to underline the fractious nature of their relationship. This use of humour is deployed in a way that Cicero would have approved of. Cicero argued that humour was best employed at the beginning and the end of a speech (Glover, 2011). By using emotion at the beginning the audience is drawn into the speech and given some preparation for what is to come – in this case a detailed censure of the government.

The second and third elements of the speech, the use of sharp wit and the turning of an opponent's words against them were exemplified by Smith's use of Thatcher's line about Lawson being a good neighbour. Another example occurred when Smith attacked Lawson over inflation and interest rates. Smith cited Lawson's claim that a rise in inflation was a 'temporary blip' (*Hansard*, 1989, vol. 157, col. 248), which Smith used to attack the government's economic credibility: 'as interest rates blip higher and higher for longer and longer, is it any wonder that people are losing confidence in Conservative economic policy?' (*Hansard*, 1989, vol. 157, col. 248).

This speech was an attack on the government, using pathos in the form of humour and logos in the form of detailed evidence. It was a ceremonial speech in that its main purpose was to censure the government over divisions within it and its alleged economic incompetence. Unlike the Westland speech there was not a specific charge of rule breaking, but rather a general claim that the government was doing badly. Like the Westland speech the point of the speech was not deliberation but harrying and discomforting.

Conference

Smith was not a good party conference speaker (Brivati, 2000; Dewar, 2000). Whilst he was widely acknowledged as a proficient Commons performer, that style was of little use in a party conference. The House of Commons is a small and noisy space. Dewar writes that the 'crowded, tight amphitheatre with its packed benches allowed [Smith] to establish a rapport with his audience, even to dominate. The Commons is volatile. The audience is alive, built in. Those who are there do not sit and listen. They participate' (2000: viii). It is not too much to say that as a rule a party conference hall is the polar opposite. There have certainly been times when the audience at the Labour Party conference has been active and wanted to participate – one just has to watch footage from say Kinnock's speech in 1985 where he confronts Militant Tendency. However, a party conference hall is certainly very far from the 'crowded, tight amphitheatre' of the House of Commons. As a rule there is little room for improvisation in a party conference speech, and Smith's talent for demolishing (Dewar, 2000) his opponents just did not fit with either the party conference situation or indeed with his conciliatory leadership style. Dewar argues that in the House of Commons Smith 'fed off interventions' (2000: ix) from the opposing benches. No such sustenance was available when he faced the Labour Party conference as leader. It is therefore perhaps not surprising that his performances at the Labour Party's conference have gone largely unremembered. In fact, in his edited collection of Smith's speeches Brian Brivati writes that Smith 'did not make great Labour conference speeches and we do not reproduce any here for that reason' (2000: 165).

This omission from Brivati's collection of speeches is notable, especially since one of Smith's main legacies as Labour leader was the introduction of OMOV, something which required the support of a reluctant party conference in 1993. However, Brivati argues that in this context John Prescott's ramshackle, but passionate, rhetoric had more impact (Brivati, 2000; Stuart, 2005). Indeed, it is arguable that backroom deals, some heavy arm-twisting and brinkmanship was far more important than any amount of rhetorical power in the conference hall.[1] Nevertheless, whilst Smith's speech at the 1993 party conference in support of OMOV may have had a limited impact, it is still worth examining for its approach to rhetoric.

In contrast to the two parliamentary speeches examined above, the third example of Smith's oratory was deliberative in nature. Smith needed the support of the Labour Party conference and here was a situation where a speech could and needed to make a difference to the outcome of a deliberative process, something which is a rare event indeed in the House of Commons.

According to Edward Corbett and Robert Connors (1999) deliberative rhetoric is about appealing to people to do or not to do something, or to accept or reject a certain view. In doing so there are two grounds on which one can make such an appeal. The first is based on it being the worthy (*dignitas*) or the good (*bonum*) thing to do. The second is based on it being the most useful or advantageous (*utilitas*). *Dignitas* and *bonum* are based on what is good in and of itself; *utilitas* is based on what is good for us. Hence the orator can appeal to people to choose one path over another because it is the 'right thing to do'; or because one will derive more concrete benefits from one cause of action than another.

Smith's speech to the 1993 Labour Party conference on OMOV was firmly based on *utilitas*. He argued that implementing OMOV for leadership and candidate selection and for voting at the party conference would help recruit more members, particularly those trade unionists who pay the political levy and are thus indirect members of the party. Giving more power to individual members would encourage such indirect members to convert to direct membership. He further argued that this would be of benefit to everybody involved because a direct membership of the Labour Party would not be as a replacement for the indirect membership via a trade union, but a complementary addition to trade union membership. In addition he argued that the reforms would lead to more women MPs. A final point was that adopting OMOV would show that the party was serious about reform, not only of the party, but also of the UK. Hence, OMOV was a central plank in the party's strategy to win power. This last element also featured in Smith's first speech as leader on 18 July 1992. In this speech he said of OMOV:

> I believe that the public are more likely to trust us with power if we convince them we will share that power with them by widening democracy. But if we are to convince them of our democratic credentials we must modernise the democracy of our own party. That is why I believe we must base our internal democracy on the principle of one member, one vote, and not on the basis of block votes. (Quoted in Brivati, 2000: 173)

Hence, Smith's entire appeal on OMOV was based on *utilitas*. OMOV was not to be supported because it was the right thing to do morally speaking, but because it was a means to other ends, such as winning power and strengthening the party's membership organisation. This should not really come as a surprise. Smith, ever the pragmatist, was never likely to make an appeal on the basis of abstract morality. That would not fit with his pragmatic approach to politics, nor his middle style of rhetoric stemming from that pragmatism. Hence, even though the style of rhetoric was very different (deliberative rather than judicial or ceremonial) there was a consistency in his approach to rhetoric which is based on evidence and pragmatism.

Public

Many of the comments made about Smith's performance at the Labour Party conference can also be applied to his other public speeches – that is, this was not an area that played to his strengths. Smith's main talent was as a cut-and-thrust debater, not as a set-piece speaker. Nor was he 'a natural phrase maker' (Dewar, 2000: viii) and his speeches outside the Commons were not 'sprinkled with one liners quoted again and again' (Dewar, 2000: x). Dewar argues that for Smith 'a speech was an exercise in persuasion and logic' (2000) and that his 'technique at the bar was to lead the jury to the wanted conclusion by dissection of the evidence and picking over the bones to justify his client's case' (2000: viii). The problem was that this style did not make for good television. Whilst the careful attention to detail and steady marshalling of evidence certainly worked both in the courts of law and the Commons, this approach did not lend itself to the production of ten-second sound bites which had become an increasingly important feature of politics news reporting since the 1980s. As early as 1985 *Time* magazine commented that 'TV's formula these days is perhaps 100 words from the reporter, and a "sound bite" of 15 or 20 words from the speaker' (Barnhart and Metcalf, 1997: 269). There is clearly not much room for persuasion or picking over bones in a fifteen or twenty-word sound bite. The very nature of persuasion and logic is that the listener needs to be willing to follow the speaker on a journey through to the end, a task Smith seems to have been particularly well suited to undertake. However, this is a process which takes time and time is not a luxury televised news reporting is very often willing to grant a subject. This was clearly a problem for Smith's style of rhetoric and something which was very likely to have become increasingly problematic – especially should he have been successful in becoming prime minister.

Nevertheless, whilst his performance outside the Commons may not have been his strength it is clearly still an important field to examine in understanding the rhetoric of any politician. Perhaps the most well-known speech Smith made outside the Commons was his last, given on the evening of 11 May 1994. In it he famously concluded by asking for 'the opportunity to serve'.

This speech fell firmly into the ceremonial category of rhetoric, although there was also a deliberative aspect to it in that it was clearly designed to convince the audience to support Labour. As Corbett and Connors write: 'Ceremonial discourse sometimes shades into deliberative discourse ... in praising someone, [orators] were suggesting, indirectly at least, that the audience go and do likewise' (1999: 126). The speech had three main aims: first, to censure the government and point out their failed policies, especially on skills and education; second, to show how Labour's approach is better for the country; third, to convince the representatives from business and industry that Labour's approach is the right one for them and thereby get their support. The ceremonial aspects of the speech were fairly straightforward and constituted an uncomplicated attack on the Conservative Party followed by unfavourably contrasting their failed approach to Labour's own. So, he started the speech by criticising the government's alleged focus on low wages and poor conditions as a means to competitiveness. He contrasted this approach, which can always be undercut by someone else in the developing world, with Labour's focus on skills and education (Brivati, 2000). Hence his criticism of the Conservative Party was not based on an appeal to abstract ideas such as Labour's moral superiority, but was rather based on arguing that Labour's approach would be more successful and beneficial to the audience.

This approach is continued in the deliberative parts. As with the OMOV speech to the Labour Party conference Smith employed *utilitas* rather than *bonum* and *dignitas*. He did not argue that Labour's approach was better than that of the Conservative Party as measured by some abstract principle of what constitutes moral superiority. Instead he presented the argument that Labour's principles of social justice and care for the environment were values that would be beneficial for business and industry. One example of this was when he said that 'No business can be successful without reference to the people it employs or the community in which it survives' (quoted in Brivati, 2000: 277–8). Later he said 'it will be in your interest to respect our social rights and to give power to your people, and to clever and intelligent people working in your companies and in your industries' (quoted in Brivati, 2000: 279). Smith was pushing Labour values by arguing that from a purely pragmatic and self-interested point of view they were better for business and industry than the alternative.

It is also worth observing that Smith based his appeal to the audience almost exclusively on logos with very little room for pathos. When Smith had used pathos in the past, something he certainly did do, it tended to be driven by his fondness for cutting wit. That would almost certainly not be appropriate in an audience where, as he acknowledged towards the end, some may not be 'totally committed to our cause' (quoted in Brivati, 2000: 280). Employing his sharp wit worked well in the Commons, but would be inappropriate for a partly sceptical audience. Instead he presented the practical, pragmatic case for why Labour was the right choice for business. This was consistent with Smith's general approach to oratory: the careful and detailed marshalling of the evidence, rather than an appeal to emotion or abstract principles.

Evaluating John Smith's oratory

Based on the above it would be fair to say that Smith's oratory was generally understated, sticking to the middle style: competent and well structured and without extravagant flourishes. He based his speeches far more on logos than pathos. His speeches were well crafted and often based on the careful presentation of evidence, with, when the situation warranted it, the occasional introduction of barbed wit. In other words, when pathos was used it was mainly in the form of sharp humour, rather than pulling the heartstrings.

Ethos was an important element in Smith's rhetoric, especially, as we have seen, in his best parliamentary speeches. He consciously cited his background as a lawyer to both underscore his own credibility and put his opponents in a bad light. His credibility was based on the idea of being a professional doing a job, not merely a self-interested politician. Smith was cast in the position of prosecutor; the government as the suspect in the dock; and the benches behind him, the media and the watching voters being the jury.

Taken together Smith's oratory has had a somewhat mixed legacy. It is clear from the above that his main oratorical home was the Commons, to which his style was ideally suited. His successes in that forum were illustrated by the painful impact they had on several government ministers. He had been noted as a competent and hard working minister within the party for some time (Stuart, 2005), but it was his harrowing of Conservative ministers in the second half of the 1980s which truly brought him to the attention of the media. On 14 February 1986 the *Guardian* ran an article under the headline 'Why Labour is Betting on John Smith' in which Alan Rusbridger wrote:

> It is not true to say that the Westland affair has made his name, for there have been many who have had their eye on him ever since the work he did on the Devolution Bills 10 years ago. But his nimble and ruthless pursuit of both Mr Brittan and Mrs Thatcher over the past six weeks has certainly brought him slap bang centre stage with the arch lights burning.

This article was followed up later in the year with a profile entitled 'Rising Star of the Opposition' (*Observer*, 2 November 1986). In this article Smith himself is quoted saying that it was only that year, the year of his Westland success and after sixteen years in Parliament, that he had 'been noticed outside it'. On 10 March 1986 *The Times* referred to Smith as the opposition's second most effective politician (after David Owen).

There is no doubt that Smith's skills in the House of Commons greatly benefitted his career at this time. In 1979 he came twelfth in the Shadow Cabinet elections (Stuart, 2005). In late October 1986 he had moved up to second place (*Observer*, 2 November 1986; Stuart, 2005). In mid-1987 Smith then reached the highest point in his career when he was made Shadow Chancellor. This is clearly a significant achievement in a relatively short period of time, and one to a considerable extent driven by Smith's successes in the Commons. His advance was not just down to his debating skills, but they clearly made a significant impact, especially considering the power Labour MPs used to enjoy in electing the Shadow Cabinet.

However, the extent to which this was also truly beneficial for Labour is less certain. Clearly, having people on the front bench capable of taking the battle to the other side is a good thing for a party, and Smith's two 'Parliamentarian of the Year' awards were evidence of his success in this area. There was, though, also a downside to this. Smith's success in the House of Commons and the accolades he achieved in the late 1980s stood in some contrast to the parliamentary achievements of Labour's leader, Kinnock, in the same period. According to Stuart (2005) the performance of the two men during the Westland affair opened up a rift between them, which would only grow bigger as time went on. Stuart writes that:

> [A]s Smith received his award ... it would hardly have been possible to have listened to the citation's reference to 'a cloud of elevated eloquence' without reflecting that had he been up to the relatively straightforward task of taking advantage of an open goal, Neil Kinnock, rather than John Smith, should have been collecting the award. (Stuart, 2005: 139)

The House of Commons is an unforgiving place and Martin Westlake concludes that Kinnock 'not only failed to embellish his parliamentary reputation but had actively damaged it. His critics within the party would later point to the Westland debate as an example of Kinnock's inability to strike the killer blow' (Westlake, 2001: 391). By contrast 'Smith's star had now risen to a point where he now looked and sounded like a future leader of the Labour Party' (Stuart, 2005: 139). The contrasting fortunes of the two senior Labour Party figures severely damaged their working relationship: 'From Westland onwards, the two men kept their distance. Smith, bound by loyalty to his party, refused to challenge Kinnock openly ... Kinnock meanwhile, refused to confront his indispensible subordinate. It set the pattern of the relationship between the two men for the next six years' (Stuart, 2005: 140).

Clearly Smith did not use his oratorical skills to deliberately undermine Kinnock's leadership, but they did seem to have had that effect. Neither, or perhaps both, of them are to blame for their poor working relationship, but it seemed that their differing performances in the Commons at least partly explained their deteriorating relationship. It has been argued that the poor relationship between the two caused significant damage to the party's electoral prospects: 'Gould told *The Observer* the relationship between "Kinnock and Smith was awful – it was key to the defeat in 1992"' (*Observer*, 15 October 1998).

It would be wrong to suggest that Smith's oratory was to the detriment of the Labour Party. However, oratory is by definition a personal thing – it is the use of language by an individual to persuade an audience of the strengths of that individual's position. Hence, even if that position is held on behalf of a collective, for example, a party, it stills appears that the success of oratory accrues more to the individual than the collective. In the case of Smith, his oratory was used to attack the Conservatives, and his success in doing so benefitted him greatly, but did not necessarily benefit the party as a whole to the same extent as it did Smith. Not because he was selfish in his use of his skills, but rather because of the very personal nature of oratory.

There are also signs that Smith's oratory had its weaknesses. It is noted by Stuart that when Smith faced John Major his skills did not necessarily work as well as they sometimes had. After a speech on economic policy by Smith, Major replied:

> The right hon. and learned Member for Monklands, East (Mr. Smith) made his usual forceful speech – both forceful and his usual speech. It was good music hall. He has become the Jasper Carrott of parliamentary debate. For all the humour, however, it was an empty speech. It was empty of policy, it made no serious attempt to diagnose the problem, and it provided no solutions whatsoever. On the one single issue on which he was questioned by my hon. Friend the Member for Northampton, North (Mr. Marlow) it was not until some minutes had passed and someone had whispered to him that he actually provided the answer. (*Hansard* HC, vol. 159, cols. 200–1, 31 October 1989)

According to Stuart: 'Major had spotted one of Smith's few potential weaknesses as a parliamentary debater – the danger of being seen as too frivolous' (Stuart, 2005: 161). Indeed, Smith's oratory faced other problems. It was noted above that one of Smith's strengths was his use of ethos, in the form of his background as a lawyer. He was able to present himself as a dedicated professional doing a job, and place the government in the position as the accused in the dock. This approach could however also be seen as a weakness. As was suggested earlier, the role of the lawyer is to defend the position of their client regardless of the merits of that position, something that fits with the confrontational nature of the Westminster system. The downside is that the actual commitment of the lawyer to their client's position may often be fairly limited. So, Alan Rusbridger wrote in 1986:

> Does Mr Smith's ruthless pragmatism mean that he believes in nothing? There are those who would tell you yes. His Tory friends, for example, who see it as a positive virtue. 'I don't think that he is ideological in any way. You get the impression he could speak with equal confidence for the other side on any issue'. It's that legal training. (*Observer*, 14 February 1986)

After Smith became leader it was commented in *The Times* that there 'is no perceived drama in his oratory which leads to the belief that he (like the Prime Minister) has no strength of feeling underlying what he says' (*The Times*, 16 November 1993). This lack of ideological zeal may not have been true, but his style of oratory does seem to have laid him open to such a criticism.

Once he became leader Smith's strength in the Commons seemed to have slowly developed into a subject of criticism. The piece in *The Times* quoted above went on to say that Smith was 'incapable of changing tone sufficiently to match his audience, and is, consequently, much better in small groups or in the House of Commons where his acerbic wit shows through' (*The Times*, 16 November 1993). In fact, once Smith became leader of the Labour Party the fact that his particular style of oratory was less suited to situations outside of the Commons started to get noticed. As John Watkins pointed out in the *Observer* (1 October 1992): 'The speaker who is effective in the Commons is not always so at the conference.' His focus on the Commons also lessened his impact with the media. Stuart (2005: 313) mentions Smith's 'extreme caution' in accepting interviews; that because he was 'such a House of Commons man, Smith was not always au fait with what was happening outside Westminster' (2005: 316); and that 'perhaps he was failing to recognise the growing importance of the media ... and such a stance would have been impossible to maintain as Prime Minister' (2005: 317).

Finally, it is worth noting that regardless of how good an orator a party leader is, the impact of such oratory can be limited, perhaps especially if it is (excessively) focused on just one arena as Smith's was. It has been noted that the undoubted unpopularity of the Conservative Party after 1992 was less to do with Smith than something more fundamental: 'The public mood, moving on tides deeper than the reach of any man to alter is utterly tired of incumbent ministers ... Mr Smith's oratory could hardly speed the waves, any more than Major's could resist them' (Hugo Young in the *Guardian*, 19 May 1994).

Conclusion

Smith was not an exuberant or flamboyant orator. Indeed, if 'oratory' is sometimes associated with the rousing speeches of Tony Benn, Michael Foot and Kinnock, then the more neutral 'rhetoric' is probably more appropriate for Smith's style. Smith favoured the carefully crafted speech based on solid evidence and a masterly command of the facts – laced as appropriate with sharp and occasionally devastating wit. There may be some doubts about how well his style would have gone down in the role of prime minister, demanding as it does a far greater focus on the world beyond Parliament than is the case of other front-bench posts. Nevertheless, in his natural environment he was a successful orator, even if that success did not always translate well to the outside world and damaged his relationship with Kinnock. Smith was robbed of the opportunity to prove himself as prime minister, and hence we will never know how he would have coped with the diverse oratorical demands of that role.

Notes

1 See Stuart (2005: 320–39) for a description of the tortuous process that led to OMOV being accepted.

10

The oratory of Tony Blair

Mark Bennister

A minimum to be expected from a political leader is the ability to make a few memorable remarks that seem to sum up what the leader and the party stand for, and the kind of meaning we might find in existence. (Horne, 2001: 101)

Tony Blair led the Labour party for thirteen years, turned its fortunes around, and achieved the distinction of three successive general election victories – something that had eluded all his predecessors as Labour leader. If Blair's party leadership were judged solely on electoral performance, his would be a remarkable record. His predominance was built on the successful utilisation of the institutional resources at his disposal and his own personal skill. Blair played to his strengths; he was a gifted communicator, telegenic, populist in his rhetoric and skilled at demonstrating empathy at key moments. Comfortable in a range of settings, Blair's oratory was an important function of his 'political skill' and set a new benchmark for the contemporary party leader – applauded after his final Commons performance, dominant at the party conference and a consummate media operator. He was utterly convinced of his own powers of persuasion, not by berating or battering his opponents inside and outside the party, but by more subtle coaxing and bravura performances. His oratory differed from the traditional Labour firebrand, rootless in terms of his background in the party he came to the leadership with little factional baggage.

Blair's painstakingly constructed speeches, particularly to party conferences, were intended to reach well beyond the Labour Party audience and defined how Blair was perceived and presented (and gained the upper hand in his struggle with Gordon Brown). Messages were simplistically diluted to capture the main thrust of the speech, fuelling criticism of style over substance. Yet his 'amateur thespianism' increasingly grated – oratory can turn audiences off and lose its power to engage and ultimately persuade audiences. He was mocked as 'messianic' and 'deluded'. Over time he became more isolated, often as he opined 'in a majority of one', he gave up trying to please all people inside and outside the party. This was reflected in his valedictory speaking tour in 2007, when freed from the constraints of office-seeking, he rose beyond party politics in a personalised projection of his leadership.

This chapter provides a critical analysis of the Blair oratory. It argues that his party leadership can be divided into three distinct oratorical phases: as opposition leader; as prime minister before 2003; and after 2003. The chapter will consider what rhetorical devices Blair used and to which audiences. How did the Blair oratory differ and what impact did it have on both the Labour Party and his leadership? Did Blair create a rhetorical style that set him apart from previous Labour leaders and create a new standard against which future leaders would be judged? The chapter is divided into four sections. First it considers Blair's style of speech, the tools and techniques used. Second it explores the impact of Blair's oratory on the Labour Party, the impact on organisation and policy and the key aspect of the annual conference speech. Third, much of Blair's oratory was directed at the audience beyond the party and this section looks at the extra-party influence of the words and delivery. This includes public meetings, media performances and as a predominant prime minister. Fourth, oratory is a key tool in heresthetics – the ability to outmanoeuvre opponents both inside and outside the party. To what extent could Blair rely on his oratorical skills to defeat oppositional forces?

It is striking that amongst the plethora of material (of varying quality) on Blair and the Blair premiership there is little that deals directly with his oratory. By contrast his oratory has been portrayed, imitated and mocked regularly on film and television. Bearing in mind how important and influential his oratorical performances were this is a surprising omission, more so when one considers the interactional nature of contemporary political leadership whereby skill in communication is an essential feature. Of course, many authors make reference to the Blair form of speech in analyses of the New Labour years (Mullin, 2010; Rawnsley, 2001; 2010) and others include Blair in broad studies of contemporary rhetoric (Glover, 2011; Leith, 2011). Norman Fairclough (2000) and Jonathan Charteris-Black (2005; 2012) have applied critical discourse analysis and 'comparative keyword analysis' to Blair's speeches, providing helpful linguistic dissections of rhetorical speech construction. But apart from Alan Finlayson's Leverhulme-funded work on political rhetoric, there is little systematic study of the impact and influence of Blair's political oratory.[1] This chapter contains an overview of the Blair style of oratory and offers some analysis of the impact and influence of his public utterances. Acknowledging the difficulty in generating any meaningful measurement of the impact of Blair's oratory, this chapter naturally only scratches the surface, but provides a basis for further investigation.

Style of speech

Oratory, and in particular the rhetoric used in communication, plays a key part in placing the individual as the embodiment of the government (or party). Prime ministers enhance personal capacity not just by the things they say, but by the way they say them too. Oratory, speech and the use of rhetoric – the art of speaking well in public – are important tools in the projection of personalised leadership (Charteris-Black, 2012). Aristotle, as all scholars of rhetoric will recognise, identified three different lines of argument or persuasive tools: ethos, logos and pathos. Sam Leith (2011: 47) crudely describes them as follows:

> Ethos: 'Buy my old car because I'm Jeremy Clarkson.' Logos: 'Buy my old car because yours is broken and mine is the only one on sale.' Pathos: 'Buy my old car or this cute little kitten with a rare degenerative disease will expire in agony for my car is the last asset I have in the world and I am selling it to pay for kitty's medical treatment.'

Applying these to Blair's leadership we see that in common with other contemporary leaders, ethos (the appeal from character) and pathos (the emotional appeal) proved more obvious tools than logos (argument based on fact). Furthermore classical rhetoricians identified three main types of speech: the deliberative (to make political decisions), forensic (to evaluate past action) and epideictic (to praise). Blair, in common with other contemporary politicians, tended to engage in deliberative or epideictic speaking.

Ethos: vote for me I'm Tony Blair

Early on, Blair cultivated an image of himself as an 'ordinary person'. 'I think most people who know me know that I'm a pretty normal guy' was a phrase Blair used in his first electoral campaign in 1997 and then repeated many times over the next ten years (Blair in Foley, 2000: 178). Foley attributes this in 1997 to the New Labour strategy of promoting the person Blair, most evident in the party election broadcast on 24 April 1997 which 'fused Blair's private life with his public face':

> By coming to know him as a person, the public could come to know the reasons for his mission, to appreciate the authenticity of his shared empathy, and to associate with a common impulse to make things better in practical and unthreatening ways. (Foley, 2000: 180)

To successfully do this, Blair needed to draw on his thespian roots and 'pretensions to be a pop star' at Fettes School and St John's College, Oxford (Powell, 2010: 52). His background helped to foster a confidence and natural attention-seeking public demeanour (Naughtie, 2001: 9). These 'thespian skills' and his 'extraordinary persuasive and presentational skills' – being telegenic, persuasive and able to project sincerity – helped Blair to win his party's leadership in the first place (Seldon, 2007: ix–xiv). Blair, as he himself said, chose the Labour Party rather than being born into it, and as King notes he was:

> [T]he perfect leader for the Labour Party in the 1990s ... He was young. He was classless. He was squeaky clean. He had no ties to the trade union movement. He carried virtually no ideological baggage. (King in Theakston, 2002: 307)

Yet his ethos had to be worked at. The glottal stops and flattened vowels, deployed to downplay his public school accent, were derided as 'mockney'. William Hague reflected that Blair desperately tried to be all things to all audiences: 'In Labour party magazine it was announced that "Tony's favourite food is fish and chips. He gets a takeaway from his local chippy whenever he is at home in his constituency." In the Islington Cookbook his favourite food was "fresh fettuccine garnished with an exotic sauce of olive oil, sun-dried tomatoes and capers"' (*Guardian*, 26 April 2002). Alongside working at his ethos, Blair had also to learn the art of public speaking, graduating from a nervous reader of texts to a highly accomplished performer. Blair recalled reading a prepared text to his new constituency party after the 1983 general election and his subsequent humiliation at the hands of Dennis Skinner and others (Blair, 2010: 45). Blair swiftly learned that the performance became as crucial as the words. An excruciating early performance as Shadow Employment Minister on BBC News in October 1987 confirms how he developed his performance skills (BBC, 1987).

As biographical analysis has suggested, such style – the emotional thespianism of Blair – relates to the personality of the leader and, to a lesser extent, a desire to contrast with the previous incumbent. The repudiation of the previous leader creates distance and contrast with the previous incumbent. Often a more domineering prime minister is followed by one who is less so, or vice versa. Blair proved a younger and more charismatic alternative to John Major, and to previous Labour leader John Smith. He also contrasted with the more strident approach of Neil Kinnock. Blair sought to distance himself from the traditional tribalism of Labour party politics (McAnulla, 2012). With Alistair Campbell's guidance Blair appeared on several popular television shows in which he could present himself in a relaxed, apolitical context, unmediated by the interpretations of journalists or media commentators (Campbell, 2010).

Language and argument are the main weapons available to the leader of the opposition. Blair set out his leadership style: he would lead his party while his opponent Major followed his. The high rhetoric that Blair used to good effect to undermine Major set him on a path of personalised leadership (Foley, 2002). Commentary regarding his leadership performance shifted during his early months as party leader: 'Last year I was Bambi. This year I'm Stalin. From Disneyland to dictatorship in twelve short months' (Blair, 1995, in McAnulla, 2012). In marked contrast to Kinnock's more bombastic approach, Blair sought to engender trust with the electorate deploying a softer style of rhetoric to reach out beyond traditional Labour votes. Critical to this leadership was the projection of the leader as the embodiment of a changed 'new' Labour Party. In his oratory in opposition he worked at presenting a statesman-like appeal, exuding self-confidence and competence. Blair was greatly helped early in his premiership by the way the plaudits flowed: 'telegenic and comes across as likeable, idealistic, intelligent, persuasive and sincere, personifying New Labour's cross-class appeal' (Foley, 2000: 101; Theakston, 2002: 310). It was this use of sharp, pithy rhetoric that defined the Blair oratory. From the 'people's princess' (Diana's death 1997), 'hand of history' (Good Friday Agreement), 'forces of conservatism' (1999 conference speech), 'no reverse gear' (2003), many of Blair's speeches were conveniently distilled, paraphrased and condensed. Fitting in with the (post)modern vogue for short attention spans and media-friendly instant quotes Blair immediately fitted, and embodied, the mould for the contemporary leader.

Such tools enabled Blair to swiftly develop a deliberate and calculated relationship with the electorate. In both the 1997 and 2001 election campaigns the leader was central to the message that party strategists were seeking to convey to the electorate. Blair proved particularly adept at utilising this shift towards television-based, personality-centred campaigning, and exemplified the move from the partified to the presidential in terms of style (Poguntke and Webb, 2005). In common with Margaret Thatcher, he did not talk about what *'we'* the party might do but about what *'I'* Tony Blair would do (Finlayson, 2002). This personalisation became more apparent further into his leadership and certainly post-Iraq, he rarely (if ever) dispelled or downplayed the perception that he was the exclusive author of party policy and direction (McAnulla, 2012). Blair made much more of his autonomous position, taking a robust and bullish position on Iraq. His position and rhetoric was much more risk-orientated for a political leader.

To 'mirror popular conversational norms rather than those of the political class' Blair used colloquial phrases, everyday expressions and informal discourse (Charteris-Black, 2005: 146). As such, the speaker is placed as a member of the audience being addressed. For Fairclough, Blair's capacity to anchor the public politician in the normal person was a key component of his success. He memorably used such ethos to nullify accusations of wrongdoing regarding Bernie Ecclestone's £1 million donation to the Labour Party: 'I think most people who have dealt with me think I am a pretty straight sort of guy, and I am' (*Independent*, 17 November 1997). In contrast to the evasions and posturing of general politics, Blair initially at least demonstrated the capacity to 'reassert constantly his normal, decent, likeable personality' (Fairclough, 2000: 7). This was most evident in his epideictic response to the death of Princess Diana, combining articulation of collective feeling with personalised and informal language (Finlayson, 2002). This personalised discourse aimed to reduce the space between leader and electorate or mass audience and was essentially built of a relationship between the leader and followers, based on language. Despite searching for the right words and response on many subsequent occasions he never quite scaled these heights of personalised empathy. Ethos, then, is not simply a device Blair used to get his message across. Personal character was the very substance of his argument (Finlayson and Martin, 2008).

Logos: vote for me – it's the only sensible option

Blair may have been reluctant to acknowledge or recognise Labour Party history as he sought to articulate the reinvention of the party, but he claimed to have learned his oratory from Benn. Campaigning for Cherie Blair in Thanet North in 1983, with Blair watching, Benn provided him with an early blueprint for public speaking: confidence; humour; thread; and argument.

> I had never heard him speak before that night. I sat enraptured, absolutely captivated and inspired. I thought: if only I could speak like that. What impressed me was not so much the content – actually I didn't agree with a lot of it – but the power of it, the ability to use words to move people, not simply to persuade, but to propel. (Blair, 2010: 36)

So while Blair saw the key to great oratory in emotional terms, he recognised the importance of logos, an argument based on fact. His speechwriter Peter Hyman saw this intent in his speech construction: 'As a trained barrister he believes his duty is to make an argument with a beginning, a middle and end, and one that holds up to scrutiny' (Hyman, 2005: 9). Yet rarely do modern political leaders present a full argument and are able to expose their audience to the technique of logos. Conference speeches and keynote speeches in the House of Commons are the only occasions when the full range of argument can be deployed in logical, or seemingly logical, terms. Although Blair had speechwriters, who worked closely with him, he insisted on writing all these speeches of significance himself. The process was painful; Jonathan Powell called conference speechwriting a long-winded and miserable process which only ever came together at the last minute (Powell, 2010: 51).

> Although [Jonathan] Powell employed talented speechwriters such as Peter Hyman and subsequently Phillip Collins, Blair felt he needed to pen his own words – in long-hand. 'He would get up at 4 o'clock in the morning and write in his underpants, then we'd have to dash downstairs and give it to the Garden Girls [the Number 10 secretaries] to type up … it was complete misery for the rest of us'. (Katz, 2008)

The teamwork in office was less about writing the words and more about gathering policy ideas together. Many speeches however did need to be written by others, which can cause an obvious dislocation between the words and the speaker. To be convincing as an orator the speaker has to not only believe the words, but demonstrate the perception of belief. Hyman recounts the time soon after the 1997 election when Blair tore up Hyman's prepared speech as inappropriate for the audience. Blair's experience of being slow-handclapped at the Women's Institute in 2000, when he did deliver an inappropriate and badly drafted text, exposed the dangers of misjudging an audience. Blair though had an almost messianic belief in his own powers to persuade, and the recognition that his words needed to convince sceptical audiences and propel them towards his worldview infused his speechwriting. Despite his reliance on ethos, Blair did at times resort to the argument and believed that the country could be changed fundamentally by persuasion and cajoling, not bludgeoning (Hyman, 2005: 6).

Pathos: vote for me or we're all doomed!

Ethics and morality featured strongly throughout Blair's premiership and attention is constantly drawn to the moral and religious conviction that underpinned Blair's life. Bold rhetorical statements appeared regularly creating dividing lines between good and evil, right and wrong. A conflict narrative was developed in which in Blair's world you were either with him and his crusade or against him. This came to the fore most notably in Blair's second term of office, one dominated by foreign policy issues whereby he sought to 'conceptualise the world as a struggle between good and evil in which his particular vocation is to advance the former' (Seldon, 2005: 700). Such 'conviction rhetoric' led to a greater decisiveness on the international stage than domestically (Charteris-Black, 2005; Stephens, 2004).

Yet the performance was key, the Blair speech became a major set-piece event replete with tension, a backstory and dramatic Pinteresque pauses. His use of rhetoric, absence of verbs, emotional syntax and impassioned delivery became essential features. There was much of the lay preacher style in his speeches and he appeared to thrive on the messianic adulation, particularly at annual Labour Party conferences. There are two takes on this aspect of Blair's leadership. Former Labour MP Leo Abse's entertaining psychoanalytical study of Blair tells us that 'exhibitionism is a genetic condition required in any budding politician's CV' but 'Blair's persistent display of mimetic talents … reveals even for a politician, exhibitionism in an unusually undisguised and exotic form' (Abse, 2001: 78). According to Abse, his 'narcissism' on the political stage, stemming from his unfulfilled thespian forays at Oxford and his search for identity, may have turned off some. Blair was mocked by the satirists at *Private Eye* who cast him as a domesticating Anglican vicar for announcing during the Northern Ireland peace talks in 1998: 'A day like today is not a day for sound bites, really. But I feel the hand of history upon our shoulders' (Leith, 2011: 225).

However, others saw Blair's oratory as well suited to the times. For instance, Philip Stephens described Blair's difficult 2003 post-Iraq speech as 'uncompromising in its demands for further modernisation and unrepentant about the decision to go to war yet simultaneously respectful of his critics', an 'effortless mastery of the art' of the leader's address (Cook, 2002: 222; Stephens, 2004: 363). By 2005, Blair had become more resolute in his foreign policy and had made his commitment to the alliance with the United States in Iraq and Afghanistan and to a new domestic security agenda. Although shaken by the July 2005 tube bombings, he had expected such an attack, and was aware that young British males had been a potential threat: 'the attack was a tactical surprise, but not a strategic surprise' (intelligence officer quoted in Seldon, 2007: 376). Anthony Seldon described the words in response as an example of Blair's oratory at its finest (also a good example of antithesis in deliberative speechwriting):

> When they try to intimidate us, we will not be intimidated. When they seek to change our country or our way of life by these methods, we'll not be changed. When they try

to divide our people or weaken our resolve, we will not be divided and our resolve will hold firm. (Blair, quoted in Seldon, 2007: 377)

Blair's statements and speeches on terrorism were unequivocal. He drew clear lines between good and evil, and he told the Labour Party a week after the London attacks: 'In the end, it is by the power of argument, debate, true religious faith and true legitimate politics that we will defeat this threat' (Blair, 2005a). Blair in his post-Iraq phase became increasingly reliant on pathos, to provide the emotional means to confront the terrorist threat.

Impact on the Labour Party: modernisation, modernisation, modernisation

Blair's oratory was key to the way the party was remoulded as New Labour, aligning the party with a 'young', 'modernising' and 'new' nation, using his communication skills to repackage the product as 'acceptable', 'fresh', 'optimistic' and 'dynamic'. His leadership image was carefully constructed to present him as not only more 'efficient and skilled than anyone else', but also as 'one of us', emphasising his 'extraordinary ordinariness' (Finlayson, 2002: 590). If Blair was central to repackaging the party, he was also key to managing it. Almost immediately on his election as party leader in 1994 he asserted himself on the party. 'The greatest historical claim of Blairism beyond Blair might well be Blair's style of bold, authoritative party leadership. He, perhaps more than anyone popularised the idea that a party has to be dominated by an audacious party leader to be electorally successful' observed Richard Heffernan (2007: 165). This was based on 'vertical communication' from leaders to members, whilst discouraging 'horizontal communication' between activists and members. This 'control freakery' was by design, as Labour's chief polling strategist wrote 'the leadership ran the party by having a … single chain of command leading directly to the leader of the party … [and by having] one ultimate source of campaigning authority … the leader' (Gould, 1998: 240). Blair not only had an impact on the language and discourse of the party, but on the structural relationship between followers and the leader.

Never a great Commons man

Blair was not a big fan of the House of Commons. He was uninterested in parliamentary reform, his attendance in Parliament was patchy, and his accountability limited to Prime Minister's Question Time (which he cut to once a week from 1997) and, after great pressure, twice yearly appearances in front of select committee chairs at the Liaison Committee. Philip Norton (2008: 97) suggested that Blair was 'detached' and did not understand Parliament. Indeed, Blair himself appeared to concur: in his final Question Time performance he admitted that he had 'never been a great House of Commons man' (*Hansard*, 27 June 2007). Yet he was aware of how the institutional resource of leading the party in the Commons could be utilised to bolster his own personal capacity. Blair's speech on Iraq on 18 March 2003 was one such occasion. Blair wished to 'summon the strength to recognise the global challenge of the 21st century, and meet it' and to 'stand up for what we know to be right', 'to have the courage to do the right thing' (*Hansard*, 18 March 2003). Blair had wavering Labour backbenchers and a sceptical public to persuade. Motivated by the need to reduce the back-bench rebellion in the Commons, Blair delivered a powerful and impassioned speech, one that media commentary credited with limiting the size of the rebellion (Toye, 2011). Blair took the decision on as a personal one – one that he, as prime minister, alone had to take. He also hinted that if the vote had gone against him in the Commons he would resign. Blair was unequivocal in the same speech:

> To retreat now would, I believe, put at hazard all that we hold dearest ... to tell our allies that at the very moment of action, at the very moment when they need our determination, Britain faltered: I will not be party to such a course. (*Hansard*, 18 March 2003)

This deliberative speech – concerned with the evaluation of future policy with a view to taking a decision – marked a staging post in Blair's rhetorical leadership style as the embodiment of personalised, ethical and conviction-based leadership. It was Blair attempting to persuade the audience that he was right by convincing them that he 'had the right intentions' and was 'thinking right' (Charteris-Black, 2012: 142–164).

The more regular joust at Prime Minister's Questions (PMQs) gave Blair a platform to display his particular brand of leadership. It fitted Blair's short televisual attention span – a half hour slot to rally the troops, bash the opposition and make the headlines. Blair, of course, was helped in the Commons by the large parliamentary majorities of the first two terms and the weakness of the Conservative opposition. Although William Hague gained some plaudits for his Commons performances, Iain Duncan Smith was a disaster and Blair easily saw off Michael Howard. Only when David Cameron became leader in 2005 did Blair face a real challenge across the dispatch box. But by then the number of oppositional forces within the Parliamentary Labour Party (PLP) had also risen (government whips labelled these the dissidents, dismissed and disgruntled). Brown's supporters were by now mobilising in earnest as increasing numbers of MPs were either removed to the back benches, or overlooked for promotion. As such Blair faced tougher parliamentary battles in his third term.

Perhaps more important than his (often infrequent) appearances in the Commons were his performances in PLP meetings.[2] His presence ensured a high attendance and he treated the PLP to bravura performances and a string of stirring rallying calls. His relaxed, apparently consultative manner in meetings impressed Alan Howarth MP who, having crossed the floor, was well placed to compare the formality of Conservative 1922 Committee meetings with the shirt-sleeved informality of Blair at the PLP (Bennister, 2012). Even as the malcontents in the party agitated and the wheels began to fall off, he had the meetings enthralled. As Chris

Mullin records in his diary entry for 7 November 2005, Blair, rather than seek compromise with a fractious party over the introduction of 90-day detention, took on his critics in the PLP:

> The Man was on sparkling, amazing form. I haven't seen him so good since he talked us (or most of us) into invading Iraq. The mood was revivalist. Billy Graham couldn't have done better. One after another people spoke up to say they had seen the light and were now more than ever convinced of the One True Path. Of the critics there was no sign. (Mullin, 2010: 47)

Conference adulation

Blair was a powerful and impressive public speaker. He was comfortable in a variety of settings: the conference speech; parliamentary question time; impromptu question and answer sessions. His party conference speeches were forensically analysed throughout his thirteen years as Labour Party leader. The speeches defined how Blair was perceived and presented and the presidential epithet is well placed when considering the impact of, and attention to, these speeches. Many were spun to dilute a message into a simple headline or sound bite to capture the main thrust of the speech. For example, 'The 21st century will not be about the battle between capitalism and socialism but between the forces of progress and the forces of conservatism' (BBC, 1999); 'The state of Africa is a scar on the conscience of the world' (*Guardian*, 2001); and 'I can only go one way, I've not got a reverse gear' (BBC, 2003).

Getting the party to bend to his will was a constant source of frustration for Blair, but one that he felt he could achieve using his brand of oratory whether behind the closed doors of the PLP or in the public performances of the set-piece conference speech. Blair sought to set the policy agenda, put internal and external rivals in their place and inspire the troops when he spoke at the Labour Party annual conference. He took on big themes and rather than focus on the short-term task of defeating a political foe, he had a broader outlook in his rhetoric: 'So now in turn, we have to change again – not step back from New Labour but step up to a new mark, a changing world is setting for us. The danger of government is fatigue; the benefit, experience' (Blair, 2005a). He was also adept at using humour in his speeches to deflect and diffuse, as in his 2006 conference speech to deal with his wife's alleged criticism of Gordon Brown: 'At least I don't have to worry about her running off with the bloke next door.' These conference speeches again emphasise the personalised nature of the Blair premiership, decisions (or even regrets) were couched in the singular rather than the collective: 'Every time *I've* ever introduced a reform in government, *I* wish in retrospect *I* had gone further' (emphasis added).

Blair's 2005 conference speech is a good example of how he sought to articulate broad themes and the way the Labour Party should respond to them – the new post-9/11 security agenda; globalisation; Africa. Blair in 2005 still spent most of the speech aiming his sights at critics in his own party and sending broader messages to the television audience, with only a cursory mention of the opposition parties ('never underestimate the Tories; never overestimate the Liberal Democrats'). Blair had fought a tough and often personally bitter election campaign in May, as confirmed by his political secretary Sally Morgan: 'The last one [2005 general election] was horrible, the last one was just foul, because it was all about Iraq, people calling you liar all the time, it was very wearing' (Bennister, 2012: 148). Blair was preoccupied as a world and domestic leader, as demonstrated by the events of July 2005. Between 5 and 7 July Blair had travelled to Singapore for last minute lobbying for the London 2012 Olympic bid, returned to host the G8 Summit at Gleneagles in Scotland, then had to handle the London bombings on the morning of 7 July. With such a tumultuous few months and the backdrop of continued opposition to the Iraq War, it is no surprise that Blair's speech in September 2005 should range far and wide to articulate a broader 'progressive' agenda.

The impact of the conference speech is more obvious in the early years of leadership as party leaders seek to entrench intra-party authority. Blair's impact can now be seen, with the benefit of hindsight, on the way Cameron conducted and presented himself. In this respect Cameron's performance without notes at the 2005 party conference secured his selection as leader: 'More than any of the other candidates, he understood, possibly because of his PR experience, that his appearance had to be a pitch not a speech' (Bale, 2010: 275). Cameron was eager to cast himself in the modern mould of leadership (Bennister and Heffernan, 2012). Although he qualified the epithet 'heir to Blair', he used smooth, confident, oratory and familiar rhetorical devices to 'recalibrate' the Conservative Party towards the centre much as Blair had done before him. Other senior Conservatives, such as Michael Gove, were gushing in their admiration for Blair's presentational and policy direction.

Blair and external projection: the spin cycle

The focus on the prime minister and party leader has been significantly enhanced by the advent of television (Heffernan, 2006; Mughan, 2000). When the prime minister makes a formal speech or even merely an off-the-cuff utterance in public, it is represented as the 'official' government position and recorded as such. The prime minister's words are therefore very powerful and subject to the most intense scrutiny and analysis. Blair's success was derived from his communication style in the contemporary mediatised arena. It was based on a fundamental understanding of the importance of constructing messages that are persuasive in modern communication media. In spite of Blair's keenness for the argument to win the day, the sound bite and emotional appeal were more prevalent, conscious that his words would be distilled into bite size chunks he became adept at deploying the modern media principles of 'brevity, clarity and simplicity' (Charteris-Black, 2005: 143). His style was new in that his language (drawn from developments in the United States) merged the discourse of party politics with the discourse of ordinary people – divergent prior to his leadership. Blair's persuasive discourse was based on reason and simplicity.

News media strategies were central to the electoral success of New Labour. Blair's advisors were acutely aware that while the language deployed by Blair was import-ant, so too was the medium through which it was communicated. Without being able to manage and manipulate the news media, the rhetoric and oratory of Blair would have little impact.

> An interest in process journalism, magnifies the modern Prime Minister, placing him centre stage in key political processes and with Blair centre stage a communications strategy was devised to project a positive image focused on the leader. News manage-ment strategies were part and parcel of Labour's promotion of Blair, and helped to fetish-ize the Prime Minister, reflecting the fact that leaders are increasingly the per-sonification of their parties. (Heffernan, 2006: 582)

Blair, as Heffernan points out, used his office as a 'bully-pulpit' to embody the party approach. Prime ministerial speeches and media briefings were part of the process of centralised policy agenda-setting. 'Blair's policy preferences, among them marketis-ing the public services, using public-private partnerships to modernise, say the NHS, forwarding the respect agenda and fighting the war on terrorism' were established by authoritative public and private statements from the centre (Heffernan, 2006: 592). Labour's victories would also strongly be seen as personal victories for Blair, fur-ther strengthening his legitimacy and practical power as prime minister (McAnulla, 2010). This not only reinforces the 'hollowing out' of the party – whereby the lead-ership's preferences become the party's – but also creates space between the leader and party rivals (and malcontents).

Such management and manipulation backfired, for 'in time, Blair's very facility with language and his eagerness to persuade were themselves perceived as a prob-lem, ironically undermining his persuasiveness' (Kane and Patapan, 2010: 384). His autonomous position, detached and aloof from the party, made him vulner-able. Heavy criticism eventually compelled Blair to moderate the actions of his spin machine, but the damage to credibility had been done. By the end of his premiership some MPs 'had moved from not believing Blair's speeches to not bothering to read them' (Stothard, in Kane and Patapan, 2010: 385). Blair had travelled from being a seemingly honest source in tune with the public to being cast as 'Bliar', whose every word could not be believed by fellow ministers, party and public alike. The reliance on ethos to bolster trust in 1997 had become counterproductive by 2007, largely as a result of his misplaced 'ethical discourse' on military intervention in Iraq.

Blair, heresthetics and the politics of manipulation

Political leaders work hard to occupy the 'established ground of political right' (Kane, 2001: 38). The maintenance of this occupation is enhanced by the ability to manoeuvre and manipulate without seeming to betray core values. William Riker called this art 'heresthetics' (Kane, 2001: 38). More specifically, heresthetics refers to the 'deliberate attempt to structure political situations so that opponents will either have to submit or be trapped' (Hargrove, 1998: 32). Manipulation and manoeuvres to put opponents on the defensive are played out by the contemporary leader in the public representation of leadership image and continual or perpetual campaigning. Oratory is critical to this manipulation, as Riker explained:

> The herestetician uses language to manipulate people. He talks to them, asking them questions and telling them facts; he utters arguments, giving reasons for believing his arguments are true; and he describes social nature, importing to his description the exact twist that leads others to respond to nature as he wishes. (Riker, 1986, in Finlayson and Martin, 2008: 451)

Accounts of meetings with Blair always emphasise what a charming man he was and how he had the ability to leave everyone in the room with the impression that they agreed with him. Powell (2010: 54) called this his 'constructive ambiguity'. His manners were impeccable and he used subtlety and charm to persuade (particularly Cabinet colleagues) that his was the right path to follow.

> Prescott would often storm into Number 10 intent on a fight. After the application of the Blair schmooze, he would find himself saying: 'Christ, Tony, I came in here disagreeing with you – and now we're in agreement'. (Rawnsley, 2010: 57)

Blair's approach to manipulating and manoeuvring opponents around did not of course extend to Brown whose volcanic temperament appeared immune to the Blair schmooze. Blair was also less congenial across the dispatch box, belittling in particular Hague and Smith during their time as opposition leaders. Amongst numerous examples, the following stands out:

> The Prime Minister (Tony Blair): It is not the hopeless misjudgements of the Leader of the Opposition [William Hague] over the Conservative party that should worry people; it is his misjudgement over Bank of England independence ... As Leader of the Opposition he may be a joke, but as Prime Minister he would be a disaster. (*Hansard*, 24 November 1999)

Heresthetics point two ways: creating and maintaining a dominant leadership image and setting the political agenda to deny opponents policy or political space. Leadership styles vary across time and space. The relationship between leadership and style and its cousin 'image' are 'as important in contemporary politics as they are misunderstood' (Gaffney, 2001: 120). Politics goes beyond the process in that leaders now place a greater importance on finding ways to 'connect with the wider public through images: appearance, behaviour, modes of speech and so forth' (Finlayson, 2002: 587).

Blair's use of heresthetics is obvious too in his policy occupation of the centre ground or 'political issue space transformation' (Finlayson and Martin, 2008: 452). New Labour was able to deny political opponents the space to develop. The shift to occupy the 'common ground' saw New Labour 'embrace and subsequently advocate the moral and material benefits of the market order' (Beech and Lee, 2008: 191). Blair championed this shift to make Labour work within the economic framework bequeathed by Thatcherism (Heffernan, 2001). The result was a policy convergence between the two main parties that left little or no place for the opposition Conservative Party to go. The connection with Thatcher went beyond the policy realm, with Blair making a conspicuous attachment to Thatcher when he was opposition leader as a 'useful device to embarrass the Prime Minister' (Foley, 2002: 199). The priority of office seeking over policy seeking shaped the party's acceptance of the political shift into enemy territory. Policy initiatives in education, crime and health gained the support of the Conservatives. In education this was no surprise as policy ideas such as specialist schools and academies, league tables and the school inspection regime had all originated under the previous Conservative governments. Indeed, by 2007, both parties shared a commitment to public services reform based on market based solutions; personalisation of services through competition and contestability; and a foreign policy rooted in the strengthening of the trans-Atlantic alliance over further EU integration (Beech and Lee, 2008: 193).

Blair was particularly adept at changing the terms of the argument and 'restructuring the political space'. 'It [heresthetics] is also a matter of political argument, involving presentation of a situation in a particular light, affording it a new definition and associating it with a motivating emotion' (Finlayson and Martin, 2008: 452). Blair did this to good effect in his final speech to party conference in 2006:

> Through constituting an ethos of paternal authority and a valedictory epideictic model Blair 'rose above' the present question of his leadership and recast the issue space as concerning the meaning of the past and its implications for the future; the question ceased to be 'should Blair be leader now' and became 'since Blair's leadership meant these particular things in the past what should leadership be like in the future?' And on that question Blair sought to stamp his answer. (Finlayson and Martin, 2008: 459)

Conclusion

Blair's oratory had a profound impact on the Labour Party and the external face of electoral politics. He was responsible for the establishment of a new political discourse, associated with New Labour. He articulated and embodied this discourse. Yet he also personalised the position of party leader, particularly in the later part of his premiership; he was attracted to policy arenas that heightened his personal standing. By steering a course towards 'high' politics (defence, foreign policy, constitutional reform) and away from 'low' politics' (domestic affairs – education, health, law and order) he enhanced his position and distanced himself from his rivals:

> These areas reinforce the statecraft aspect of the leader's role. They emphasise the difference between the status of presidents and Prime Ministers and that of other members of the government. They also usually provide good photo opportunities and a chance to escape the low-life intrigue of party politics. (Elgie, 1995: 9)

Blair was increasingly driven by a moral imperative (the pathos to add to his evident ethos), creating oratory enthused with a sense of a moral missionary striding the world stage, yet he remained a leader embattled and frustrated by the 'obstinate obsolescence of domestic politics' (Stephens, 2004: 174). The performance mattered for Blair. His legal training and, albeit limited, acting career combined to make him a powerful persuader and an impressive public speaker. Presentation and single-minded belief were hallmarks of his public persona (though he always saw good leadership as epitomised by strength of resolve and character). Displays of humility were rare, as for Blair any demonstration of weakness was a sign of poor leadership. Such rhetorical dominance has a downside; the use of language to restructure the space can tip a leader into a demagogue who 'flatters their constituency, singing their praises while demonising their opponents' (Uhr, 2005: 96). For John Uhr, the 'demagogue is the political cheat who tries to fool all the people, all the time' (Uhr, 2005: 96). As Blair's rhetoric began to grate (and he was lampooned and satirised for his over-the-top pathos), those critics who saw such demagoguery in his speeches came to the fore, to the extent that he appeared to be revered more by Conservative Party elites than Labour.

Blair's oratory can be divided into three phases: as opposition leader; as prime minister before 2003; and after 2003. He developed his public persona and established the language of New Labour in opposition. Up to 2003 his external facing oratory reflected the dominance of a leader aspiring to be presidential and utterly in control of his party and the policy agenda. After 2003, he became more moralising in tone; decisions were his and his alone. Less interested in attempting to please all people all the time he developed as an autonomous party leader. Finally freed from having to garner extra-party votes or intra-party support he could speak his mind in 2007, without the pressures of office-seeking.

Blair set the bar high, the performance, delivery and emotion turned a Blair speech into an event. He always trumped the 'clunking fist' performance of Brown at party conference, had the PLP in his hand and could still turn on the style after leaving office at the Chilcott Iraq Inquiry. He can now command large appearance fees for his public speaking. Before Blair, oratory was firmly rooted in traditional public speaking and Labour leaders had to live up to a grand tradition. Blair changed the nature of Labour oratory; he was a political communicator rather than a speaker. The succession of bland party leaders that followed him, struggling to provide oratory that resonates and inspires, may yet cause commentators and researchers to cast Blair in a better light in years to come.

Notes

1 The research, including academic resources and a speech repository, can be found at www. britishpoliticalspeech.org/.
2 The importance of the leader's address to the parliamentary party is evidenced by Thatcher's famous description of the miners' leaders as 'the enemy within', made to a supposedly 'private meeting' of the 1922 committee, but reported fully in *The Times* the next day (Toye, 2011: 185).

11

The oratory of Gordon Brown

Judi Atkins

Gordon Brown entered Parliament as MP for Dunfermline East (later Kirkcaldy and Cowdenbeath) in 1983. He rose quickly through the party ranks to become Shadow Chief Secretary to the Treasury in 1987, and was soon marked out as a face for the future (Mandelson, 2010). Brown's impressive parliamentary performances while filling in as Shadow Chancellor in 1988 dramatically increased his profile, and he was subsequently appointed to that position in July 1992. The sudden death of John Smith on 12 May 1994 triggered a contest for the Labour leadership, in which Brown was initially expected to stand against Tony Blair. However, following a meeting with Blair at the Granita restaurant in Islington, Brown withdrew from the leadership race in favour of his rival. The details of this meeting are still contested, but the tensions it created would resurface many times in the years ahead (Driver and Martell, 2006).

New Labour won a landslide general election victory in May 1997, after which Brown was appointed Chancellor of the Exchequer. Broadly speaking, his first six years in this role were a success, the highlights of which were his decision to grant independence to the Bank of England and his thwarting of Blair's plans to take Britain into the single European currency (Seldon and Lodge, 2011). However, the rivalry between the two men intensified from 2003, and Brown began positioning himself to take over the party leadership. Following several coup attempts by his supporters, Brown eventually became prime minister on 27 June 2007. Although his premiership started well, his hesitation over whether to call a general election in the autumn of 2007 fatally undermined his credibility. From this point on, Brown was plagued by a series of problems, of which the most personally damaging were the fiascos over the 10p tax rate and the nationalisation of Northern Rock (Seldon and Lodge, 2011: 98). While Brown's decisive response to the banking crisis of 2008–9 gave his popularity a much-needed boost, this improvement was not to last, and Labour suffered a heavy defeat in the May 2010 general election (Seldon and Lodge, 2011).

Circumstances notwithstanding, the question arises of why Brown, whom Ed Balls described as Labour's 'most successful chancellor' (quoted in Porter *et al.*, 2010), experienced such a troubled premiership. For scholars such as Anthony

Seldon and Guy Lodge (2011) and Kevin Theakston (2011), Brown's difficulties stemmed largely from his personal weaknesses, among which were limited
emotional intelligence, a lack of an overarching vision, and poor communication
skills. However, the impact of Brown's rhetorical style has so far been neglected,
and the present chapter seeks to rectify this oversight by examining his oratory
in the three arenas between 1992 and 2010. In so doing, it argues that although
Brown's logos-based rhetoric served him well as (Shadow) Chancellor, it seriously hampered his effectiveness as prime minister. This role requires the ability to create a connection with voters through appeals to pathos, and Brown's
failure in this respect damaged his public image and his party's electoral prospects alike.

Labour in opposition 1992–96

As Shadow Chancellor, the primary purpose of Brown's contributions to parliamentary debate was to challenge the economic policies and strategy of John
Major's government. To this end, he marshalled factual evidence from a range of
sources, including the speeches of key opposition figures (Brown, 1992, col. 310;
1994, col. 609) and the Conservative Party's 1992 general election manifesto
(Brown, 1992, col. 308; 1994, col. 610). These quotations were intended to highlight the discrepancy between the government's words and actions, and thus to
undermine its credibility. Brown also used statistics to attack the Conservatives'
record, inviting MPs to 'look at the scale of the problems that the Chancellor
should have dealt with ... the longest recession since the 1930s, £30 billion lost
output, unemployment rising for many months to come' (Brown, 1992, col.
311). This extensive use of factual evidence indicates that Brown's parliamentary
oratory was characterised mainly by appeals to logos. However, it also contributed to his ethos, as the ability to draw on a variety of sources can demonstrate a
speaker's competence.

Brown's contributions to parliamentary debate also revealed his sense of humour,
which he sometimes employed to mock his opponents. For instance, in making the
case that Conservative policy was based not on economic strategy but on the judgement of Norman Lamont, he asserted: 'Every day is judgment day – the Chancellor's
judgment – Norman's wisdom. That is the basis of economic policy – unsound
before breakfast, unsound before lunch and unsound before dinner' (Brown, 1992,
col. 315). This extract exemplifies the techniques of *anaphora* – 'repetition of the
same word at the beginning of successive clauses' – and *tricolon*, the use of a three-
part pattern for emphasis (Lanham, 1991: 11, 154), both of which are present in
Brown's oratory throughout his career.

To enhance Labour's credibility as an alternative government, Brown outlined
his party's solutions to the problems facing Britain at that time. On unemployment,
for instance, he proposed the introduction of an environmental task force for young

people, which would be paid for through a 'windfall tax on the excess profits of the privatised utilities' (Brown, 1994, cols 606–7). For Brown, the windfall tax was justified because the utilities had increased their profits by 50 per cent despite the recession. However, he claimed, the government was 'not prepared to act in relation to the privatised utilities … because too many people in the Conservative party benefit from those profits'. Here, Brown employed *antithesis* to contrast Labour's willingness to act 'on behalf of the consumers of this country' with the Conservatives' desire to protect vested interests (Brown, 1994, cols 606–8). This strategy of identifying, magnifying and exploiting 'dividing lines' with his opponents (Mandelson, 2010: 111) was another consistent feature of Brown's oratory, and indeed facilitated his swift rise to the top of the Labour Party.

Brown's parliamentary oratory is primarily deliberative and, as such, reflects the adversarial nature of that institution. In contrast, conference speeches are instances of *epideictic*, or ceremonial, rhetoric that are designed to affirm a party's identity and values, and to inspire the faithful (Finlayson and Martin, 2008). Thus, in this setting, Brown sought to reassure delegates that although modernisation had involved tough choices for Labour, the party had 'emerged stronger for it, with policies that combine the need for discipline and prudence with our burning passion for social justice' (1996). Using *antithesis*, he juxtaposed Labour's approach with the 'crude, free market ideology' of the Conservatives (1996). This enabled him to undermine his opponents and to demonstrate that, despite the changes it had undergone, Labour remained true to its core values. Brown was largely successful in achieving the latter aim because, although a leading figure of the party's New Right, he 'had a real feel for, and more sympathy with, the longer-standing traditions of the Labour movement' than did Blair (Thorpe, 2008: 243). As a result, the ideological pairing of Brown and Blair was largely able to keep the different factions within the party under control. In fact, Labour sometimes played on its unity to discredit the Conservative Party (see, for instance, Brown, 1996), which at the time was engaged in bitter in-fighting over the issue of Europe.

Central to Labour's modernisation strategy was its desire to establish a reputation for economic competence. It founded its approach on a belief in globalisation which, for Brown, demanded a 'platform of stability from which opportunity and dynamism will flourish' (1996).[1] This commitment to economic stability constituted, he said, a rejection of the 'stop-go [and] inflationary booms' of the Thatcher era in favour of 'careful long-term investment [and] a dedication to equality and social justice' (1995). It also represented a break with the 'tax and spend' policies of 'Old' Labour. As Brown put it, 'I want our Labour government to be remembered not as a big spender, but as a wise spender' (1995). This prudent, disciplined approach quickly earned him the sobriquet 'the Iron Chancellor', which came to symbolise his power and indeed lay at the core of his political identity.

An important feature of Brown's conference speeches is his use of metaphor. In his 1995 address, for instance, he employed conflict metaphors to remind delegates that 'the war against inflation is a Labour war and is an essential part of our battle against insecurity and unemployment'. Here, Brown implied a positive evaluation by representing his party – the agent of conflict – as heroic, and its policies 'as if they were part of a military campaign'. Such representations are intimately linked to attributes like courage, strength and determination, which appeal to the emotions of an audience. Construction metaphors, meanwhile, encourage favourable evaluations of the speaker by communicating an 'optimistic and socially purposeful outlook' (Charteris-Black, 2005: 90, 14, 122). An appeal to ethos of this kind is present in Brown's assertion that 'we will build our future – the Labour future – on a solid foundation of a just and efficient economy' (1995).

There are a number of themes that recur in Brown's oratory throughout his career. Among them are modernisation, economic prudence and 'the politics of potential' (Lee, 2009: 31), the latter of which found expression in Brown's vision of 'a new Britain, vibrant with new energy, awash with opportunity, alive with compassion' (1995). The son of a Church of Scotland minister, Brown also made frequent use of the language of morality and religion.[2] In 1994, for instance, he told Parliament that accusations of sleaze were symptomatic of a 'breakdown in ethics at the heart of government' (Brown, 1994, col. 611), and later claimed that 'only a Labour government will bring moral purpose and economic responsibility to the running of this country'. Indeed, Brown argued, Labour was uniquely placed to do this because 'we stand where we always have stood, not on the shifting sands of political expediency, but on the solid rock of social justice' (1995).[3] Taken together, these themes served to inspire the party membership, undermine the Conservatives, and demonstrate to the public that Labour was fit to govern. While instrumental to New Labour's 1997 victory, however, many of these ideas would come back to haunt Brown in later years, as we will see below.

The first two terms 1997–2004

In May 1997, the new Chancellor transferred control over interest rates to the Bank of England in a move that signified 'our determination to break from the short-termism of the past and to establish long-term confidence … and monetary stability' (Brown, 1997a, col. 303). With regard to fiscal stability, Brown pledged that New Labour would adhere to Conservative spending plans for two years and, in his first Budget, announced a comprehensive review of government spending (Brown, 1997a, col. 314). In making his case for these measures, Brown drew primarily on economic statistics and factual evidence. He also referred repeatedly to fairness, prudence and the *antithesis* between 'the many' and 'the few', which enhanced his ethos of economic competence while reassuring the left that New Labour remained true to socialist values. In these respects, Brown's oratory benefitted his party, and in fact contributed to its second general election victory in 2001. However, the comprehensive spending review and the subsequent 'public spending agreements' gave Brown a hitherto unprecedented degree of influence across the policy spectrum, which he would later exercise in his efforts to undermine Blair's premiership (Rawnsley, 2001: 147; 2010: 78).

Brown's first Budget of the second term was focused on 'building a Britain of greater enterprise and greater fairness' (Brown, 2002, col. 586). A substantial portion of his Statement was devoted to New Labour's achievements since 1997, which he contrasted with the failures of the previous Conservative governments. In particular, he juxtaposed the 'cautious assumptions' underpinning New Labour's economic policy with the 'imprudent assumptions' of the early 1990s that 'contributed to the boom and bust that did so much damage' (Brown, 2002, col. 579). However, the centrepiece of this Budget was Brown's proposal to 'raise UK national health spending ... on average by 7.4 per cent in real terms each year'. This pledge marked the end of New Labour's fiscal caution and ushered in a period of high spending, which Brown labelled prudence 'for a purpose' (Brown, HC Deb., 17 April 2002, col. 592). According to Seldon and Lodge, this new approach was designed to increase Brown's standing within the Labour Party in anticipation of becoming prime minister (2011). It also coincided with an escalation in his hostility towards Blair which, at that time, was played out in the dispute over foundation hospitals.

In 1998 Brown gave an interview to the BBC's *On the Record*, which focused on welfare reform, macroeconomic policy and Economic Monetary Union (EMU). Here, he returned to themes from his 1997 Budget Statement – notably economic stability and his long-term approach to the economy – which he again contrasted with 'the boom and bust of the past'. As we would expect, Brown's responses relied primarily on factual evidence, though he reiterated his commitment to equality of opportunity by saying: 'I believe the Government itself has a responsibility, a direct duty to promote equality of opportunity, in employment, in education and right throughout the economy' (BBC, 1998a). Brown made frequent use of repetition in television interviews, which on this occasion was apparent in his replies to questions on tax and benefit reform. However, it was less evident in the section dealing with EMU, where Brown ruled out entry until his five economic tests had been met. This position was diametrically opposed to that of the pro-European Blair, and Brown's ability to set the agenda on the issue demonstrated the extent of his influence over New Labour policy.

Meanwhile, Brown's appearance on *Breakfast with Frost* in December 2001 focused on his commitment to increase investment in the National Health Service (NHS). As in that year's Budget Statement, Brown supported his argument by quoting the recommendations of the Wanless Report on long-term health trends. While this appeal to logos was characteristic of Brown's oratory, his limited use of *antithesis*, and the near-absence of references to the dividing lines between New Labour and the Conservatives, are significant departures that perhaps reflect David Frost's gentler interviewing style. Also noteworthy is Brown's use of humour, which was evident in his comment that the birth of his first child would enable him to 'say more about the needs of children … from the point of view of prudence, or any other name that we choose, if it's a girl' (BBC, 2001a). However, this rare attempt to connect with the public was overshadowed by Brown's assertion that 'what Tony Blair and I have said to each other really is a matter for us', which triggered renewed media speculation about the existence of a 'deal' between them (BBC, 2001b).

Like his Budget Statements, Brown's conference speeches in this period made extensive use of *antithesis* to positively evaluate New Labour and undermine the Conservatives. They were also heavy on policy and spending announcements, though in his 1997 address Brown linked the government's modernisation agenda to 'Labour's enduring values'. In this, Brown claimed, New Labour was following in the footsteps of Keir Hardie and Aneurin Bevan, two great modernisers who had also applied their party's ideals to 'new circumstances and new challenges'. This legitimation strategy was intended to appeal to both the New Right and the traditionalist wings of the party, and thus to unite them behind New Labour's programme. It also contributed to Brown's ethos as a man of principle, which he reinforced with his use of religious language[4] and his claim that his approach to economic modernisation 'is not about image, it is about substance'. Brown's closing line equated Labour values – which, incidentally, were also his personal values – with British values, and thus enabled him to appeal simultaneously to his party and to the public. As such, it is unsurprising that they featured heavily in his conference speeches and interviews throughout his political career.

So far, Brown's oratory, with its emphasis on policy and appeals to logos, was consistent with his position as Chancellor. However, his 2003 conference speech was widely seen as a statement of his own leadership ambitions at a time when Blair's position was vulnerable following the Iraq War (Rawnsley, 2010). This address encompassed a range of issues beyond the economy, such as foreign affairs and international development, and in this respect it was more akin to a party leader's speech than that of a Chancellor of the Exchequer. Brown also elaborated his personal philosophy, employing journey metaphors to 'represent himself as a "guide", his policies as "maps" … and to create solidarity' by constructing his hearers as travelling companions (Charteris-Black, 2005: 46). Thus, he attributed his party's success in government to 'taking the Labour road – often the hard road – being true to our Labour values'. Significantly, 'taking the Labour road' was equated with following Brown's policy programme, which conferred a positive evaluation on both his record as Chancellor and his prospective leadership. Brown closed his speech with a direct challenge to Blair's authority, asserting: 'This Labour Party – best when we are boldest, best when we are united, best when we are Labour.' This phrase exemplifies *anaphora* and *tricolon* but, more importantly, caricatured Blair's famous alliterative line 'at our best when at our boldest' (2003). In so doing, it brought the animosity between the 'Blairites' and 'Brownites' into the open, and thus shattered New Labour's carefully constructed image of a united party.

Brown's pitch for the Labour leadership 2005–6

Brown opened his 2005 Budget Statement with the boast that 'Britain is today experiencing the longest period of sustained economic growth since records began in the year 1701'. As such, he continued, it was vital to maintain stability and growth while 'putting Britain's hard-working families first' (Brown, 2005a, col. 257). To support his claims, Brown drew on economic data and government-commissioned reports and, as in previous years, he exploited the dividing lines between New Labour and the Conservatives. After warning that a loosening of the fiscal stance would 'repeat the pattern of past governments at this stage ... [and] risk a return to the high inflation, high interest rates, stop-go and short-termism of the past and put long term stability at risk', Brown proposed a modest fiscal tightening, a move he described as the 'prudent course for Britain' (Brown, 2005a, col. 266). He thus cemented his reputation for economic competence, which helped New Labour to an historic third general election victory at a time when Blair's personal popularity was waning.

In 2006 Brown delivered his tenth Budget, and he legitimated his economic strategy by noting that 'the last Chancellor to deliver ten Budgets in a row was Nicholas Vansittart in 1822'. Moreover, he claimed, his was 'the only Government in British history to be entering the tenth consecutive year of uninterrupted economic growth', a statement he supported with an array of economic statistics (Brown, 2006a, col. 287). Again using *antithesis*, Brown contrasted Britain's current prosperity with the difficulties it had faced under the Conservatives, and he reminded Parliament that 'I have said before: no return to boom and bust' (Brown, 2006a, col. 288). To enable Britain to meet the challenges ahead, Brown argued, more investment was needed. In particular, he pledged to increase spending on schools, families and Britain's infrastructure – investment that was possible 'because of the stability that we have achieved' (Brown, 2006a, col. 290). Thus, as Seldon and Lodge observe, Brown continued his 2002 strategy of spending increasing sums of money to 'pave his way with gold flagstones into Number 10' (2011: xviii).

On 30 September 2004, Blair told journalists that 'If I am elected [in May 2005], I will serve a full term. I do not want to serve a fourth term' (quoted in Rawnsley, 2010: 280). This announcement sparked intense speculation about the date of Blair's departure, which was to gradually erode his authority and power. At the same time, it strengthened Brown's position, and he used his 2005 conference speech to present himself as Labour's leader-in-waiting. To this end, he attempted to inspire delegates and enhance his ethos by listing some of the government's achievements – among which were the introduction of the winter fuel allowance for those aged over sixty and the creation of two million jobs – and by asserting that his policies had made New Labour 'the natural party for economic strength in our country today'. Brown then told his audience that 'the next election must and will be new Labour renewed against a Conservative party still incapable of renewal' (Brown, 2005b). *Prima facie*, this statement appears to be another instance of Brown using *antithesis* to ridicule the Conservatives. However, his reference to the next election is curious, given that New Labour had won a third term of office less than five months previously. As such, it is perhaps better understood as a call for Blair to stand down – 'new Labour renewed' under a new leader. Brown's subsequent pledge to travel around the UK in the next twelve months, 'to discuss the economic, social and constitutional changes we need to build for the future' (2005b), did nothing to dispel this impression. Indeed, writes Andrew Rawnsley, Brown's supporters were 'determined that they would have Blair out of Number 10 by the next year' (2010: 348).

The central theme of this speech was Brown's core values and motivations, which he conveyed primarily through personal anecdotes. In particular, he described how his parents had given him his 'moral compass', the idea that 'in return for what we received we had a duty to put something back'. This principle, he continued, was vivified in 'our duty and determination as parents, as neighbours, as citizens, that every child can fulfil their potential and that no child is left out'.[5] Brown then employed *antithesis* to contrast this commitment with the injustice of the Thatcher era, when 'one child in every three born in our country was born into poverty', and he invited delegates to 'reflect for a moment on the talent wasted, the loss of what might have been' (2005b). Such a direct appeal to pathos was a departure from Brown's usual factual style, but it afforded him an effective means of uniting his audience behind his avowed mission of ending child poverty, and ultimately behind his prospective leadership.

New Labour's 2006 party conference took place shortly after Brown's allies had orchestrated a failed coup against Blair. Brown saw this occasion as an opportunity to 'seal his dominant position' (Rawnsley, 2010: 405), and to this end he set out his agenda for government. At the heart of this approach was Brown's belief in the politics of potential, which was expressed in a commitment to increase spending on education. This, he claimed, would enable Britain to succeed in the global economy by 'engaging the creative talents of all' (2006a). Brown again refused to confine himself to economic issues, and he addressed policy areas ranging from immigration and Britishness to social housing and health. In so doing, notes Rawnsley, Brown 'pounded out points like a machine gun and pummeled his audience into clapping' (2010: 405), a technique he employed regularly in his conference speeches, though with varying degrees of success.

Instead of making appeals to logos, Brown justified his approach by recounting anecdotes about the everyday experiences of ordinary people – the devout Muslim mother he had met in Luton, and the 'responsible young couple' unable to afford their first home (see Atkins and Finlayson, 2013). He also sought to enhance his ethos by speaking again about his 'moral compass' and, in a thinly veiled dig at Blair, he contrasted his belief in 'politics as service' with those who 'see politics simply as spectacle'. However, the high point of Brown's speech was his assertion that he 'would relish the opportunity to take on David Cameron' (2006a), which was well received by party members and consolidated his position as the next Labour leader.

The theme of leadership also dominates the two interviews selected to illustrate Brown's public oratory at this stage of his career. Brown gave the first of these to *The Andrew Marr Show* shortly after New Labour achieved poor results in the May 2006 local elections (BBC, 2006a). After describing this experience as a 'wake-up call' for the party, Brown argued that New Labour had to recognise that 'the world is changing as a result of globalisation [and] terrorism' and, in particular, that 'the new agenda is security, law and order as well as stability and economic growth'. In order to meet these challenges, he continued, the party had to renew itself for the future, primarily by appealing to a 'larger and wider group of people across the country'. Here, Brown did not explicitly equate 'renewal' with a change in the Labour leadership, a point Marr picked up on with a question about Blair's departure. In response, Brown claimed that 'the vast majority of people want what Tony Blair ... has said that he wants to achieve and that is a stable and orderly transition' (BBC, 2006a). However, he refused to be drawn on the details of when Blair would stand down or on the recent Cabinet reshuffle, and he instead reiterated his previous statements about the transition and the challenges facing Britain in the future. Thus, on this occasion, Brown used repetition not for emphasis, but to deflect awkward questions about the party leadership.

Brown gave another interview to the BBC at the beginning of September 2006, following an unsuccessful attempt by his supporters to remove Blair as leader. This incident dominated the discussion, which Brown took as an opportunity to repair his tarnished image. To this end, he distanced himself from the abortive coup by describing it as 'completely ill-advised', and repeatedly asserting that 'Tony will make his decision in his own way'. Brown also welcomed a leadership election, saying that 'I've got no difficulty, and certainly there's no personal issue about other people standing' (BBC, 2006b). Here, Brown attempted to present an image of collegiality to dispel concerns about his private behaviour; in Marr's words, that he was 'somebody who is very controlling, who bears grudges, who's difficult to get on with'. For the same reason, Brown again invoked his 'moral compass': the notion that 'you work hard, you take responsibility, you treat people fairly, you work with people, and ... you don't walk by on the other side' (BBC, 2006b). However, the episode seriously damaged Brown's reputation, with an ICM poll for the *Guardian* placing him seventeen points behind David Cameron for his ability to work with colleagues and eight points behind for trust (Glover, 2006). It also revealed the disjunction between Brown's public persona and the private individual, which for many was exemplified by the 'bigot' incident that occurred during the 2010 general election campaign.

Brown as prime minister 2007–9

Despite the concerns of some Labour MPs about his fitness to lead, Brown became prime minister on 27 June 2007. In his first debate on the Queen's Speech, and in accordance with the rhetorical conventions of Parliament, Brown drew on factual evidence and economic statistics to highlight Labour's achievements and to justify its policy agenda for the year ahead. Among these initiatives were proposals to raise the education leaving age to eighteen and to promote social housing. On the latter, Brown quoted the words of three Conservative figures to demonstrate that their policy was 'confused, contradictory and not thought through' (Brown, 2007c, col. 29), and thus to undermine their credibility. However, the relative absence of new ideas in the government's legislative programme meant that Cabinet members 'increasingly felt that they were drifting without any clear sense of direction' (Seldon and Lodge, 2011: 56), a problem that was to plague Brown throughout his premiership.

The 2008 Debate on the Address came just three months after disaffected Labour MPs launched an unsuccessful bid to unseat Brown. It also gave Brown his first – and last – opportunity to 'outline a full legislative programme before the general election in 2010' (Seldon and Lodge, 2011: 203). Thus, Brown introduced legislation to abolish child poverty and to 'give, for the first time, young people who qualify the right to apprenticeships' (Brown, 2008, col. 31). The key issue at this time was the global financial crisis, to which Brown responded by announcing measures to ensure that 'no hard-working family who demonstrate to their bank a willingness to pay can or should face the fear of repossession of their family home' (Brown, 2008, col. 34). He then used *antithesis* to contrast Labour's approach with that of the Conservatives, asserting that 'we will invest to take the action necessary for the economy, whereas [Cameron's] party refuses to make the necessary investment' (Brown, 2008, col. 37). However, despite Brown's efforts, his legislative programme was seen as 'more of a shopping list than a coherent new agenda'. This, together with the lack of new initiatives in such key areas as education (Seldon and Lodge, 2011), did nothing to dispel concerns that the Brown government had run out of ideas.

Labour's 2007 party conference took place against the backdrop of speculation about whether Brown would call an autumn general election. The early months of his premiership had been marked by terrorism, flooding, and an outbreak of foot-and-mouth disease, and Brown claimed that 'the resilience of the British people' in the face of these challenges had been 'powerful proof of the character of our country' (Brown, 2007a). By implication, Brown's robust response to these events demonstrated the strength of his leadership, enabling him to portray himself as 'father of the nation' (Rawnsley, 2010: 501). He further enhanced his ethos by reiterating his commitment to govern by a 'moral compass' and his belief in the politics of potential. Faced with the possibility of a general election, however, Brown attempted to broaden Labour's appeal by outlining a distinctly populist agenda. Most controversially, he expressed an ambition to '[draw] on the talents of all to create British jobs for British workers' (2007a), which upset many on the left of the party.[6] Those on the right, meanwhile, were concerned by the absence of an overarching narrative. Nonetheless, the speech was well received by the media, which concluded that Brown was ready to fight an election (Seldon and Lodge, 2011).

In the event, Brown did not call an election until 2010, a decision that not only revived concerns about his character, but did irreparable harm to his ethos of strength and competence (Rawnsley, 2010). The 2009 party conference took place three months after a second coup against him, and he therefore faced an uphill struggle to win back the support of his party. Unsurprisingly, Brown's speech was dominated by the economic crisis, and he attempted to bolster his position by reminding his audience that his decisive action had prevented Britain from sliding into a 'great depression'. In contrast, he argued, 'the Conservative Party were faced with the economic call of the century and they called it wrong' (2009). For this reason, he continued, they were unfit to govern. In anticipation of the general election, Brown presented an array of new policies, among which were free social care and an expansion of free childcare. However, claim Seldon and Lodge, 'few believed Brown's claim that the money was available to fund all the new commitments he had announced', while his reluctance to talk about reducing the country's budget deficit 'made him appear hopelessly out of touch and badly damaged his own economic reputation' (2011: 332, xxix).

The economic crisis was the focus of Brown's interview with the *BBC Politics Show*, which followed the second recapitalisation of Britain's banks in November 2008. When asked about the cause of the crisis, Brown replied that 'the inflation and the problems we had were not generated themselves in Britain ... this is a global problem that started in America' (BBC, 2008b). By this time, Brown's record as Chancellor was coming under increasing scrutiny – not least the failure of his tripartite structure of financial regulation[7] – and his claim to have abolished boom-and-bust was now seen as the height of hubris. In an attempt to salvage his reputation, Brown criticised the Conservatives' 'do nothing' approach as 'lacking in compassion as well as irresponsible'. After all, he claimed, 'not to give real help now would cause more damage later' (BBC, 2008b). Brown then employed *antithesis* to contrast this stance with Labour's proactive approach, which comprised a range of measures to support savers and homeowners. However, these policy-focused responses 'conveyed no sense that he empathised with voters' immediate and everyday struggles to pay their mortgages and grocery bills' (Rawnsley, 2010: 537). Thus, Brown's use of logos prevented him from establishing an emotional connection with his audience and, despite his skilful management of the financial crisis, damaged his standing in the eyes of the public.

A key element of Brown's political philosophy that this chapter has so far only touched on is Britishness. Since November 1997, Brown made his case for British values on a number of occasions (see Lee, 2006), one of which was a Radio 4 interview in 2009. Here, Brown argued that Britain needed 'a stronger national sense of purpose' to bind people together, and thus to enable them to meet the challenges of globalisation (BBC, 2009; Brown, 2006b). For Brown, citizenship involves reciprocal rights and responsibilities that will 'protect and enhance the British way of life' and, moreover, will strengthen Britain's communities (BBC, 2009; Brown, 2007b).

This pairing had assumed greater importance since the financial crisis; indeed, he claimed, 'people would now I think agree more than ever that wealth should help more than the wealthy, they agree that people have responsibilities to others who are in difficulty' (BBC, 2009). With these words, Brown appealed to the authority of 'the people', both to support his claims and to shape his ethos by demonstrating that he was in touch with their views (Atkins and Finlayson, 2013). This populist rhetorical strategy is present throughout the interview and, unusually for Brown, predominates over logos-based reasoning. Nevertheless, such appeals are present in Brown's references to the work of liberal historians and philosophers,[8] which in turn contributed to an ethos of erudition.

After rejecting definitions of Britishness founded on 'race' and ethnicity, Brown advocated dialogue as the best means of identifying common ground between 'people from different communities in different parts of Britain' (BBC, 2009). This commitment to inclusivity was perhaps intended to dispel Brown's controlling image, though it soon became clear that his list of British values – 'tolerance, liberty, fairness', and reciprocal rights and responsibilities – was very much a reflection of his personal beliefs.[9] Nonetheless, Brown's repeated linkage of his own values to Labour values, as well as to British values, enabled him to portray himself as a man of principle who was in touch with both his party's roots and the moral instincts of the electorate.

Brown's resignation 2010

On 3 January 2010, three days before a third abortive coup against him, Brown made an appearance on *The Andrew Marr Show*. The main topic of discussion was inevitably the economy, which Brown described as the 'defining issue of the election' and the 'decision of the decade' (BBC, 2010a). This alliterative pair appeared twice in the interview, and it is likely that it was Brown's scripted sound bite for the occasion. Brown subsequently employed alliteration and *antithesis* to distinguish his economic strategy from that of the Conservatives, saying: 'I believe in an age of aspiration ... I'm afraid the Conservatives have gone for an age of austerity and that means that the majority of hardworking families suffer as a result.' To support this argument, Brown outlined his government's proposals for promoting economic recovery and protecting the public services, but this appeal to logos served only to highlight his inability to connect with voters. He also sought to enhance his ethos by appealing to his experience of 'manag[ing] this country through good times and difficult economic times'. Here, Brown perhaps intended to demonstrate that he was better equipped than his rivals for 'the next stage, which is moving from recession to growth, to high levels of growth and high levels of employment, giving people new jobs' (BBC, 2010a). However, this strategy was double-edged, as it 'stamped Brown as the candidate of the status quo in what was a change election' (Rawnsley, 2010: 728).

On 18 April 2010, Brown made another appearance on *The Andrew Marr Show* (BBC, 2010a). This interview came shortly after the first televised leaders' debate of the general election campaign, at which Brown had appeared 'mannered and stilted' in comparison with his more charismatic opponents (Seldon and Lodge, 2011: 450). Brown acknowledged his image problems, telling Marr that 'I lost on presentation, I lost on style. Maybe I lost on smiling'. However, he continued, 'I didn't try to be something I'm not. I'm not certainly trying to be the king of presentation or PR style'. With this in mind, Brown attempted to portray himself as a more substantial politician than his opponents, to which end he made frequent appeals to logos and listed policy initiatives from Labour's manifesto. After all, he argued, 'the issue is surely this: What are the best policies for the country? Who can best equip us for the future?' (BBC, 2010b). However, Brown's decision to emphasise substance over style in the leaders' debates and television interviews was a serious miscalculation. As Kathleen Hall Jamieson explains, 'television invites a personal, self-disclosing style that draws public discourse out of a private self and comfortably reduces the complex world to dramatic narratives' (1990: 84). This style contrasts with Brown's predominantly logos-based rhetoric which, though highly effective in Parliament, was poorly suited to a television audience. Indeed, his inability to make effective appeals to pathos was all too apparent in the leaders' debates, where he suffered through comparisons with his opponents – both of whom were able to establish a rapport with the public by gazing steadily at the camera and speaking in clear, everyday language (Rawnsley, 2010: 734). This poor performance was mirrored at the ballot box, and in May 2010 Labour registered its second-worst general election defeat since 1918 (Seldon and Lodge, 2011).

Conclusion

In conclusion, it is clear that Brown's ability to marshal factual evidence in the three arenas under consideration made him a highly effective (Shadow) Chancellor. It also contributed to his 'Iron Chancellor' image which, according to one of his friends, he 'has worked very hard to cultivate … He thinks it gives him authority' (quoted in Beckett, 2009b). Indeed, Brown's frequent repetition of such phrases as 'prudence with a purpose' and 'no return to boom and bust' served to enhance this ethos and, moreover, 'transform[ed] Labour's prospects by making its economic policies sound authoritative' (Beckett, 2009b). Brown further strengthened his position by employing *antithesis* to exploit dividing lines with the Conservatives, a technique that proved highly effective in Parliament and facilitated his rise through the party ranks. In Roger Liddle's words, 'the way to the top [of the Labour Party] has always been through brilliant attacks on the Tories'. However, he continues, 'there comes a point when it is necessary to speak to the country as well as the party' (quoted in Mandelson, 2010: 153), as Brown was to discover when he took over the premiership in 2007.

It soon became apparent that Brown's logos-based oratory was ill-suited to the role of prime minister, which requires the use of pathos to engage with and inspire the electorate. As Rawnsley explains, 'modern politics demands from leaders the ability to make – or at least fake – an emotional connection with voters. Tony Blair had that capacity to excess, which made it even more starkly obvious that Gordon Brown could not do it' (2010: 537). Such a connection is primarily established through television, a medium with which Brown often appeared uncomfortable; indeed, he once told Peter Mandelson that 'I'm good at what politics used to be about, about policies ... But now people want celebrity and theatre' (2010: 14). And yet, Brown could cut a commanding figure on the world stage. In this context, write Seldon and Lodge, he was 'capable of speaking with brilliance and passion', and it was here that he delivered the most powerful oratory of his time as prime minister (2011: xxxi).[10] While this is attributable in part to the coherence of Brown's international agenda, the fact remains that if he had only been able to make the same emotional impact in a domestic context, then he might have enjoyed a less troubled – and ultimately more successful – premiership.

Notes

I am very grateful to the Editors for their helpful comments on an earlier draft of this chapter. I also wish to acknowledge the financial support of the Leverhulme Trust (grant no. F/00 3910 – How the Leader Speaks).

1 At this time, key New Labour figures represented globalisation as an 'unstoppable force' to which governments needed to adapt (Blair, 2010). Indeed, as Anthony McGrew correctly points out, this representation played an important role in the rationalisation of New Labour's programme of modernisation and renewal (2004).
2 Moral language also played a central role in the oratory of Blair, notably in relation to New Labour's anti-social behaviour policies and the Iraq War of 2003. For discussion, see Atkins (2011: chs 8 and 9).
3 Here, Brown drew on the 'Parable of the Wise and Foolish Builders', which appears in Luke 6:46–9 and Matthew 7:24–7.
4 In this address, Brown repeated his 1995 claim that 'we stand where we always did – not on the shifting sands of political expediency, we stand on the solid rock of social justice'. Moreover, his peroration contained the statement 'no more the rich man in his castle, the poor man at the gate' (1997b), which paraphrased a line from the hymn *All Things Bright and Beautiful*.
5 Here, Brown again employed the techniques of alliteration, *anaphora, tricolon* and *antithesis*, which occur frequently in his oratory.
6 Similarly, in 2005, Brown told his party conference that 'we will work to ensure that British inventions can and will mean British jobs in British companies for British workers'. That this statement passed without comment is perhaps indicative of the media's more favourable disposition towards Brown during his time as Chancellor.
7 This structure comprised the Financial Services Authority (FSA), the Treasury and the Bank of England (Lee, 2009).

8 Specifically, Brown referred to the historians Gertrude Himmelfarb and Thomas
   Babbington Macaulay, and to the philosophers John Rawls and Adam Smith.
9 A further concern is that Brown conflates Britishness and British history with Englishness
   and English history. As a result, his conception of Britishness is fundamentally flawed
   (Lee, 2006; 2009: ch. 5).
10 To support this claim, Seldon and Lodge cite Brown's speech on development to the UN
   General Assembly on 31 July 2007, his address to the US Congress on 4 March 2009,
   and his presentation to the 'TED' Global conference in Oxford on 22 July 2009 (2011:
   xxxi).

12

The oratory of Ed Miliband

Andrew S. Crines

Introduction

Ed Miliband's style of communication is prone to variable success. For example he was most effective in communicating a convincing narrative during his keynote speeches to the 2012 and 2013 Labour conferences, yet this success only occasionally translates to the media or the Commons. This is because his conference successes were heavily dependent upon his ethos and his political persona, which enlivened his sympathetic audience. Both speeches were also textured frequently by pathos which was designed to provoke specific reactions from his audience, such as applause or discontent with the Conservatives. However his use of logos was often limited. Indeed, he would eschew logos whilst embracing his ethos- and pathos-driven arguments.

Because of the internal impact it had within the Labour Party this chapter will focus on Miliband's 2012 conference speech. This can be seen as a watershed moment in which he spelt out his post-New Labour ideological vision, under the moniker of One Nation Labour. Rhetorically it is also worthy of examination because of the distinctive means by which Miliband drew upon the modes of persuasion. His ethos was central to the persona he constructed. To do so he presented his family's story and how his upbringing helped inform his Labour values. This emphasised his trustworthy character and credible set of values which he linked to Labour's long-standing commitments to social justice, equality and national solidarity. He used these to texture his arguments for ideological renewal, simultaneously drawing on his own experiences thereby constructing and using his political persona. By doing so he was then able to embody a clear political vision which proved appealing. Nonetheless it must be noted that this style of communication is problematic outside of the conference chamber because it depends upon a sympathetic audience.

In fact, the electorate is less convinced by ethos-driven arguments that lack substantial doses of logos or pathos. For media interviews Miliband tends to rely excessively upon his own character without providing depth of logical argument, thus harming his credibility with the mainstream viewer. For example he would often aim to 'tell you who I am' (Watt, 2012) rather than provide a more logos-based answer to a specific issue. Moreover, in the Commons he is often defeated because of his overreliance on a supportive audience to make his cases which makes him appear uncertain. Indeed, the combative arenas of the media and the Commons are often harmful to Miliband's style of communication because he is unable to simply rely on his ethos or persona. Thus, although Miliband delivers effective conference speeches to supportive audiences that does not translate well to other arenas. This holds his message and its broader impact back and prevents him from being a 'classic orator' in the style of Harold Wilson, Neil Kinnock or Tony Blair. However given he has driven forward an ideological shift in the Labour Party through the use of his conference speeches and his rhetorical style he can be credited with some impact as an orator.

Securing the leadership

It is first worth considering how Miliband became leader and the effect it had on his political ethos and persona. When Gordon Brown resigned as Labour leader following the result of the 2010 general election, there was a broad expectation that David Miliband would emerge as the leader (Kirkup and Prince, 2010). This was because he was seen as the successor to Blair's political legacy and the candidate most likely to challenge the Conservative Party. He was also the first to make it formally known that he wanted to succeed Brown and that his renewal strategy would be predicated around extending New Labour under the banner of Next Labour (Smith, 2010). He also enjoyed the tacit support of Blair, however the former leader was cautious about voicing this publicly (Grice, 2010). Thus it appeared as though the trajectory David Miliband was on would take him to the leadership.

Yet this seemingly clear and certain path was unexpectedly disrupted by his brother, Ed. He was the younger of the two, he had shown less inclination towards the leadership, and so it seemed unlikely he would be the new Labour leader. Nonetheless, he went on to snatch victory from his brother because he gave opponents to the next stage of New Labour a more credible alternative than the other candidates. He did so by critiquing New Labour's record over Iraq 'which he attributed partly to a lingering Cold War mentality that Britain always had to support America militarily in any global conflict', that Blair and Brown had 'over-privileged financial services at the expense of other industries', and 'he also expressed his opposition to top-up fees for university students, alluded to errors on various civil liberties issues (such as ID cards) and lamented the disdain with which Party treated the trade unions' (Dorey and Denham, 2011: 298). In fact, '"the world has changed", Ed Miliband insisted, which obviously meant that New Labour also had to change accordingly' (Dorey and Denham, 2011: 298). Whilst David Miliband had made it clear he believed Labour's renewal would revolve around extending New Labour further, Ed Miliband argued this was a mistake and that renewal necessitated a more traditional embrace of classic social democracy, thus negating the need to present a 'new' vision for Labour renewal. This message helped Miliband junior gain the support of the unions, which proved sufficient for him to secure the majority of votes needed to defeat his brother. His was a classical form of Croslandite Labourism more associated with the Gaitskellite right during the 1950s, 1960s, 1970s and 1980s. However, as Peter Dorey and Andrew Denham argue, 'that such principles and policies were variously being denounced by his opponents (both inside the Party and beyond) as extremist, or as signifying a reversion to Old Labour, "does show how political debate has narrowed in this country", he lamented' (Dorey and Denham, 2011: 302).

Miliband's early leadership was something of a slow burner. He did not immediately put forward a clear vision for Labour, nor did he clearly explain why (and where) he wanted to lead the party. This led to a rhetorical disconnect between himself and the electorate which helped the Conservative-led Coalition dominate the political agenda. Both David Cameron and George Osborne attacked his political persona for stabbing his brother in the back (Cameron, 2011), claimed that he was 'left wing and weak' (*Huffington Post*, 2011), and that he had declining support with the electorate (Das, 2011). Because Miliband's communication skills are often driven by consensus and co-operation they appear less certain than those of Cameron in a combative arena. Moreover, given Miliband was seen as an ideological ally of Brown during the New Labour years it was possible for his opponents to include him in their attempt to blame Brown for the consequences of the financial crisis (Blackburn, 2010; Burns, 2010). Given the Coalition's political objectives are articulated through the rhetoric of deficit reduction in the national interest (Crines, 2013a) this placed Miliband on the wrong side of the political narrative. Put simply, Miliband's early period of leadership lacked a compelling direction or narrative.

Nevertheless, in 2011 Miliband's uncertain leadership appeared to be transformed following the revelations of malpractice at the *News of the World*. The allegations surrounding phone hacking became a political scandal when the closeness of Cameron with Rebekah Brooks was revealed. This, coupled with Cameron's decision to hire the former editor of the scandal-hit newspaper Andy Coulson as Director of Communications, provided Miliband with an opportunity to go on the offensive. Miliband's performance in the debate in the Commons over the phone hacking scandal added significantly to his political capital, as he effectively summed up the mood of the House and set the political agenda in relation to the withdrawal of News Corporation's bid for a controlling stake in Sky television. By doing so he was able to present himself as a credible leader of the opposition who could seemingly embody the revulsion felt by politicians and the public alike. This also provided him with a chance to begin articulating a broader message with his newfound voice and credibility (Hayton, 2011).

Constructing Ed Miliband's political persona

Because Miliband uses his personal persona to articulate his political messages it would be useful to consider how it has developed. Rhetorically speaking, Miliband is quite distinctive in his use of the modes of persuasion. Whilst an orator may often use their ethos to convince an audience of their arguments, Miliband instead uses pathos and his persona to attempt to convince the audience of his ethos. Through pathos he constructs arguments by using narratives drawn from his family history and the experiences of those he has met, whilst logos is infrequently used to texture those arguments. Utilising his background whilst aiming to attract more credibility is a key component of his rhetoric because it is how he strives to convince the audience that he is a capable leader. In part this is because of the precarious position he was in after securing the leadership (without majority support amongst his MPs or party members), leading him to strive to convince the Labour Party that he is a competent leader. It is a narrow technique that allows him to avoid intra-party conflicts or challenges to his leadership, however it is effective only within the confines of the Labour movement and so this can be problematic in terms of convincing the broader electorate of this message.

The strategy of appealing to the party through his ethos is a response to the issues he faced in the early period of his leadership. As stated earlier the unexpected nature of his victory means his ethos was yet to be fully established. Also harmful to Miliband's ethos was the artificial construction of his political persona by his Conservative opponents. This further damaged his leadership credibility and political character. Indeed, between 2010 and 2012 he was characterised as 'Red Ed' (Montgomerie, 2011) and likened to Wallace from *Wallace and Gromit* (Crampton, 2012), both attacks designed to erode his credibility and portray his character as unsuitable for national leadership (Crampton, 2012). Although Miliband later aimed to reduce their potency by mocking them – his father 'would've loved the idea of "Red Ed"' (Miliband, 2012) – it was useful shorthand for his political opponents who wished to argue Labour had moved further leftwards and away from its more successful and centrist New Labour past (Nelson, 2013). This also created some political space for Cameron to claim a degree of ownership over Blair's legacy, which even included using Blair's historic arguments over public sector reforms against Miliband at Prime Minister's Questions (PMQs) (*Total Politics*, 2012). Moreover, the association with the left and the role of the unions in securing his leadership undermines Labour's broader electoral strategy because of the historical associations with doctrinaire arguments, industrial action and electoral failure. Put simply, this negative persona argued Miliband represented Labour's socialist 'radicalism' (Bagehot Blog, 2010).

This was a problem for Miliband because to be linked with an electorally harmful Old Labour image associates him with the politics of ideological division. These political issues were coupled with an overarching attempt to undermine his ethos by associating him with figures of fun. In fact, the association with Wallace linked him with 'the hapless, twitty inventor whose ideas rarely go according to plan' (Gaffney and Lahel, 2013: 6). Moreover, the charge that he is a 'geek' (Kite, 2010) heightened the sense that he was distant from the average voter. Also the perception that he 'shafted his brother' (Cowley, 2012) risked giving credence to the argument that he lacked moral standing. Such attacks all strove to construct a negative political persona, that of a weak leader and an outsider who would not be suitable to be prime minister (Deedes, 2012; Hansan, 2012). In summary the political persona which had been rhetorically constructed by his opponents was a potentially significant electoral liability.

As a consequence Miliband needed to develop an ethos-based alternative which would be moderate, in touch with the electorate, and able to keep Labour united. By doing so he hoped to render 'Red Ed' and 'Wallace' inert whilst demonstrating he understood the needs of the electorate. To do this however he needed to have the Labour movement united and on his side. Given the manner of his leadership victory and the lack of a credible narrative it appeared that this could not be guaranteed. Indeed, although increasingly in retreat the Blairite faction of the party remained uncertain about his leadership. Thus, Miliband used the 2012 conference as a platform to begin building on the leadership ethos he demonstrated during the phone hacking scandal debate and to secure the active rather than tacit support of the Labour Party and its supporters.

Articulating One Nation Labour

The 2012 Labour conference is vital in seeing how Miliband sought to articulate a convincing narrative for himself whilst simultaneously ideologically renewing Labour. In the weeks leading up to the conference he did this by giving media interviews to the *Andrew Marr Show* and the *New Statesman* where he talked about what he believed in. Alan Johnson wrote an article about Miliband for the *Guardian* entitled 'Ed Miliband, Show Us You Have What it Takes to be Prime Minister', and Richard Behr wrote an article for the *New Statesman* on Miliband's charismatic leadership (Gaffney and Lahel, 2013: 7–8). These pre-conference outputs were directed towards the Labour Party in order to lay the foundations for the Miliband's ethos-driven positive persona. Moreover, Michael Sandel's lecture at the conference 'illustrated Miliband's relationship with academics and their use of academic phraseology' which 'are helpful if used with care' (Gaffney and Lahel, 2013: 11). Miliband also engaged with a Labour fringe event on Europe which 'illustrated his presence at conference' (Gaffney and Lahel, 2013). These strove to give Miliband a positive profile with the conference before delivering his keynote speech. As Gaffney and Lahel rightly argue this gave the overarching impression that 'the conference was being inhabited by Ed Miliband' (Gaffney and Lahel, 2013: 12).

His keynote speech at the conference was instrumental in presenting both his positive persona and a new ideological direction to both his supporters and doubters. His One Nation vision sought to ideologically renew Labour by arguing a new and convincing case for social democracy that would be post-New Labour and post-financial crisis. It was a speech that constructed his ethos, his 'likable persona', and emphasised long-standing emotive values that would be appealing to the Labour rank and file. The speech, which was delivered 'without an autocue, notes or tele-prompter' (Gaffney and Lahel, 2013: 12), introduced his political vision and values because he needed to grow his character and credibility with the audience. To do that he first emotionalised his family story by telling the conference how they came to Britain following the Second World War: 'Both of my parents came to Britain as immigrants, Jewish refugees from the Nazis. I know I would not be standing on this stage today without the compassion and tolerance of our great country. Great Britain' (Miliband, 2012). He also argued that he was 'a person of faith, not a religious faith but a faith nonetheless. A faith, I believe, many religious people would recognise. So here is my faith. I believe we have a duty to leave the world a better place than we found it' (Miliband, 2012). To grow this dimension of his ethos he used pathos to emotionalise his family story because he wanted his audience to trust his character and to show that he was a credible Labour leader because he empathised with those in need.

Throughout the speech he drew from his background to explain his values, yet he would often critique the record of his opponents on economic management by saying they represented groups and policies that not only undermine economic growth but subvert the values he articulated. He also critiqued his opponents' ideological adherence to privatisation and the model of competition, saying 'here's what I hate most of all. It's that the whole way they designed this NHS reorganisation was based on the model of competition that there was in the privatised utility industry, gas, energy and water' (Miliband, 2012). In fact, he goes on to blame such interest groups for the flaws in how the economy is constituted by arguing that large corporations and energy companies do not create a fair economy and that this results in two nations (Miliband, 2012). He would tie that critique to his ethos saying 'this is who I am. This is what I believe. This is my faith' (Miliband, 2012). Centrally to developing the logos of his One Nation argument he uses the Aristotelian technique of 'witnesses'. These are stories and experiences derived from members of the public who he argues are facing the consequences of harsh economic difficulties. He uses these 'witnesses' to legitimise his argument by saying their experiences represent 'two nations' in modern Britain.

> You know I think of the young woman I met at a youth centre in London earlier this year. She was brimming with hopes and ambitions for the future. She was full of life. She was full of desire to get on and do the best for herself. And then she told me her story. She'd sent off her CV to 137 employers and she'd not had a reply from any of them. Many of you in this audience will know people in the same position. Just think how that crushes the hopes of a generation. I want to talk to her, to a whole generation of young people who feel that Britain under this Government is not offering them a future. (Miliband, 2012)

By describing the experiences of such 'witnesses' Miliband is able to imply that he is in touch with the needs of the electorate, thereby growing his ethos. Put simply, this technique helps to demonstrate that he understands the plight faced by ordinary people while simultaneously curtailing the negative persona constructed by his political opponents about his distance from the everyday lives of people in the UK.

Miliband also used pathos to tap into the Olympic spirit of unity and to link this to his vision of One Nation. Given the success the UK enjoyed at the 2012 Olympics this was an attempt to associate himself with any residual feel-good factor (something also seen in the 2012 conference speeches of Cameron and Nick Clegg).

> You see the problem isn't the British people, just think about the Olympics and Paralympic games. It was a triumph for Britain. And why did we succeed? We succeeded because of the outstanding volunteers, the Games Makers who are here with us today, all 70,000 Games makers. They put a mirror up to Britain and showed us the best of ourselves. (Miliband, 2012)

He went on to connect the successes at the Olympics with the solidarity of the nations within the UK. He argued that 'if you think about the people of Scotland and the Olympic games, they weren't cheering on just the Scottish athletes of Team GB, they were cheering on all the athletes of Team GB' (Miliband, 2012). Given the UK was represented through 'Team GB' he argued it symbolised the sense of togetherness that the nations of the UK shared during the Olympics, which he later argues is fundamental in understanding One Nation Labour.

However, to ensure his argument had an element of logos and ethos he also briefly drew upon Benjamin Disraeli's original speech. Indeed, bearing in mind the longevity of One Nation Conservatism articulated chiefly through *Sybil* it is unsurprising Miliband should acknowledge it in his own speech. He used pathos to dispel the connection with the Conservatives, saying:

> He was a Tory. But don't let that put you off, just for a minute. His speech took over three hours to deliver, don't worry, don't worry, and he drank two whole bottles of brandy while delivering it. That is absolutely true. Now look, I just want to say, I know a speech that long would probably kill you. And the brandy would definitely kill me. But let us remember what Disraeli was celebrated for. (Miliband, 2012)

Rhetorically speaking he used humour by reminding the audience that the original was a three-hour speech, the large amount of alcohol consumed and that his audience need not fear a repeat. This transformed its acknowledgement into a moment of pathos and simultaneously growing his ethos. He argued the values which underscored Disraeli and his two nation critique 'has echoed through British history' (Miliband, 2012). In fact, Miliband argued Disraeli articulated 'a vision of a Britain where patriotism, loyalty, dedication to the common cause courses through the veins of all and nobody feels left out. It was a vision of Britain coming together to overcome the challenges we faced. Disraeli called it "One Nation"' (Miliband, 2012). This pathos-driven approach to advancing his argument taps into romantic conceptions of British national unity. Despite the controversies surrounding nationhood it was a strong argument because the conference was receptive to the idea of social and economic solidarity. Indeed, Miliband argued that the situation facing the nation today is similar to that which Disraeli critiqued.

Yet simply to acknowledge Disraeli's One Nation values was not sufficient. Nor was it enough to simply use them to attack contemporary neo-liberalism. Rather, Miliband needed to connect the ideas with the long-standing aspirations of the Labour Party, thereby claiming ownership of one of the Conservative Party's key ideological traditions. To do this he suggested that the Attlee administration borrowed from the values of One Nation in order to rebuild Britain in 1945. 'We heard the phrase again as the country came together to defeat fascism. And we heard it again as Clement Attlee's Labour government rebuilt Britain after the war' (Miliband, 2012). The ideals of social solidarity, unity and equality were elements that he claimed he shared with both Disraeli and Clement Attlee through One Nation, saying 'That is my vision of One Nation. That is my vision of Britain. That is the Britain we must become' (Miliband, 2012). By linking Disraeli's ideas with one of Labour's most effective administrations Miliband was able to present 'One Nation Labour' as descended from one of the party's proudest achievements.

Another part of claiming ownership of Disraeli's One Nation idea was to draw attention to the Conservative Party's current ideological composition. Miliband sought to show that the Conservatives had abandoned One Nation ideas and instead embraced the politics and economics of individualism. To do that he attacked Cameron's leadership, saying 'You can't be a One Nation Prime Minister if all you do is seek to divide the country. Divide the country between north and south. Public and private. Those who can work and those who can't work' (Miliband, 2012). By arguing that Cameron's party no longer believed in One Nation Conservatism, Miliband was able to appeal to moderate floating voters who voted Conservative in 2010. He used ethos to demonstrate empathy with their concerns, saying:

> I understand why you voted for him. I understand why you turned away from the last Labour government. This Government took power in difficult economic times. It was a country still coming to terms with the financial crisis. A financial crisis that has afflicted every country round the world. I understand why you were willing to give David Cameron the benefit of the doubt. (Miliband, 2012)

He also used logos to argue that the Coalition had failed to deliver the economic success those voters expected. 'I think we've had long enough to make a judgement. Long enough to make a judgement because they turned a recovery into the longest double dip recession since the war. Because there are more people looking for work for longer than at any time since the last time there was a Conservative government' (Miliband, 2012). Miliband is using limited logos and ethos to appeal to the moderate voter as a means of convincing them to return to Labour. More broadly Miliband also argued that 'the British people', rather than the institutional causes of the crisis, were taking the brunt of the Coalition's economic policies and the programme of spending cuts: 'Now look around you, you know the problem is the British people are paying the price of this government's failure' (Miliband, 2012). Indeed, he used ethos and logos to argue:

> not because there hasn't been pain and tax rises and cuts affecting every family in this country. Not because they didn't want to cut borrowing. They did. Not because your services aren't getting worse. They are. But because if you stop an economy growing, then it leaves more people out of work claiming benefits, not paying taxes. (Miliband, 2012)

He argued that such policies consolidate the two nations identified by Disraeli and that in order to be a One Nation prime minister such divisions would need to be combatted. For Miliband, the economic record was evidence that the Coalition had not delivered prosperity and that the government needed to be changed. 'If the medicine's not working you change the medicine. And friends, I'll tell you what else you change. You change the doctor too. And that is what this country needs to do' (Miliband, 2012). To win these voters back Miliband also aimed to highlight Labour's moderate policies. In fact, claiming a degree of parity with One Nation Conservatism would make it harder for the Conservatives to argue Labour was dominated by the left. Thus, Miliband used logos to critique the record of the Coalition and to connect his ideas of One Nation Labour with his audience. However in order to provide a positive argument it was necessary for him to demonstrate the ideological value of One Nation to Labour's broader ideological renewal. To do that he used logos to argue Labour could not return to Old or New Labour because the party needed a broader appeal to attract the support of the centrist voter. He posited the question:

> what does it mean to the Labour Party to be One Nation? It means we can't go back to Old Labour. But so too it is right to move on from New Labour because New Labour, despite its great achievements, was too silent about the responsibilities of those at the top, and too timid about the accountability of those with power. (Miliband, 2012)

Old Labour was seen as a dogmatic electoral liability whilst New Labour was no longer relevant following the financial crisis. Rather Miliband argued Labour had to be 'the party of south just as much as the party of the north. And we must be the party as much of the squeezed middle as those in poverty. There is no future for this party as the party of one sectional interest of our country' (Miliband, 2012). This represented an ideological shift because 'we must be a One Nation party to become a One Nation government, to build a One Nation Britain. And here's how we are going to take these steps to do that' (Miliband, 2012). To advance his argument he drew from ethos and logos to link the values of One Nation to the Labour Party on three key components.

The first component of One Nation Labour is providing social welfare for those unable to work due to disabilities and providing training for those who can. Here he uses pathos and logos to make the argument that social welfare should be targeted towards those in need. Indeed, Miliband argued that a One Nation government has a responsibility to provide social care for its citizens (Miliband, 2012). 'You see I think it is incredibly important that to be One Nation we must show compassion and support for all those who cannot work. Particularly the disabled men and women of our country' (Miliband, 2012). Nonetheless, he also argued that cuts would mean reducing public services because current public spending settlements necessitated reductions to expenditure. He subsequently downplayed the logos of his argument by using pathos to argue that 'those with the broadest shoulders will always bear the greatest burden. I would never cut taxes for millionaires and raise them on ordinary families. That is wrong, that is not being One Nation' (Miliband, 2012). This simultaneously enabled Miliband to argue Labour was retaining its pathos-driven commitment to social justice whilst accepting the logic of some cuts to spending.

The second component of One Nation Labour was education reform. He again used pathos to argue that 'to be a One Nation economy you have got to use all the talents of all of our young people' (Miliband, 2012). He went on to argue that a significant number of young people have been left idle because they did not attend university. He critiqued New Labour's emphasis on a university education as the main route to success by arguing vocational qualifications have equal value. He again used a 'witness' and pathos to relate his argument to the audience. 'I remember when Chris and I were at Haverstock. I remember at Haverstock school, my comprehensive, the kids who were good at passing exams, who were academic, they could go to university and the world would just open up for them like it did for me' (Miliband, 2012). He used a combination of this witness and pathos to justify a change in policy emphasis, saying 'for a long time our party has been focused on getting 50% of young people into university. I believe that was right. But now it's time to put our focus on the forgotten 50% who do not go to university' (Miliband, 2012). Succinctly, he argued New Labour had created an imbalanced skillset in the economy which needed to be addressed. His solution was textured with both pathos and logos which was 'a new gold standard qualification so they know when they are taking that exam they have a gold standard vocational qualification, a new Technical Baccalaureate' (Miliband, 2012). This would provide skills and training both through schools and in the workplace thereby producing 'a qualification to be proud of' (Miliband, 2012). Miliband also argues this would be possible by drawing the private sector into the One Nation project. 'Because when the public sector is having a contract with a private sector company, it is not just buying goods and services, it must be about building One Nation together. Public and private sectors joining together to do it' (Miliband, 2012).

The third component of One Nation Labour was economic reform. For this dimension Miliband again used pathos to argue that 'we need a One Nation economy and the first big mission of the next Labour government is to sort out our banks' (Miliband, 2012). This appealed to his audience because the banking sector was strongly critiqued by Labour for its role in the financial crisis. But he argued the reforms went beyond preventing a future financial crisis. Rather he used pathos to argue that the banking sector was excessively orientated around itself and that 'we need banks that serve the country not a country that serves its banks' (Miliband, 2012). Indeed, he suggested that bankers were 'more interested in playing the international money markets' rather than aiding the British economy (Miliband, 2012). Thus, he argued that One Nation Labour would 'ensure that the high street bank is no longer the arm of a casino operation' thereby making them less able to compete internationally (Miliband, 2012). The reliance on pathos in critiquing the banking sector was designed to appeal to his immediate sympathetic audience therefore he did not use an argument predicated upon logos.

After outlining the three areas above, he went on to again use pathos in his over-arching critique of the Conservatives' approach to governing by attacking Michael Gove's vision of education. To do this he first used ethos and himself as a 'witness' to critique Conservative education plans, saying Gove 'wanted to bring back two-tier academic exams. I remember what that was like. O-levels and CSEs one whole group of young people written off. We are not going back to those days. Michael Gove who has contempt for vocational qualifications' (Miliband, 2012). This pathos-driven attack was designed to solicit applause but also to argue that Gove symbolised 'a choice of two futures' (Miliband, 2012). He constructed these as either a narrow elite or a One Nation education policy tied to a One Nation economy (Miliband, 2012). By structuring his attack in this way he was able to engineer a reaction from his audience, however the absence of logos prevented him from presenting a clearer critique.

As the speech began to conclude Miliband drew increasingly upon his persona and rhetorical ethos. He used these to argue the case for an outward-looking country. 'My vision of One Nation is an outward looking country. A country which engages with Europe and the rest of the world. I am incredibly proud to be the son of immigrant parents. I am incredibly proud of the multi-ethnic diverse Britain' (Miliband, 2012). Although he was using the ethos attributed to him by his family's background, the logos of his argument was economic because in order to trade Britain would be at a disadvantage if its influence was reduced. However, his broader argument concerning immigration was premised around his own experiences as the son of immigrant parents. For this argument his ethos as the descendant of an immigrant family textured his arguments with pathos, before arguing that immigration reform is also a significant part of developing a One Nation economy and society. This approach sought to detach his arguments from those who premise their arguments using nationalism and 'alien others' because he was the son of an immigrant family calling for greater controls. Using logos he concedes that immigration is valuable because of the benefits it brings Britain. 'To make that vision work for our country, immigration must work for all and not just some. And friends, too often in the past we have overlooked those concerns, dismissed them too easily' (Miliband, 2012). He went on to critique the consequences of Labour dismissing immigration, arguing some immigrants have been used to undercut other workers. Indeed, he continues arguing 'we will stop recruitment agencies just saying they are only going to hire people from overseas. And we will end the shady practices, in the construction industry and elsewhere, of gang-masters. So we need a system of immigration that works for the whole country and not just for some' (Miliband, 2012). By using this approach Miliband is able to use his ethos to call for controls to immigration, pathos to celebrate Britain's openness, and logos in arguing the economic case for reforms.

The final arguments he used to legitimise One Nation revolved around the Union and the sense of shared values. To do so he used pathos to remind his audience that because England, Scotland, Wales and Northern Ireland constituted 'Team GB' the Union plays a significant part in constructing a sense of shared identity and solidarity.

> If you think about the people of Scotland and the Olympic games, they weren't cheering on just the Scottish athletes of Team GB, they were cheering on all the athletes of Team GB. That's what the SNP don't understand. And why would a party that claims to be left of centre turn its back on the redistribution, the solidarity, the common bonds of the United Kingdom? (Miliband, 2012)

In fact, he argues that One Nation Labour is predicated upon solidarity with the nations of the UK because of the sense of shared identity. He used pathos to attack those calling for an independent Scotland because it is a significant part of the UK's 'soul'. He argues that the case for the Union is evident 'not just in pounds and pence but in the soul of our nation. You see I don't believe that solidarity stops at the border' (Miliband, 2012). He also used pathos to critique the centre-left credentials of the Scottish National Party by arguing a progressive party should aim to maximise solidarity by remaining together rather than seeking to break away. Miliband maintained that the Union was a fundamental part of One Nation Labour and its political identity. Indeed, he argued 'It is up to us. We the Labour Party must be the people who fight, defend and win the battle for the United Kingdom' (Miliband, 2012). However, second to that was the National Health Service (NHS). Here Miliband again used a combination of pathos and ethos to defend the NHS.

> The magic of the NHS for me is that you don't leave your credit card at the door. The NHS, it's based on a whole different set of values, a whole different set of values that the people of Britain love. Not values of markets, money and exchange but values of compassion, care and co-operation. That is the magic of the NHS; that is why the British people love the NHS. (Miliband, 2012)

Those values are co-operation, care and solidarity. He critiqued the Conservatives because 'the Tories have shown in government it's something they just don't understand' (Miliband, 2012) and used pathos to strongly argue that the top-down reorganisations of the NHS represent a broken 'solemn contract with the British people, a contract that can never be repaired' (Miliband, 2012). By drawing his speech to a close in this manner he uses pathos to build it up to a crescendo. The reaction of the audience was highly positive, which helped make him appear as a strong and uniting leader and prompted positive media reporting. In fact, Miliband's final remarks draw the speech back to his persona by saying 'Britain has given my family everything. Britain and the spirit, the determination, the courage of the people who rebuilt Britain after the Second World War' (Miliband, 2012). Such emotional rhetoric is then tied to a final proposition to his audience: 'who in this generation will rebuild Britain for the future?' This is a question that is designed to inflame the positive response of his audience. He went on to use pathos to conclude that:

> Friends, it falls to us, it falls to us, the Labour Party. As it has fallen to previous genera-
> tions of Labour Party pioneers to leave our country a better place than we found it.
> Never to shrug our shoulders at injustice and say that is the way the world is. To come
> together, to join together, to work together as a country. (Miliband, 2012)

The concluding remark is also designed to consolidate the overarching message, 'One Nation: a country for all, with everyone playing their part. A Britain we rebuild together' (Miliband, 2012). It is unsurprising Miliband would conclude his speech using pathos because the purpose of his keynote is to rouse his audience and to motivate them, however it is worth noting that pathos and ethos textures much of his rhetorical approach thereby securing the support of the conference hall.

Conclusion

Miliband succeeded in presenting a positive persona to the conference through his ethos and pathos. This is an effective means of communicating with the Labour conference which has enabled him to dispel the earlier negative persona created by his opponents. His message of renewal was positively received because it was predicated on values which he argues are long-standing within Labour history, such as solidarity and equality of opportunity.

The logos of Miliband's argument is that One Nation can be created through social, economic and educational reform. These each depend upon co-operation between different sectors and service providers in British society. He also argues One Nation can be extended to the UK on issues concerning national identity and a sense of cultural and political togetherness. Nevertheless, the key issue concerning One Nation Labour appears to be communicating it beyond the conference hall. Given it is based on intellectual arguments derived from ideological theory and political history there is a risk the message may not resonate with the wider electorate.

Conclusion

The changing face of Labour oratory

Andrew S. Crines

The art of oratory is the power of successful persuasion. Through clarity of message, and awareness of the feelings of their audience, an orator can hope to elicit demonstrations of support from those they address, for example through applause. As such effective orators have three overarching considerations. They are 1) how they use their character and credibility to ensure the audience lends them their ears; 2) how they want to appeal to the emotions either through humour or other emotions; 3) and what logical premise they want to base their arguments on. These are the Aristotelian modes of persuasive rhetoric vis-à-vis ethos, pathos, logos and have been used throughout this volume to draw out how leading Labour figures persuaded their audiences.

As has been demonstrated in this volume, constructing a speech that revolves around these three modes of persuasion is not always an easy task. It must have a logical foundation: for example Harold Wilson's 'white heat' speech argued romantic allusions of socialism had little place in a quickly changing global economy based on technology and science (Crines, 2013b). It should aim to produce an emotional reaction in the audience strong enough to become a significant motivator in soliciting support for the message. Wilson used this technique by creating a sense of fear of irrelevance should Labour fail to rise to the challenge he set before them. Put simply, the idealised romanticism of Labour's past was insufficient to deal with the realities of a world dominated by two technologically-driven superpowers (Wilson, 1963). Because Wilson's renewal argument was advanced in the early stages of his leadership his case for an embrace of scientific socialism was rhetorically premised more on his newness (ethos) and represented a break from the immediate and divisive past.

It is also important to note, as we have in this volume, that orators draw asymmetrically from these modes of persuasion depending on the expectations of their audience and the specific requirements of the particular arena. Indeed, the orators we have featured in this volume faced a range of audiences such as the party at conference, their fellow parliamentarians in the Commons, and the wider public through the media and/or open meetings. How they used the modes of persuasion would, therefore, be predicated upon the reaction they wished to solicit from a specific audience. Each of the audiences considered here had different expectations and political needs, thus each required different styles of speech in order to resonate.

A key finding of this volume is that as part of this process each of the orators used their ideological perspective to inform their arguments and convince the audience of their message. Within that, the broadly defined 'left' tended to draw from emotive perspectives, whilst the social democratic right gravitated more towards pragmatic, logical appeals. In the case of this volume 'the left' was represented mostly by Aneurin Bevan, Barbara Castle, Tony Benn and Michael Foot; whilst the social democratic right included Hugh Gaitskell, Harold Wilson, James Callaghan, Neil Kinnock, John Smith, Tony Blair, Gordon Brown and Ed Miliband. How these ideological identities were constructed is beyond the scope of this volume, however these have been thoroughly explored elsewhere (Crines, 2011; Cronin, 2004; Fielding, 1997; Jones, 1996; Thorpe, 2008). Each tradition fought for prominence in the party by arguing their case to partisan audiences both at constituency and conference level, as well as to the electorate through open meetings, radio and television. Each claimed to represent the interests of Labourism, so how both traditions communicated is worth briefly considering.

The overarching style of the moderate/radical left tended to be more romantic and emotion-driven because of the inclination to draw from past battles and future causes as a means of challenging 'the establishment'. Such refrains would often be given centre stage in their rhetoric thereby justifying socialist thought. For example Bevan's rhetoric emotively confronted opponents by challenging their intellectual or moral integrity, especially on issues which he passionately believed in. This was evident in his advocacy of a National Health Service (NHS) where he argued 'not even the apparently enlightened principle of the "greatest good for the greatest number" can excuse indifference to individual suffering. There is no test for progress other than its impact on the individual' (Bevan, 1952b: 167–8). For Bevan, this was an emotional issue which therefore led to, even demanded, emotionally charged rhetoric – even if such rhetoric would sometimes act as a barrier if it lacked logic. Castle used rhetoric in a similar fashion by drawing on feelings of past injustices caused by a lack of social security provision for the poorest in society. For example, when talking about welfare provision before 1945, she argued that 'there was no welfare state, and people had to rely mainly on the Poor Law – that was all the state provided. It was very degrading, very humiliating. And there was a means test for receiving poor relief' (Castle, 2000). Here she used fear to warn her audience of possible consequences if Britain's welfare state ceased to provide universal support. Neither of these orators drew heavily on logos, but both were still highly effective because of their powerful pathos and ethos. Succinctly, both these forms of emotive appeals sought to justify state welfare by either attacking their opponents or portraying an alternative in a highly undesirable way.

Both Benn and Foot also used emotional rhetoric to appeal more to the romanticism of their cause. This was often achieved by drawing on historical movements or individuals who appear to give credence to their argument of a longer running opposition to 'the establishment'. Benn often used the Parliamentarians during the Civil War and the Levellers to show how direct action can be effective in opposing unchallenged political power (Benn, 1979: 31–2), and by connecting their cause to the problems facing Britain today Benn was attempting to link their past success to his hope of future victories. He argued the Levellers 'represented the aspirations of working people who suffered under the persecution of kings, landowners and the priestly class, and they spoke for those who experienced the hardships of poverty and deprivation' (Benn, 2011). By doing so Benn is claiming that opposition to elites is a long-standing tradition that is still active at the rank and file level of the Labour Party and within the broader working classes, and so by adopting a similar approach the Labour movement could achieve its aims more directly. Foot also drew in historical events to texture his arguments by using stories drawn from past causes to argue their enduring relevance. Often Foot would rest his arguments on the liberal idealism developed by theorists such as William Hazlitt. He argued that Hazlitt 'was an idealist who knew that present enemies must be fought here and now, tooth and nail, on their own ground' (Foot, 1981f: 28). Foot used pathos-driven arguments based on moral causes and collective opposition rooted in class conflict, liberal socialism and the rank and file. Broadly speaking each of these approaches textured the rhetoric of the moderate left with emotive and intellectual romanticism, but failed to connect logically with the audience (or electorate). This represented something of a barrier between their argument and the electorate because theirs was a rhetorical method predicated on foreknowledge which became dated with the swift passing of time, whereas the social democrats used rhetoric rooted more in the present.

Because the social democrats tended to draw more heavily on more forward-looking arguments they appeared more pragmatic and logical. The social democratic right also tended to prioritise electoral victory at the expense of socialist romanticism. To that end the social democrats were more willing to change aspects of Labour's historic *raison d'être* in order to appear in touch with the concerns of the electorate. This gives the social democratic rhetoric a greater sense of logos. Such is the case of Gaitskell whose rationalism relied on logical arguments. These sought to convince the electorate to reach their own conclusions based on evidence and argument rather than emotional appeals (Butler and Rose, 1960). Such a logical approach subscribes to a core oratorical technique of genuine persuasion over manipulation through the presentation of facts. As stated earlier Wilson's pragmatism as leader could be rhetorically effective, particularly when striving to move Labour beyond the divisions of the 1950s. Indeed, a fundamental aspect of Wilson's rhetorical strategy was through logos, although the devaluation episode undoubtedly undermined his ethos. It is also interesting to note that the social democrats demonstrated a stronger sense of economic realism, or at least a willingness to accept the constraints of a capitalist economy. For example Callaghan's broad acceptance of the International Monetary Fund's (IMF) terms in 1976 reflected the perceived need for new economic policies, which he also argued reflected the wishes of the electorate (Callaghan, 1976c). He argued that the country could no longer afford ideological indulgencies such as those devised through Stuart Holland's Alternative Economic Strategy (Holland, 1978), and that wage restraint and changes to spending priorities were needed.

Between 1979 and 1982 the Labour Party was overcome by a pathos-driven debate centred on left-wing romanticism, however logos-driven social democratic attacks on the left subsequently came into the ascendency with Kinnock's modern-isation agenda. This was predicated upon accepting the changed nature of society and the consequences of a denationalised industrial sector. Kinnock used the conference arena to show that logical arguments were necessary in order to regain office. His fail-ure to do so can be attributed to his inability to carry that message of modernisation to the electorate. His successor, Smith, also used logic to argue that electoral victory was possible only with further reforms. Thus 'One Member, One Vote' was designed to replace the trade union 'block vote' and, in so doing, radically reform the relation-ship between the party and the unions. Combatting pathos-driven romanticism was also a significant aspect of the Blair reforms, that saw Clause IV as an idealistic piece of Labour history which had no place in a party aiming to convince the electorate of their economic logos. Thus, although many at the rank and file level of the move-ment argued it was a symbolic part of Labour's history (Cronin, 2004; Shaw, 1996), the logos of the argument won out. Following Blair, Brown's logos was premised on technical and economic issues. Despite the attempts to articulate a convincing nar-rative of inclusive Britishness, his logos represented a shift away from renewal and towards fiscal management and economic competence. By doing so a rhetorical bar-rier fell between the leadership and the electorate, which made him appear distant. This is a barrier which Miliband is seeking to remove by presenting Labour as a rein-vigorated party with a clear macro-vision. However, given this strategy is targeted towards internal renewal it has limited salience with the electorate beyond, drawing a line under New Labour and the Blair/Brown divisions. Thus, the Miliband strategy is open to the accusation of having limited logos beyond the confines of the party and so, at the time of writing, appears unconvincing to the wider electorate.

Broadly speaking, throughout Labour's post-war history the moderate left and social democratic traditions represented the windows through which the orators featured here spoke to attract the support of their chosen audience. This created ideological divisions that led to internal battles and electoral defeats. Ultimately, the social democrats proved more effective because their rhetoric appeared to better reflect the sentiments of the broader electorate. The moderate left failed to resonate with the electorate because it appeared to be too idealistic and romantic, whilst the social democrats revolved their rhetoric around the present and the prosaic.

It is also important to note that the arenas we have considered in this volume have of course changed over the post-war period. The media has become less deferential and more omnipresent; the Labour conference is less about debating resolutions and more about showcasing established policies and personalities; the Commons is more a combative arena than a debating chamber, and is a place for the leader to rally the back benchers. These reflect the broader changing nature of debate in British politics. This means oratorical styles and rhetorical strategies have also had to change, although the importance of clarity surrounding the message remains vital. To briefly summarise the growth of the media sound bite means that politicians are less able to develop complex arguments through in-depth interviews, while speeches are reported in sound bite form. A clear message of modernisation/reform/change dominates whilst nuanced arguments about ideological theory have little place. This is because a succinct message tends to be clear whilst longer argument may become hazy. Also at the conference the speaker is expected to present a coherent vision of how Labour's values will inform policies by giving an overarching narrative ahead of providing more specific details supported by their own ethos. The older power of the conference to affect the policy formulation process has been reduced to the point where resolutions carry little or no significant weight upon that process. Thus the focus upon conference today is more about presenting an inspiring message that is textured by logos. Meanwhile the objective of Prime Minister's Questions (PMQs) has culminated in the 'Punch and Judy' caricature of parliamentary debate. Yet, the Commons still presents an opportunity for orators to garner support for their arguments with the media because a poor performance risks a negative press whilst a good performance tends to avoid such criticism and may win some plaudits. The Commons also enables the speaker to gain the support of fellow MPs, whilst attacking the arguments of opponents. As a result, although the arenas have changed in character over the course of the post-war period their significance to effective oratory and rhetoric remains.

This volume has contributed to the emerging debate on rhetoric by focusing on the oratory of leading Labour figures. We have concluded that the modes of persuasive oratory are each asymmetrically employed by the speakers throughout the post-war period within various changing arenas and political contexts. Whilst the debates change, as the arenas adapt, and the expectations of the electorate evolve, the style of oratory has changed too. Bevan's pathos-driven appeals at conference gave way to Blair's more concise logos-orientated media sound bite. Yet the importance of clarity remains. Indeed, clarity may be even more important in today's Labour politics because of, rather than despite, the changing nature of the arenas. A strong conference performance demonstrates competence; effective parliamentary oratory showcases the support of the party; a clear message given to the media can persuade the electorate. An effective performer attracts the support of their audience, be that the movement, the Commons or the electorate. This demonstrates the vital importance of clear rhetoric and effective oratory, and how it can produce political success.

Bibliography

Abrams, F. (1997) 'Blair: I think I'm a pretty straight sort of guy', *The Independent*, 17 November 1997.

Abse, L. (2001) *Tony Blair: The Man Behind the Smile*, London: Robson Books.

Adams, J. (1992) *Tony Benn: A Biography*, London: Macmillan.

Adonis, A. (2006) '30 Years On, Callaghan's Words Resonate', *Guardian*, 17 October 2006.

Alderman, K. (1992a) 'The Leader of the Opposition and Prime Minister's Question Time', *Parliamentary Affairs*, 45:1, pp. 66–76.

Alderman, K. (1992b) 'Harold Macmillan's Night of the Long Knives', *Contemporary British History*, 6:2, pp. 243–65.

Althusser, L. (2008) 'Ideology and Ideological State Apparatus', in *On Ideology*, London: Verso, pp. 1–60.

Anderson, B. (1986) 'BL: One way street to a Tory crash', *The Times*, 10 March, p. 12.

Andrews, L. (2008) *Bevan Assembly Act*, 21 May 2008. Available at: www.leightonandrews. com/2008/05/bevan-assembly-art.html. Accessed 24 May 2012.

Aristotle (1991) *The Art of Rhetoric*, London: Penguin.

Aristotle (2004) *Rhetoric: Book I*, Chapter 2, 15 March 2004. Available at: http://rhetoric. eserver.org/aristotle/rhet1-2.html. Accessed 2 November 2013.

Assinder, N. (2002) 'Barbara Castle: A Dynamic Firebrand', *BBC News*, 3 May 2002. Available at: http://news.bbc.co.uk/1/hi/uk_politics/1967264.stm. Accessed 7 March 2012.

Atkins, J. (2011) *Justifying New Labour Policy*, Basingstoke: Palgrave Macmillan.

Atkins, J. and Finlayson, A. (2013) '"… A 40-Year-Old Black Man Made the Point to Me": Everyday Knowledge and the Performance of Leadership in Contemporary British Politics', *Political Studies*, 61:1, pp. 161–77.

Atkinson, M. (1984) *Our Masters' Voices: The Language and Body-language of Politics*, London: Routledge.

Bagehot Blog (2010) 'Ed Miliband is Elected Labour Leader by the Union Vote', *The Economist*, 25 September 2010. Available at: www.economist.com/blogs/bagehot/2010/09/ed_ miliband_0. Accessed 3 December 2013.

Bale, T. (2010) *The Conservative Party From Thatcher to Cameron*, Cambridge: Polity.

Barber, M. (1996) 'New Labour, 20 Years On', *Times Educational Supplement*, 11 October 2006.

Barber, M. (2007) *Instruction to Deliver*, London: Politico's.

Barnhart, D. and Metcalf, A. (1997) *America in So Many Words: Words That Have Shaped America*, Boston: Houghton Mifflin.

BBC (1969) 'A Year in the Life: Craghead: 1968–1969', BBC 2, 5 October 1969.

BBC (1972) 'Women in Politics', BBC Radio 4, 14 January 1972.

BBC (1987) 'Interview with Tony Blair', BBC 1, 20 October 1987.

BBC (1995) *The Wilderness Years*, BBC 2, 18 December 1995.

BBC (1998a) 'Gordon Brown Interview', *On the Record*, 23 March 1998. Available at: www.bbc.co.uk/otr/intext/gordon_brown.22.3.98.html. Accessed 26 September 2011.

BBC (1998b) 'Aneurin Bevan: Labour's Lost Leader', BBC News, 1 July 1998. Available at: http://news.bbc.co.uk/1/hi/events/nhs_at_50/special_report/120208.stm. Accessed 11 May 2012.

BBC (1999) 'Tony Blair's speech in full', *BBC News*, 28 September 1999. http://news.bbc.co.uk/1/hi/uk_politics/460009.stm.

BBC (2001a) 'Gordon Brown Interview', *BBC Breakfast with Frost*, 2 December 2001. Available at: http://news.bbc.co.uk/1/hi/programmes/breakfast_with_frost/1687984.stm. Accessed 26 September 2011.

BBC (2001b) 'Labour "Pact" Back in Spotlight', 3 December 2011. Available at: http://news.bbc.co.uk/1/hi/uk_politics/1688097.stm. Accessed 6 October 2011.

BBC (2003) 'Blair vows no reverse on reform', *BBC News*, 30 September 2003. http://news.bbc.co.uk/1/hi/uk_politics/3149164.stm.

BBC (2006a) 'Gordon Brown Interview', *BBC Sunday AM*, 7 May 2006. Available at: http://news.bbc.co.uk/go/pr/fr/-/1/hi/programmes/how_euro_are_you/4981972.stm. Accessed 27 September 2011.

BBC (2006b) 'Gordon Brown Interview', *BBC Sunday AM*, 10 September 2006. Available at: http://news.bbc.co.uk/go/pr/fr/-/1/hi/programmes/sunday_am/5332438.stm. Accessed 27 September 2011.

BBC (2008a) 'Wilson Had Alzheimer's When PM', 10 November 2008. Available at: http://news.bbc.co.uk/1/hi/health/7720200.stm. Accessed 1 October 2011.

BBC (2008b) 'Gordon Brown Interview', *BBC Politics Show*, 3 November 2008. Available at: http://news.bbc.co.uk/go/pr/fr/-/1/hi/programmes/politics_show/7741358.stm. Accessed 27 September 2011.

BBC (2009) Interview conducted by Matthew d'Ancona as part of his Britishness series, BBC Radio 4, 31 March 2009. Available at: www.york.ac.uk/ipup/projects/britishness/brown.html. Accessed 27 September 2011.

BBC (2010a) 'Gordon Brown Interview', *The Andrew Marr Show*, 3 January 2010. Available at: http://news.bbc.co.uk/go/pr/fr/-/1/hi/programmes/andrew_marr_show/8438431.stm. Accessed 27 September 2011.

BBC (2010b) 'Gordon Brown Interview', *The Andrew Marr Show*, 18 April 2010. Available at: http://news.bbc.co.uk/go/pr/fr/-/1/hi/programmes/andrew_marr_show/8628337.stm. Accessed 27 September 2011.

BBC (2012) 'Ed Miliband Interview', *The Andrew Marr Show*, 30 September 2012. www.youtube.com/watch?v=xTFf7ROZHWg.

Beckett, A. (2009a) *When the Lights Went Out: Britain in the Seventies,* London: Faber.

Beckett, A. (2009b) 'Where Did It All Go Wrong for Gordon Brown?', *Guardian*, 3 June 2009. Available at: www.guardian.co.uk/politics/2009/jun/03/gordon-brown-scandal-unpopularity-election. Accessed 23 January 2012.

Beech, M. (2004) 'New Labour', in Plant, R., Beech, M. and Hickson, K. (eds) *The Struggle for Labour's Soul: Understanding Labour's Political Thought since 1945,* London: Routledge, pp. 86–102.

Beech, M. and Lee, S. (2008) *Ten Years of New Labour,* Basingstoke: Palgrave Macmillan.

Benn, T. (1979) *Arguments for Socialism,* London: Penguin.

Benn, T. (1988) *Out of the Wilderness: Diaries 1963–1967,* London: Arrow Books.

Benn, T. (1989) *Against the Tide: Diaries 1973–1976,* London: Hutchinson.

Benn, T. (1994a) *Years of Hope: Diaries, Papers and Letters 1940–1962,* London: Hutchinson.

Benn, T. (1994b) *The End of an Era: Diairies 1980–90,* London: Arrow Books.

Benn, T. (2011) 'The Levellers and the Tradition of Dissent', *BBC News,* 17 February 2011. Available at: www.bbc.co.uk/history/british/civil_war_revolution/benn_levellers_01. shtml. Accessed 15 November 2013.

Bennister, M. (2009) 'Tony Blair as Prime Minister', in Casey, T. (ed.) *The Blair Legacy,* Basingstoke: Palgrave Macmillan, pp. 165–77.

Bennister, M. (2012) *Prime Ministers in Power: Political Leadership in Britain and Australia,* Basingstoke: Palgrave Macmillan.

Bennister, M. and Heffernan, R. (2012) 'Cameron as Prime Minister: The Intra-Executive Politics of Britain's Coalition Government', *Parliamentary Affairs,* pp. 1–24.

Bernstein, G. (2004) *The Myth of Decline: The Rise of Britain Since 1945,* London: Pimlico.

Bevan, A. (1945) 'Speech to Labour Activists', *Wales Online,* 29 September 2009. Available at: www.walesonline.co.uk/news/wales-news/2010/09/29/swansea-university-sets-up-archive-of-political-speeches-91466-27360600. Accessed 24 May 2012.

Bevan, A. (1946) *Speech to the National Federation of Building Trades Operatives.* Available at: www.britishpathe.com/video/nye-bevan-speech. Accessed 13 May 2012.

Bevan, A. (1950) 'Mr Bevan on Mr Churchill', *The Times,* 6 February 1950, p. 3.

Bevan, A. (1952a) 'Labour Must Take the Offensive', *The Times,* 27 October 1952, p. 2.

Bevan, A. (1952b) *In Place of Fear,* London: Simon & Schuster.

Bevan, A. (1957a) 'One Sided Nuclear Ban Rejected by Labour', *The Times,* 4 October 1957, p. 10.

Bevan, A. (1957b) *Report of the Labour Party Conference 1957,* London: The Labour Party.

Bevan, A. (1959) *Report of the Labour Party Conference 1959,* London: The Labour Party.

Black, L. (2001) '"The Bitterest Enemies of Communism": Labour Revisionists, Atlanticism and the Cold War', *Contemporary British History,* 15:3, pp. 26–62.

Blackburn, D. (2010) 'Miliband turns Brownite', *The Spectator,* 18 June 2010. Available at: http://blogs.spectator.co.uk/coffeehouse/2010/06/miliband-turns-brownite/. Accessed 1 December 2013.

Blackledge, P. (2013) 'Left Reformism, the State and the Problem of Socialist Politics Today', *International Socialism: A Quarterly Journal of Socialist Theory,* 139. Available at: www.isj. org.uk/?id=903. Accessed 1 November 2013.

Blair, T. (1996) *Speech given at Ruskin College, Oxford,* 16 December 1996.

Blair, T. (2002) *Speech to the Labour Party Annual Conference,* 1 October 2002.

Blair, T. (2005a) *Speech to Labour Party Annual Conference,* 16 September 2005.

Blair, T. (2005b) *Speech to the Labour Party Annual Conference,* 27 September 2005.

Blair, T. (2010) *A Journey,* London: Hutchinson.

Blumler, J.G. and McQuail, D. (1968) *Television in Politics: Its Uses and Influence,* London: Faber & Faber.

Bogdanor, V. (2007) 'Social Democracy', in Seldon, A. (ed.) *Blair's Britain 1997–2007,* Cambridge: Cambridge University Press, pp. 164–182.

Bowie, R. (1974) *Suez 1956*, Oxford: Oxford University Press.

Braddon, R. (1963) *Suez: The Splitting of a Nation*, London: Collins.

Brivati, B. (1996) *Hugh Gaitskell*, London: Richard Cohen.

Brivati, B. (1999) 'Hugh Gaitskell', in Jefferys, K. (ed.) *Leading Labour: From Keir Hardie to Tony Blair*, London: I.B. Tauris, pp. 97–115.

Brivati, B. (2000) *Guiding Light: The Collected Speeches of John Smith*, London: Politico's.

Brivati, B. (2008) *Hugh Gaitskell*, Oxford: Oxford University Press.

Broad, M. and Daddow, O. (2010) 'Half-Remembered Quotations from Mostly Forgotten Speeches: The Limits of Labour's European Policy Discourse', *The British Journal of Politics and International Relations*, 12:2, pp. 205–22.

Brookshire, J.H. (1995) *Clement Attlee*, Manchester: Manchester University Press.

Brown, G. (1971) *In My Way: The Political Memoirs of Lord George Brown*, London: Gollancz.

Brown, G. (1992) *Autumn Statement*, HC Deb 18 November, vol. 214 cols 307–17.

Brown, G. (1994) *Debate on the Economy*, HC Deb 23 November, vol. 250 cols 601–12.

Brown, G. (1995) *Speech to the Labour Party Conference*, 2 October 1995.

Brown, G. (1996) *Speech to the Labour Party Conference*, 30 September 1996.

Brown, G. (1997a) *Budget Statement*, HC Deb 2 July, vol. 297 cols 303–16.

Brown, G. (1997b) *Speech to the Labour Party Conference*, 29 September 1997.

Brown, G. (2001) *Budget Statement*, HC Deb 7 March 2001, vol. 364 cols 295–309.

Brown, G. (2002) *Speech to the Commons*, 17 April 2002, cols. 579, 586, 592.

Brown, G. (2003) *Speech to the Labour Party Conference*, 29 September 2003.

Brown, G. (2005a) *Budget Statement*, HC Deb 16 March 2005, vol. 432 cols 257–69.

Brown, G. (2005b) *Speech to the Labour Party Annual Conference*, 26 September 2005.

Brown, G. (2006a) *Budget Statement*, HC Deb 22 March 2006, vol. 444 cols 287–302.

Brown, G. (2006b) *Speech to the Labour Party Annual Conference*, 25 September 2006.

Brown, G. (2006c) *Speech to the Fabian New Year Conference*, 14 January 2006.

Brown, G. (2007a) *Speech to the Labour Party Annual Conference*, 24 September 2007.

Brown, G. (2007b) *Speech at a seminar on Britishness at the Commonwealth Club, London*, 27 February 2007.

Brown, G. (2007c) *Debate on the Address*, HC Deb 6 November, vol. 467 cols 23–34.

Brown, G. (2008) *Debate on the Address*, HC Deb 3 December, vol. 485 cols 26–39.

Brown, G. (2009) *Speech to the Labour Party Conference*, 29 September 2009.

Brown, G. and Straw, J. (2008) *The Governance of Britain*, London: HM Stationery Office.

Burns, J. (2010) 'British Labour Party Looks to Rebuild', *New York Times*, 16 May 2010. Available at: www.nytimes.com/2010/05/17/world/europe/17britain.html?_r=0. Accessed 1 December 2013.

Butler, D. and Rose, R. (1960) *The British General Election of 1959*, London: Macmillan.

Callaghan, J. Uncatalogued Papers, Bodleian Library, Oxford.

Callaghan, J. (1968a) *Speech to the House of Commons, Hansard*, 27 February 1968.

Callaghan, J. (1968b) *Speech to the House of Commons, Hansard*, 18 March 1968.

Callaghan, J. (1971) *James Callaghan on the Common Market*, London: Labour Committee for Safeguards on the Common Market.

Callaghan, J. (1974) *Speech to the Cooperative Party Annual Conference*, 13 April 1974.

Callaghan, J. (1976a) *Report of the Seventy Fifth Annual Conference of the Labour Party*, London, Labour Party.

Callaghan, J. (1976b) *Speech to Ruskin College*, 18 October 1976.

Callaghan, J. (1976c) *Speech for Meeting at Woolwich*, 30 January 1976.

Callaghan, J. (1976d) *Statement to the Press Association*, 17 March 1976.

Callaghan, J. (1976e) *Prime Ministerial Broadcast*, 5 April 1976.

Callaghan, J. (1976f) *Speech to the Union Shop, Distributive and Allied Workers Annual Conference, Blackpool*, 25 April 1976.

Callaghan, J. (1976g) *Speech to the National Committee of the Amalgamated Union of Engineering Workers*, 19 May 1976.

Callaghan, J. (1978a) *Speech to the TUC Conference, Brighton*, 5 September 1978.

Callaghan, J. (1978b) *Prime Ministerial Broadcast*, 7 September 1978.

Callaghan, J. (1978c) *Speech to the Opening of the TGWU Building, Cardiff*, 16 September 1978.

Callaghan, J. (1979) *National Executive Committee Minutes*, 23 May 1979.

Callaghan, J. (1980) *Speech to the All Wales Rally, Brecon*, 5 July 1980.

Callaghan, J. (1986a) *Speech to the House of Commons, Hansard*, 15 January 1986.

Callaghan, J. (1986b) *Speech to the House of Commons, Hansard*, 16 April 1986.

Callaghan, J. (1987a) *Speech to the House of Commons, Hansard*, 9 March 1987.

Callaghan, J. (1987b) *Speech on Defence*, March 1987.

Callaghan, J. (1987c) *Speech to the Labour Party Conference*, September 1987.

Callaghan, J. (1988) *Time and Chance*, London: Collins/Fontana.

Callaghan, J. (1996) *Ruskin Anniversary Lecture, Institute of Education*, 15 October 1996.

Cameron, D. (2011) Prime Minister's Questions, 9 March 2011. Available at: www.youtube.com/watch?v=zMdsOqGASRE. Accessed 28 November 2013.

Campbell, A. (2010) *Diaries Volume One: Prelude to Power 1994–1997*, London: Hutchinson.

Campbell, J. (1983) *Roy Jenkins*, London: Weidenfeld & Nicolson.

Campbell, J. (1987) *Nye Bevan and the Mirage of British Socialism*, London: Weidenfeld & Nicolson.

Campbell, J. (1994) *Edward Heath: A Biography*, London: Pimlico's.

Campbell, J. (2000) *Margaret Thatcher Volume 1: The Grocer's Daughter*, London: Jonathan Cape.

Castle, B. (1959) 'Chairman's Address', in *Report of the Fifty-Eighth Annual Conference of the Labour Party, Blackpool, 1959*, London: The Labour Party.

Castle, B. (1966a) *Minister for Transport, speaking at Sunderland Town Hall*, The Labour Party: London, 18 March 1966.

Castle, B. (1966b) *Minister of Transport speaking at a Labour Party Conference at Spinners Hall, St. George's Road, Bolton*, The Labour Party: London, 17 September 1966.

Castle, B. (1968a) *Speech by Secretary of State for Employment and Productivity to the Industrial Society Conference on the new White Paper 'Productivity, Prices and Incomes Policy in 1968 and 1969', Connaught Rooms, London, May 28*, London: Department of Employment and Productivity.

Castle, B. (1968b) *Speech at opening of the new Remploy factory Acton*, London: Department of Employment and Productivity, 9 October 1968.

Castle, B. (1970) *Remploy Provides Useful Work for Willing Hands – Speech on 25th Anniversary Celebrations of Remploy Ltd*, London: Department of Employment and Productivity, 7 April 1970.

Castle, B. (1974) *Speech: Family Life in Modern Society to Conference of the North-West Group of the Council for Family Social Work, Liverpool*, 25 October 1974.

Castle, B. (1975) *Secretary of State for Social Services, speaking to Labour Party Officers, at the Salsibury Hotel, Weston Super Mare,* 27 June 1975.

Castle, B. (1980) *The Castle Diaries Volume II,* London: Weidenfeld & Nicolson.

Castle, B. (1984) *The Castle Diaries. Vol. II: 1964–70,* London: George Weidenfeld & Nicolson Ltd.

Castle, B. (1990) *The Castle Diaries: 1964–1976,* London: Papermac.

Castle, B. (1993) *Fighting All the Way,* London: Macmillan.

Castle, B. (1997) 'A Passionate Defiance', in Goodman, G. (ed.) *The State of the Nation: The Political Legacy of Aneurin Bevan,* London: Victor Gollancz, pp. 36–67.

Castle, B. (2000) *Socialism and Social Conditions in 1930s Britain,* 16 October. Available at: www.pbs.org/wgbh/commandingheights/shared/pdf/int_barbaracastle.pdf. Accessed 4 April 2012.

Charteris-Black, J. (2005) *Politicians and Rhetoric: The Persuasive Power of Metaphor,* Basingstoke: Palgrave Macmillan.

Charteris-Black, J. (2011) *Politicians and Rhetoric: The Persuasive Power of Metaphor,* Basingstoke: Palgrave Macmillan.

Charteris-Black, J. (2012) 'Comparative Keyword Analysis and Leadership Communication: Tony Blair – a Study of Rhetorical Style', in Helms, L. (ed.) *Comparative Political Leadership,* Basingstoke: Palgrave Macmillan, pp. 142–64.

Childs, S. (2008) *Women and British Party Politics: Descriptive, Substantive and Symbolic Representation,* Oxon: Routledge.

Clifford, D. (2012) 'Neil Kinnock: Out of the Wilderness', *Progress Online,* 22 February 2012. Available at: www.progressonline.org.uk/2012/02/22/neil-kinnock-out-of-the-wilderness/. Accessed 31 October 2013.

Coates, D. (1975) *The Labour Party and the Struggle for Socialism,* Cambridge: Cambridge University Press.

Cockcroft, R. and Cockcroft, S. (2005) *Persuading People: An Introduction to Rhetoric,* Basingstoke: Palgrave Macmillan.

Conroy, H. (2006) *Callaghan,* London: Haus Publishing.

Cook, R. (2002) *Point of Departure,* London: Simon & Schuster.

Coopey, R., Fielding, S. and Tiratsoo, N. (1993) 'Introduction', in Coopey, R., Fielding, S. and Tiratsoo, N. (eds) *The Wilson Governments 1964–1970,* London: Pinter, pp. 1–9.

Corbett, E. and Connors, R. (1999) *Classical Rhetoric for the Modern Times,* Oxford: Oxford University Press.

Coyte, P. and Kinnock, N. (1980) *How to Speak in Public,* London: The Labour Party.

Cowley, J. (2012) 'He's Not for Turning', *New Statesman,* 5 September 2012. Available at: www.newstatesman.com/politics/politics/2012/09/ed-miliband-he%E2%80%99s-not-turning. Accessed 3 December 2013.

Crampton, C. (2012) 'Is Ed Ugly, or Does He Just Not Look Enough Like a PM for Us?', *Total Politics,* 16 January 2012. Available from: www.totalpolitics.com/blog/289342/is-ed-ugly-or-does-he-just-not-look-enough-like-a-pm-for-us.thtml. Accessed 3 December 2013.

Crewe, I. and King, A. (1997) *The Birth, Life and Death of the Social Democratic Party,* Oxford: Oxford University Press.

Crines, A. (2011) *Michael Foot and the Labour Leadership,* Newcastle: Cambridge Scholars Publishers.

Crines, A. (2013a) 'The Rhetoric of the Coalition', *Representation*, 49:2, pp. 207–18.

Crines, A. (2013b) 'Communicating the White Heat of Technology', *Ballots and Bullets*, 28 June 2013. Available at: http://nottspolitics.org/2013/06/28/communicating-the-white-heat-of-technology/. Accessed 31 October 2013.

Critchley, J. (1990) *The Palace of Varieties*, London: Faber & Faber.

Cronin, J. (2004) *New Labour's Pasts: The Labour Party and its Discontents*, London: Pearson.

Crosland, A. (1918–1977) *Anthony Crosland Papers*, British Library of Political and Economic Science, London.

Crossbencher (1958) *Sunday Express*, 10 August 1958.

Crossman, R. (1976) *The Diaries of a Cabinet Minister Volume 2: Lord President of the Council and Leader of the House of Commons 1966–68*, London: Hamish Hamilton and Jonathan Cape.

Crossman, R. (1977) *The Diaries of a Cabinet Minister Volume 3: Secretary of State for Social Services, 1968–1970*, London: Hamish Hamilton and Jonathan Cape.

Crossman, R. (1979) *The Crossman Diaries: Selections from the Diaries of a Cabinet Minister, 1964–1970*, edited by A. Howard, London: Book Club Associates.

Dalyell, T. (2007) 'The Greatest Commons Performance', *Guardian*, 3 May 2007. Available at: www.theguardian.com/theguardian/2007/may/03/greatspeeches.

Damgaard, E. and Svensson, P. (1989) 'Who Governs? Parties and Policies in Denmark', *European Journal of Political Research*, 17, pp. 731–5.

Das, S. (2011) 'The Graphs That Should Worry Ed Miliband', *Left Foot Forward*, 15 December 2011. Available at: www.leftfootforward.org/2011/12/the-graphs-that-should-worry-ed-miliband/. Accessed 28 November 2013.

Deacon, R. (2006) *Devolution in Britain Today*, 2nd edn, Manchester: Manchester University Press.

Deedes, H. (2012) 'Labour Has the Wrong Leader. But Not the Wrong Miliband', *Mail Online*, 24 January 2012. Available at: www.dailymail.co.uk/debate/article-2091073/Ed-Miliband-Labour-wrong-leader.html. Accessed 3 December 2013.

Dell, E. (2000) *A Strange and Eventful History: Democratic Socialism in Britain*, London: HarperCollins.

Dewar, D. (2000) 'Foreword', in Brivati, B. (ed.) *Guiding Light: The Collected Speeches of John Smith*, London, Politico's, pp. 7–11.

Dictionary of the Welsh Language [Geiriadue Prifysgol Cymru] (2006) 1st edn, Cardiff: University of Wales Press.

Disraeli, B. (1845) *Sybil*, London: Henry Colburn.

Donoughue, B. (2009) *Downing Street Diary Volume Two: With James Callaghan in No. 10*, London: Pimlico.

Dorey, P. and Denham, A. (2011) '"O, brother, where art thou?" The Labour Party Leadership Election of 2010', *British Politics*, 6:3, pp. 286–316.

Douglas, R. (2005) *The Liberals: A History of the Liberal and Liberal Democrat Parties*, London: Continuum.

Dower, G.M.F. (1984) *Neil Kinnock: The Path to Leadership*, London: George Weidenfeld & Nicolson Ltd.

Driver, S. and Martell, L. (2006) *New Labour*, 2nd edn, Cambridge: Polity Press.

Dutton, D. (2006) *Douglas-Home*, London: Haus Publishing.

Elgie, R. (1995) *Political Leadership in Liberal Democracies*, Basingstoke: Palgrave Macmillan.

Epstein, L. (1960) 'Partisan Foreign Policy: Britain in the Suez Crisis', *World Politics*, 12, pp. 201–24.

Epstein, L. (1964) *British Politics in the Suez Crisis*, London: Pall Mall.

Estorick, E. (1949) *Stafford Cripps: A Biography*, London: Heinemann.

Fairclough, N. (2000) *New Labour, New Language?*, London: Routledge.

Fielding, S. (1995) '"White Heat" and White Collars: The Evolution of "Wilsonism"', in Coopey, R., Fielding, S. and Tiratsoo, N. (eds) *The Wilson Governments 1964–1970*, London: Pinter, pp. 29–47.

Fielding, S. (1997) *The Labour Party: Socialism and Society since 1951*, Manchester: Manchester University Press.

Fielding, S. (2003) *The Labour Governments, 1964–70. Vol. 1, Labour and Cultural Change*, Manchester: Manchester University Press.

Fielding, S. (2007) 'Rethinking Labour's 1964 Campaign', *Contemporary British History*, 21:3, pp. 309–24.

Fielding, S. (2010) 'Labour's Campaign: Things Can Only Get … Worse', *Parliamentary Affairs*, 62:2, pp. 653–66.

Fielding, S. and Tanner, D. (2006) 'The "Rise of the Left" Revisited: Labour Party Culture in Post-war Manchester and Salford', *Labour History Review*, 71:3, pp. 211–33.

Finlayson, A. (2001) *Making Sense of New Labour*, London: Lawrence and Wishart.

Finlayson, A. (2002) 'Elements of Blairite Image of Leadership', *Parliamentary Affairs*, 55, pp. 586–99.

Finlayson, A. (2007) 'From Beliefs to Arguments: Interpretive Methodology and Rhetorical Political Analysis', *British Journal of Politics and International Relations*, 9:4, pp. 545–63.

Finlayson, A. (2012) 'Rhetoric and the Political Theory of Ideologies', *Political Studies*, 60:4, pp. 751–67.

Finlayson, A. and Martin, J. (2008) '"It ain't what you say…"': British Political Studies and the Analysis of Speech and Rhetoric', *British Politics*, 3, pp. 445–64.

Foley, M. (2000) *The Blair Presidency*, Manchester: Manchester University Press.

Foley, M. (2002) *John Major, Tony Blair and a Conflict of Leadership*, Manchester: Manchester University Press.

Foot, M. (1960) *Tribune*, 24 October 1960.

Foot, M. (1962) *Aneurin Bevan*, vol. 1, London: MacGibbon & Kee.

Foot, M. (1973a) *Aneurin Bevan*, vol. 2, London: Davis-Poynter.

Foot, M. (1973b) *Speech to Nelson and Colne CLP*, 9 December 1973.

Foot, M. (1974a) *Speech to a Public Meeting at Taunton*, 25 January 1974.

Foot, M. (1974b) *Speech to the Society of Labour Lawyers*, 19 July 1974.

Foot, M. (1974c) *Speech at Ebbw Vale CLP*, 20 September 1974.

Foot, M. (1976) *Speech to Barrow In Furness CLP*, 25 September 1976.

Foot, M. (1978) *Speech at Finchley*, 13 September 1978.

Foot, M. (1979) *The Parliamentarians: Robin Day in Conversation with Michael Foot*, BBC 2, 25 February 1979.

Foot, M. (1980) *Speech to Liverpool Unemployment Rally*, 29 November 1981.

Foot, M. (1981a) *Interview with Robin Day*, BBC, 26 March 1981.

Foot, M. (1981b) *Weekend World*, ITV, 25 January 1981.

Foot, M. (1981c) *Weekend World*, ITV, October 1981.

Foot, M. (1981d) *Speech to Glasgow Unemployment Rally*, 21 February 1981.

Foot, M. (1981e) *Panorama*, BBC 1, 23 March 1981.

Foot, M. (1981f) *Debts of Honour*, London: HarperCollins.

Foot, M. (1982) *New Year Address to the Nation*, 1 January 1982.

Foot, M. (1983) *Weekend World*, ITV, 27 February 1983.

Foot, M. (1986) *Loyalists and Loners*, London: Collins.

Foot, M. and Bruce, D. (1949) *Who Are the Patriots?*, London: Gollancz.

Frank, B., Horner, C. and Stewart, D. (eds) (2010) *The British Labour Movement and Imperialism*, Newcastle: Cambridge Scholars Publishing.

Gaffney, J. (2001) 'Imagined Relationships: Political Leadership in Contemporary Democracies', *Parliamentary Affairs*, 54:1, pp. 120–33.

Gaffney, J. and Lahel, A. (2013) 'Political Performance and Leadership Persona: The UK Labour Party Conference of 2012', *Government and Opposition*, 48:4, pp. 461–505.

Gaitskell, H. (1959) *Report of the Labour Party Conference 1959*, London: The Labour Party.

Gaitskell, H. (1962a) 'Letter to Roy Jenkins', Hugh Gaitskell Papers, 8 May 1962, London: University College London.

Gaitskell, H. (1962b) 'Britain and the Common Market: Texts of Speeches Made at the 1962 Labour Party Conference by the Rt Hon. Hugh Gaitskell and Rt Hon. George Brown', London: Labour Party.

Gallagher, M., Laver, M. and Mair, P. (2006) *Representative Government in Modern Europe: Institutions, Parties and Governments*, New York: McGraw-Hill.

Glover, D. (2011) *The Art of Great Speeches and Why We Remember Them*, Cambridge: Cambridge University Press.

Glover, J. (2006) 'Brown Feels the Cameron Effect', *Guardian*, 22 September 2006. Available at: www.guardian.co.uk/politics/2006/sep/22/uk.polls. Accessed 12 October 2011.

Golding, J. (2003) *Hammer of the Left: Defeating Tony Benn, Eric Heffer and Militant in the Battle for the Labour Party*, London: Politico's.

Gould, P. (1998) *The Unfinished Revolution: How the Modernisers Saved the Labour Party*, London: Little Brown.

Grice, A. (2010) 'Don't Back Me for Leader, Miliband Urged Blair', *The Independent*, 2 September 2010. Available from: www.independent.co.uk/news/uk/politics/dont-back-me-for-leader-miliband-urged-blair-2068150.html. Accessed 27 November 2013.

Griffiths, J. (1969) *Pages From Memory*, London: Littlehampton Book Services.

Guardian (1986) 'Why Labour is Betting on John Smith', 14 February 1986.

Guardian (1960a) 'Mr Gaitskell Faces Uproar: Firm Line Amid Shouts and Jeers', 7 November 1960.

Guardian (1960b) 'Mr Gaitskell Faces Hecklers: Noisy Manchester Meeting', 8 November 1960.

Guardian (1962) 'Mr Gaitskell Hits Out at Dissidents: Angry Retort to Rowdy Nuclear Demonstrators', 7 May 1962.

Guardian (2001) 'Blair confronts scar on the world's conscience', 7 February 2001. www.theguardian.com/world/2002/feb/07/politics.development

Guardian (2002) 'What I learned about Tony – the hard way', 26 April 2002.

Hansan, M. (2012) 'Come on Ed, You Don't Need Tony to Win', *The Huffington Post*, 11 July 2012. Available at: www.huffingtonpost.co.uk/mehdi-hasan/come-on-ed-you-dont-need-tony_b_1665129.html. Accessed 3 December 2013.

Hansard (1942) 'General Direction of the War', *Hansard* 2 July 1942. Available at: http://hansard.millbanksystems.com/commons/1942/jul/02/central-direction-of-the-war. Accessed 11 May 2012. House of Commons Debate, London: HMSO.

Hansard (1945) *Hansard* 20 August 1945. House of Commons Debate, London: HMSO.

Hansard (1946a) 'National Health Service Bill', *Hansard* 30 April 1946. Available at: http://hansard.millbanksystems.com/commons/1946/apr/30/national-health-service-bill. Accessed 12 May 2012. House of Commons Debate, London: HMSO.

Hansard (1946b) *Hansard* 29 October 1946. House of Commons Debate, London: HMSO.

Hansard (1947a) *Hansard* 18 March 1947. House of Commons Debate, London: HMSO.

Hansard (1947b) *Hansard* 28 October 1947. House of Commons Debate, London: HMSO.

Hansard (1948a) *Hansard* 8 March 1948. House of Commons Debate, London: HMSO.

Hansard (1948b) *Hansard* 2 November 1948. House of Commons Debate, London: HMSO.

Hansard (1949) *Hansard* 21 March 1949. House of Commons Debate, London: HMSO.

Hansard (1951) *Hansard* 5 December 1951. House of Commons Debate, London: HMSO.

Hansard (1952) *Hansard* 25 February 1952. House of Commons Debate, London: HMSO.

Hansard (1956) 'Middle East', *Hansard* 5 December 1956. Available at: http://hansard.millbanksystems.com/commons/1956/dec/05/middle-east. Accessed 12 May 2012. House of Commons Debate, London: HMSO.

Hansard (1960a) *Hansard* 13 December 1960. House of Commons Debate, London: HMSO.

Hansard (1960b) *Hansard* 23 March 1960. House of Commons Debate, London: HMSO.

Hansard (1961) *Hansard* 28 June 1961. House of Commons Debate, London: HMSO.

Hansard (1971) *Hansard* 3 November 1971. House of Commons Debate, London: HMSO.

Hansard (1976a) *Hansard* 3 August 1976. House of Commons Debate, London: HMSO.

Hansard (1976b) *Hansard* 30 November 1976. House of Commons Debate, London: HMSO.

Hansard (1976c) *Hansard* 16 December 1976. House of Commons Debate, London: HMSO.

Hansard (1977) *Hansard* 23 March 1977. House of Commons Debate, London: HMSO.

Hansard (1978) *Hansard* 15 February 1978. House of Commons Debate, London: HMSO.

Hansard (1979) *Hansard* 28 March 1979. House of Commons Debate, London: HMSO.

Hansard (1982) *Hansard* 3 April 1982. House of Commons Debate, London: HMSO.

Hansard (1986) *Hansard* 27 January 1986. House of Commons Debate, London: HMSO.

Hansard (1992) *Hansard* 5 March 1992. House of Commons Debate, London: HMSO.

Hansard (2007) 'Tony Blair's Final PMQs', 27 June, Col. 330. www.parliament.uk/visiting/online-tours/virtualtours/transcripts/commons/blairs-pmqs/. House of Commons Debate, London: HMSO.

Hansard (HC Deb) (1909–2004) *The Official Report, House of Commons, 5th Series*, London: HMSO.

Hargrove, E. (1998) *The President as Leader: Appealing to the Better Angels of Our Nature*, Kansas: University Press of Kansas.

Harris, R. (1984) *The Making of Neil Kinnock*, London: Faber & Faber.

Harrison, M. (1966) 'Television and Radio', in Butler, D.E. and King, A. (ed.) *The British General Election of 1966*, London: Macmillan, pp. 125–48.

Haseler, S. (1969) *The Gaitskellites: Revisionism in the British Labour Party 1951–1964*, London: Macmillan.

Hassan, G. (2009) 'What Happens When Labour Falls from Power', *Our Kingdom*, 9 June 2009. Available at: www.opendemocracy.net/blog/ourkingdom-theme/guy-aitchison/2009/06/09/what-happens-when-labour-falls-from-power. Accessed 3 November 2013.

Hatfield, M. (1978) *The House the Left Built: Inside Labour Policy-Making 1970–1975*, London: Victor Gollancz.

Hattenstone, S. (2001) 'Comrade Kinnock', *Guardian*, 2 July 2001. Available at: http://politics.guardian.co.uk/profiles/story/0,9396,-2929,00.html. Accessed 2 March 2012.

Hayton, R. (2011) 'At Long Last, Miliband Finds His Voice ... But Now He Has to Make Sure That His Message is Heard', *Yorkshire Post*, 16 July 2011. Available from: www.yorkshirepost.co.uk/news/debate/columnists/richard_hayton_at_long_last_miliband_finds_his_voice_but_now_he_has_to_make_sure_that_his_message_is_heard_1_3579895. Accessed 1 December 2013.

Healey, D. (1989) *The Time of My Life*, London: Michael Joseph.

Heffernan, R. (1992) *Defeat from the Jaws of Victory: Inside Kinnock's Labour Party*, London: Verso.

Heffernan, R. (2001) *New Labour and Thatcherism: Political Change in Britain*, London: Palgrave Macmillan.

Heffernan, R. (2006) 'The Prime Minister and the News Media: Political Communication as a Leadership Resource', *Parliamentary Affairs*, 59:4, pp. 582–98.

Heffernan, R. (2007) 'Tony Blair as Labour Party Leader', in Seldon, A. (ed.) *Blair's Britain*, Cambridge: Cambridge University Press, pp. 143–63.

Heffernan, R. (2011) 'Labour's New Labour Legacy: Politics after Blair and Brown', *Political Studies*, 9:2, pp. 163–77.

Hennessy, P. (1997) *Muddling Through: Power, Politics and the Quality of Government in Postwar Britain*, London: Indigo.

Hennessy, P. (2000) *The Prime Minister: The Office and Its Holders Since 1945*, London: Allen Lane.

Heppell, T. (2008) 'The Degenerative Tendencies of Long Serving Governments ... 1963, 1996, 2008?', *Parliamentary Affairs*, 61:4, pp. 578–96.

Heppell, T. (2010) 'The Labour Party Leadership Election of 1963: Explaining the Unexpected Election of Harold Wilson', *Contemporary British History*, 24:2, pp. 151–71.

Heppell, T. (2012) 'Hugh Gaitskell 1955–1963', in Heppell, T. (ed.) *Leaders for the Opposition: From Churchill to Cameron*, Basingstoke: Palgrave Macmillan, pp. 33–47.

Heppell, T., Crines, A. and Nicholls, R. (2010) 'Ideological Alignments Within the Parliamentary Labour Party and the Leadership Election of 1976', *British Politics*, 5:1, pp. 65–91.

Hoggart, S. (1981) *On the House*, London: Robson Books.

Hoggart, S. (1983) *Back on the House*, London: Pan Books.

Hoggart, S. (1999) 'Blair Lays on the Therapy for the Terracotta Army', *Guardian*, 3 November 1999. Available at: www.theguardian.com/politics/1999/nov/03/politicalnews.politics. Accessed 3 March 2012.

Hoggart, S. (2008) 'Orators: The Good, the Bad and the Awful', *Total Politics*, 19 September 2008.

Hoggart, S. and Leigh, D. (1981) *Michael Foot: A Portrait*, London: Hodder & Stoughton.

Holland, S. (1978) *An Alternative Economic Strategy*, Nottingham: Spokesman Books.

Hornby, R. (1963) 'Parties in Parliament 1959–1963: The Labour Party', *Political Quarterly*, 34:3, pp. 240–8.

Horne, A. (1989) *Macmillan 1957–1986*, London: Macmillan.

Horne, D. (2001) *Looking For Leadership*, Melbourne: Viking.

Horner, D. (1995) 'The Road to Scarborough: Wilson, Labour and the Scientific Revolution', in Coopey, R., Fielding, S. and Tiratsoo, N. (eds) *The Wilson Governments 1964–1970*, London: Pinter, pp. 48–71.

Howard, A. and West, R. (1965) *The Making of the Prime Minister*, London: Jonathan Cape.

Howell, D. (1980) *British Social Democracy*, London: Croom Helm.

Huffington Post (2011) 'David Cameron Dismisses Strikes and Brands Ed Miliband as "Left Wing and Weak"', *Huffington Post*, 30 November 2011. Available at: www.huffingtonpost.co.uk/2011/11/30/damp-squib-david-cameron-strikes_n_1120175.html. Accessed 27 November 2013.

Hunter, L. (1959) *The Road to Brighton Pier*, London: Arthur Barker.

Hyman, P. (2005) *1 Out of 10: From Downing Street Vision to Classroom Reality*, London: Vintage.

The Independent (2010) 'Michael Foot: Writer and politician who rose to become leader of the Labour Party' [Obituary], 4 March. Available at: www.independent.co.uk/news/obituaries/michael-foot-writer-and-politician-who-rose-to-become-leader-of-the-labour-party-1915727.html.

Jamieson, K. (1988) *Eloquence in an Electronic Age: The Transformation of Political Speechmaking*, Oxford: Oxford University Press.

Jamieson, K.H. (1990) *Eloquence in an Electronic Age: The Transformation of Political Speechmaking*, Oxford: Oxford University Press.

Jay, D. (1980) *Change and Fortune*, London: Hutchinson.

Jefferys, K. (2000) 'The Attlee Years 1935–1955', in Brivati, B. and Heffernan, R. (eds) *The Labour Party: A Centenary History*, Basingstoke: Macmillan, pp. 68–86.

Jenkins, P. (1989) *Mrs Thatcher's Revolution*, London: Pan Books.

Jenkins, R. (2009) 'Harold Wilson', in *Oxford Dictionary of National Biography*, Oxford: Oxford University Press.

Jones, E. (1994) *Neil Kinnock*, London: Robert Hale Ltd.

Jones, M. (1995) *Michael Foot*, London: Gollancz.

Jones, T. (1996) *Remaking the Labour Party: From Gaitskell to Blair*, London: Routledge.

Kane, J. (2001) *Politics of Moral Capital*, Cambridge: Cambridge University Press.

Kane, J. and Patapan H. (2010) 'The Artless Art: Leadership and the Limits of Democratic Rhetoric', *Australian Journal of Political Science*, 45:1, pp. 371–89.

Karvounis, A., Manzo, K. and Gray, T. (2003) 'Playing Mother: Narratives of Britishness in New Labour Attitudes Toward Europe', *Journal of Political Ideologies*, 8:3, pp. 311–25.

Katz, I. (2008) 'The Inside Man', *Guardian*, 15 March.

Kavanagh, D. (2011) *Thatcherism and the End of the Post-war Consensus*, BBC History, 3 March 2011. Available at: www.bbc.co.uk/history/british/modern/thatcherism_01.shtml. Accessed 2 November 2013.

Kenny, M. and Smith, M. (1997) 'Discourses of Modernisation: Gaitskell, Blair and the Reform of Clause IV', *Journal of Elections, Public Opinion and Parties*, 7:1, pp. 110–26.

Kinnock, N. (1984) *Leader's Speech, Blackpool*. Available at: www.britishpoliticalspeech.org/speech-archive.htm?speech=190. Accessed 2 February 2012.

Kinnock, N. (1985) *Leader's Speech, Bournemouth*. Available at: www.britishpoliticalspeech.org/speech-archive.htm?speech=191. Accessed 2 February 2012.

Kinnock, N. (1987) *Leader's Speech, Brighton*. Available at: www.britishpoliticalspeech.org/speech-archive.htm?speech=193. Accessed 2 February 2012

Kinnock, N. (2011) *Speaker's Lecture on Michael Foot*, 12 July 2011. Available at: http://news.bbc.co.uk/democracylive/hi/house_of_commons/newsid_9487000/9487828.stm. Accessed 19 February 2012.

Kirkup, J. and Prince, J. (2010) 'David Miliband Favourite to be Next Labour Leader', *Telegraph*, 3 May 2010. Available at: www.telegraph.co.uk/news/election-2010/7671883/General-Elections-2010-David-Miliband-favourite-to-be-next-Labour-leader.html. Accessed 27 November 2013.

Kite, M. (2010) 'Ed Miliband: Self-confessed Maths "Geek" with Talent for Diplomacy', *Telegraph*, 25 September 2010. Available at: www.telegraph.co.uk/news/politics/labour/8025055/Ed-Miliband-Self-confessed-maths-geek-with-a-talent-for-diplomacy.html. Accessed 3 December 2013.

Kogan, D. and Kogan, M. (1982) *The Battle for the Labour Party*, Glasgow: Fortuna.

Kogan, M. (1985) *Letter to James Callaghan*, 31 July 1985. Held in Callaghan Papers.

Kynaston, D. (2007) *Austerity Britain, 1945–1951*, London: Bloomsbury.

Labour History Archive and Study Centre (LHASC) (1959) *Labour Party Annual Report 1959*, London: Labour Party.

Labour Party (1976) *Report of the Seventy Fifth Annual Conference of the Labour Party*, London: Labour Party.

Labour Party (1978) *Report of the Eighty Sixth Annual Conference of the Labour Party*, London: Labour Party.

Labour Party (1987) *Report of the Seventy Seventh Annual Conference of the Labour Party*, London: Labour Party.

Labour Party Manifesto Group Papers, Labour History Archive and Study Centre, Manchester.

Labour Party National Executive Committee (NEC) Minutes, Labour History Archive and Study Centre, Manchester.

Lanham, R.A. (1991) *A Handlist of Rhetorical Terms*, 2nd edn, Berkeley: University of California Press.

Laybourn, K. (1992) *A History of British Trade Unionism: c. 1770: 1990*, Stroud: Sutton.

Laybourn, K. (2008) 'Pacifists, Patriots and the Vote: The Erosion of Democratic Suffragism in Britain during the First World War By Jo Vellacott', *History*, 93, p. 312.

Laybourn, K. (2009) 'Trade Unionism in Britain since 1945', in Craig Phelan, *Trade Unionism since 1945: Towards a Global History*, Oxford: Peter Lang, pp. 199–230.

Laybourn, K. (2011a) 'The Independent Labour Party and the Second Labour Government 1929–1931: The Move Towards Revolutionary Change', in J. Shepherd, *The Second Labour Government: A Reappraisal*, Manchester: Manchester University Press, pp. 100–16.

Laybourn, K. (2011b) '"Histories of Labour: National and International Perspectives", by Joan Allen, Alan Campbell and John McIlroy, eds. and "Making History: Organizations of

Labour Historians in Britain since 1960", by John McIlroy, Alan Campbell, John Halstead and David Martin, eds.', *Labor History*, 52:3, pp. 347–9.

Leach, R. (2000) 'The Decline of Political Oratory?', paper for the Political Studies Association-UK 50th Annual Conference, 10–13 April 2000, London.

Leapman, M. (1987) *Kinnock*, London: Unwin Hyman.

Lee, A.M and Lee, E.B. (1939) *The Fine Art of Propaganda*, New York: Harcourt, Brace and Company.

Lee, S. (2006) 'Gordon Brown and the British Way', *Political Quarterly*, 77:3, pp. 369–78.

Lee, S. (2009) *Boom and Bust: The Politics and Legacy of Gordon Brown*, Oxford: OneWorld Publications.

Leith, S. (2011) *You Talkin' To Me? Rhetoric From Aristotle to Obama*, London: Profile Books.

LHASC *Labour Party Parliamentary Labour Party Papers*, Manchester: Labour Party.

LHASC (1965) *Labour Party Annual Report 1965*, London: Labour Party.

LHASC (1966) *Labour Party Annual Report 1966*, London: Labour Party.

LHASC (1968) *Labour Party Annual Report 1968*, London: Labour Party.

LHASC (1975) *Labour Party Annual Report 1975*, London: Labour Party.

LHASC (1976) *Labour Party Annual Report 1976*, London: Labour Party.

LHASC (1981) *Labour Party Conference Report 1981*, London: Labour Party.

LHASC (1982) *Labour Party Conference Report 1982*, London: Labour Party.

Lijphart, A. (1999) *Patterns of Democracy: Government Forms and Performance in Thirty-six Countries*, New Haven: Yale University Press.

Lovenduski, J. (2005) *Feminizing Politics*, Cambridge: Polity Press.

Macmillan, H. (1973) *At the End of the Day*, London: Macmillan.

MacPherson, H. (1994) 'Upright Rabelaisian', *New Statesman*, May 1994.

Mallalieu, J. and Gaitskell, H. (1952) 'Gaitskell Delivers New Red Letter', *Tribune*, 10 October 1952, p. 1.

Mandelson, P. (2010) *The Third Man: Life at the Heart of New Labour*, London: HarperPress.

Manifesto Group (1977) 'What We Must Do: A Democratic Socialist Approach to Britain's Crisis', *Manifesto Group*, March 1977.

Manifesto Group (1979) 'The Future of Counter-Inflation Policy', *Manifesto Group*, January 1979.

Marquand, D. (1999) *The Progressive Dilemma*, London: Phoenix.

Marquand, D. (2008) *Britain since 1918: The Strange Career of British Democracy*, London: Weidenfeld & Nicolson.

Martin, J. (2013) 'Situating Speech: A Rhetorical Approach to Political Strategy', *Political Studies*, EarlyView, doi: 10.1111/1467–9248.12039, 18 pp.

Martineau, L. (2011) *Politics and Power: Barbara Castle*, London: André Deutsch.

McAnulla, S. (2010) 'Post-political Poisons? Evaluating the "Toxic" Dimensions of Tony Blair's Leadership', Conference Paper, University of Leeds.

McAnulla, S. (2012) 'Blair', in Heppell. T (ed.) *Leaders of the Opposition: From Churchill to Cameron*, Basingstoke: Palgrave Macmillan, pp. 168–83.

McCormick, P. (1980) 'The Labour Party: Three Unnoticed Changes', *British Journal of Political Science*, 10:3, pp. 381–7.

McDermott, G. (1972) *Leader Lost: A Biography of Hugh Gaitskell*, London: Leslie Frewin.

McGrew, A. (2004) 'Globalisation', in Plant, R., Beech, M. and Hickson, K. (eds) *The Struggle for Labour's Soul: Understanding Labour's Political Thought since 1945*, London: Routledge, pp. 137–62.

McKie, D. (2005) 'Lord Callaghan', *Guardian*, 28 March 2005.

McSmith, A. (2006) 'Blair in His Own Words', *Independent*, 27 September 2006. Available at: www.independent.co.uk/news/uk/politics/blair-in-his-own-words-417732.html. Accessed 2 November 2013.

Meredith, S. (2008) *Labours Old and New: The Parliamentary Right of the British Labour Party 1970–79 and the Roots of New Labour*, Manchester: Manchester University Press.

Mikardo, I. (1988) *Back-Bencher*, London: Weidenfeld & Nicolson.

Miliband, E. (2012) *Speech to the Labour Conference*, 2 October 2012. Available at: www.labour.org.uk/ed-miliband-speech-conf-2012. Accessed 29 November 2013.

Minkin, L. (1978) *The Labour Party Conference*, London: Allen Lane.

Mitchell, J. (1963) *Crisis in Britain 1951*, London: Secker and Warburg.

Montgomerie, T. (2011) 'David Cameron Challenges Red Ed to Condemn Next Week's Public Sector Strikes', *ConservativeHome*, 23 November 2011. Available at: www.conservativehome.com/thetorydiary/2011/11/david-cameron-challenges-red-ed-to-condemn-next-weeks-public-sector-strikes.html. Accessed 3 December 2013.

Morgan, J. (1981) *The Backbench Diaries of Richard Crossman*, London: Hamish Hamilton and Cape.

Morgan, K. (1987) *Labour People: From Hardie to Kinnock*, Oxford: Oxford University Press.

Morgan, K. (1992) *Labour People: Hardie to Kinnock*, Oxford: Oxford Paperbacks.

Morgan, K. (1997a) *Callaghan: A Life*, Oxford: Oxford University Press.

Morgan, K. (1997b) *Interview with Stephen Meredith*, 17 October 1997.

Morgan, K. (1998) 'The Historical Roots of New Labour', *History Today*, 48:10, pp. 15–28.

Morgan, K. (1999) 'James Callaghan 1976–80', in Jefferys, K. (ed.) *Leading Labour: From Keir Hardie to Tony Blair*, London: I.B. Tauris, pp. 133–50.

Morgan, K. (2004) 'United Kingdom: A Comparative Case Study of Labour Prime Ministers Attlee, Wilson, Callaghan and Blair', *Journal of Legislative Studies*, 10:2/3, pp. 38–52.

Morgan, K. (2007a) 'Leadership and Change: Prime Ministers in the Post-war World – James Callaghan', Gresham College Lecture, 5 June 2007. Available at: http://xxpt.ynjgy.com/resource/data/20090601/U/gresham2007055/index.htm

Morgan, K. (2007b) *Michael Foot: A Life*, London: HarperCollins.

Mughan, A. (2000) *Media and the Presidentialization of Parliamentary Elections*, Basingstoke: Palgrave Macmillan.

Mullin, C. (2010) *Decline and Fall: Diaries 2005–2010*, London: Profile Books.

Naughtie, J. (2001) *The Rivals*, London: Fourth Estate.

Nelson, F. (2013) 'The Tories Can Steal Voters Labour Has Abandoned', *The Spectator*, 21 June 2013.

Norton, P. (2008) 'Tony Blair and the Office of Prime Minister', in Beech, M. and Lee, S. (eds) *Ten Years of New Labour*, Basingstoke: Palgrave Macmillan, pp. 89–102.

Oborne, P. (2007) *The Triumph of the Political Class*, London: Simon & Schuster.

Observer (1986) 'Rising Star of the Opposition', 2 November, 1986.

O'Hara, G. (2006) '"Dynamic, Exciting, Thrilling Change": The Wilson Government's Economic Policies, 1964–70', *Contemporary British History*, 20:3, pp. 383–402.

Olmsted, W. (2006) *Rhetoric: A Historical Introduction*, London: Blackwell.

Owen, D. (1992) *Time to Declare*, London: Penguin.

Panitch, L. and Leys, C. (2001) *The End of Parliamentary Socialism*, London: Verso.

Pearce, E. (1992) 'Labour's School Debaters Line up for Larynx Duty', *New Statesman and Society*, 5 June 1992.

Perkins, A. (2003) *Red Queen: The Authorized Biography of Barbara Castle*, London: Macmillan.

Pettitt, R. (2012) 'Me, Myself and I: "Self-referencing" in Labour Party Conference Leaders' Speeches', *British Politics*, 7:2, pp. 111–34.

Phillips, M. (1980) *The Divided House: Women at Westminster*, London: Sidwick & Jackson.

Pimlott, B. (1993) *Harold Wilson*, London: HarperCollins.

Plant, R., Beech, M. and Hickson, K. (2004) *The Struggle for Labour's Soul*, London: Routledge.

Poguntke, T. and Webb, P. (2005) *The Presidentialization of Politics: A Comparative Study of Modern Democracies*, Oxford: Oxford University Press.

Ponting, C. (1989) *Breach of Promise: Labour in Power 1964–1970*, London: Penguin.

Porter, A., Kirkup, J. and Winnett, R. (2010) 'Tony Blair's Revenge on Gordon Brown Puts Labour on Brink of Civil War', *Telegraph*, 1 September 2010. Available at: www.telegraph.co.uk/news/politics/tony-blair/7976472/Tony-Blairs-revenge-on-Gordon-Brown-puts-Labour-on-brink-of-civil-war.html. Accessed 23 January 2012.

Powell, D. (2001) *Tony Benn: A Political Life*, London: Continuum.

Powell, J. (2000) *Elections as Instruments of Democracy: Majoritarian and Proportional Visions*, New Haven: Yale University Press.

Powell, J. (2010) *The New Machiavelli: How to Wield Power in the Modern World*, London: Bodley Head.

Pugh, M. (2011) *Speak for Britain: A New History of the Labour Party*, London: Vintage.

Radice, G. (2002) *Friends and Rivals: Crosland, Jenkins and Healey*, London: Little, Brown.

Radice, G. (2010) 'Crosland and the Future of Socialism', *Policy Network*, 30 July 2010. Available at: www.policy-network.net/pno_detail.aspx?ID=3881&title=Crosland+and+The+Future+of+Socialism. Accessed 2 November 2013.

Raine, A. (1900) *Garthowen: A Story of the Welsh Homestead*, New York: A.L. Burt. Co.

Ramsden, J. (1998) *An Appetite for Power: The History of the Conservative Party since 1830*, London: HarperCollins.

Ramsey, K. (2004) 'Politics at the Water's Edge: Crisis Bargaining and Electoral Competition', *Journal of Conflict Resolution*, 48:4, pp. 459–86.

Rawnsley, A. (2001) *Servants of the People: The Inside Story of New Labour*, London: Penguin Books.

Rawnsley, A. (2010) *The End of the Party: The Rise and Fall of New Labour*, London: Penguin Books.

Reeves, R. (2007) *John Stuart Mill: Victorian Firebrand*, London: Atlantic Books.

Richards, S. (2011) 'In the Age of Twitter, the Art of Oratory is Fast on the Way Out', *Independent*, 31 May 2011.

Riddell, P. (1997) 'The End of Clause IV, 1994–95', *Contemporary British History*, 11:2, pp. 24–49.

Rose, R. (1964) 'Parties, Tendencies and Factions', *Political Studies*, 12:1, pp. 33–46.

Roth, A. (1977) *Sir Harold Wilson: Yorkshire Walter Mitty,* London: Macdonald & Jane's.

Rowland, C. (1960) 'Labour Publicity', *Political Quarterly,* 31:3, pp. 348–60.

Rusbridger, A. (1986) 'Why Labour has been betting on Smith', *The Observer,* 14 February 1986, p. 17.

Salter, P. (2009) 'Brown's Britishness', *Adam Smith Institute,* 17 April 2009. Available at: www.adamsmith.org/blog/media-and-culture/brown%E2%80%99s-britishness. Accessed 2 November 2013.

Sandbrook, D. (2008) *Never Had It So Good: A History of Britain from Suez to the Beatles,* London: Abacus.

Sandbrook, D. (2010) *White Heat: A History of Britain in the Swinging Sixties,* London: Abacus.

Sandry, A. (2011) *Plaid Cymru: An Ideological Analysis,* Cardiff: Welsh Academic Press.

Saville, J. (1980) 'Hugh Gaitskell: An Assessment', *The Socialist Register.* Available at: http://www.marxists.org/archive/saville/1980/xx/gaitskell.htm#n24. Accessed 31 October 2013.

Seldon, A. (2005) *Blair,* London: Free Press.

Seldon, A. (2007) *Blair Unbound,* London: Simon & Schuster.

Seldon, A. and Kavanagh, D. (2005) *The Blair Effect 2001–2005,* Cambridge: Cambridge University Press.

Seldon, A. and Lodge, G. (2011) *Brown at 10,* London: Biteback Publishing Ltd.

Shaw, E. (1996) *The Labour Party Since 1945,* Oxford: Blackwell.

Shea, M. (1992) 'He really must get better glasses', *The Times,* 16 November 1992, p. 16.

Shore, P. (1993) *Leading the Left,* London: Weidenfeld & Nicolson.

Short, C. (1994) 'John Smith's Qualities and Quality', *Tribune,* 27 May 1994.

Sodha, S. (2012) 'Ed Miliband is right to seek the redistribution of economic power', *New Statesman,* 25 September 2012.

Smith, A. (2010) 'David Miliband Launches Campaign on "Next Labour" Theme', *LabourList,* 17 May 2010. Available from: http://labourlist.org/2010/05/david-miliband-launches-campaign-on-next-labour-theme-full-speech/. Accessed 27 November 2013.

Smith, H. (2010) 'Lost Leaders: Neil Kinnock', *New Statesman,* 3 March 2010. Available at: http://www.newstatesman.com/uk-politics/2010/03/labour-party-kinnock-blair. Accessed 4 November 2013.

Sparks, J. (2005) *The Roots of Appalachian Christianity,* Lexington: The University Press of Kentucky.

Stephens, P. (2004) *Tony Blair: The Price of Leadership,* London: Politico's.

Stuart, M. (2005) *John Smith: A Life,* London: Politico's.

Sunday Express (1958) 'Crossbencher', 10 August.

Theakston, K. (2002) 'Political Skills and Context in Prime Ministerial Leadership in Britain', *Politics and Policy,* 30:2, pp. 283–323.

Theakston, K. (2007) 'What Makes for an Effective British Prime Minister?' *Quaderni di scienza politica,* 14, pp. 227–49.

Theakston, K. (2011) 'Gordon Brown as Prime Minister: Political Skills and Leadership Style', *British Politics,* 6:1, pp. 78–100.

Thomas, J. (1997) '"Taffy was a Welshman, Taffy was a Thief": Anti-Welshness, the Press and Neil Kinnock', *Llafur: Journal of Welsh Labour History,* 7:2, pp. 95–108.

Thomas Symonds, N. (2005) 'A Reinterpretation of Michael Foot's Handling of the Militant Tendency', *Contemporary British History*, 19:1, pp. 27–51.

Thomas Symonds, N. (2006) 'Oratory, Rhetoric and Politics: Neil Kinnock's "Thousand Generations" Speech and the General Election of 1987', *Llafur: Journal of Welsh People's History*, 9:3, pp. 65–80.

Thomson, P. (1999) *Dictionary of Labour Quotations*, London: Politico's.

Thorpe, A. (2001) *A History of the British Labour Party*, Basingstoke: Palgrave.

Thorpe, A. (2005) 'Reasons for "Progressive" Disunity: Labour and Liberal Politics in Britain, 1918–45', *Socialist History*, 27, pp. 21–42.

Thorpe, A. (2006) '"In a Rather Emotional State"? The Labour Party and British Intervention in Greece, 1944–45', *The English Historical Review*, 121:493, pp. 1075–105.

Thorpe, A. (2008) *A History of the British Labour Party*, Basingstoke: Palgrave Macmillan.

Thorpe, A. (2009) 'The Communist Party and the New Party', *Contemporary British History*, 23:3, pp. 477–91.

Thorpe, A. (2012) 'The Labour Party and the Trade Unions', Paper to the History and Policy Group, 10 March 2012. Available at: www.historyandpolicy.org/forums/union/meeting_100312.html. Accessed 1 November 2013.

The Times (1956a) 'Unity in the Middle East: The Prime Minister's Report', 14 February 1956.

The Times (1956b) 'Government Wins Vote of Confidence', 22 February 1956.

The Times (1963) 'Mr. Wilson Waves the New Banner of Revolution', 2 October 1963.

The Times (1967) 'Broadcast Call to National Pride. "We're on our own now"', 20 November 1967.

The Times (1977) 'Moderates in the Labour Party, 2: The Manifesto Group: Giving Intellectual Credibility to Policies', 30 September 1977.

The Times (1978) 'Mr Callaghan Renews Plea for 5% Pay Guideline', 5 September 1978.

Titan (1858) 'The Welsh Pulpit' in *Titan: A Monthly Magazine*, 26, January–June, pp. 345–9.

Total Politics (2012) 'Unparliamentary Language Dominates PMQs', *Total Politics*, 18 September 2012. Available at: www.totalpolitics.com/print/292922/unparliamentary-language-dominates-pmqs.thtml. Accessed 3 December 2013.

Toye, R. (2010) 'The Rhetorical Premiership: A New Perspective on Prime Ministerial Power since 1945', Parliamentary History, 30(2): 175–92.

Toye, R. (2011) 'The Rhetorical Premiership: A New Perspective on Prime Ministerial Power Since 1945', *Parliamentary History*, 30:2, pp. 175–92.

Toye, R. (2013) *Rhetoric: A Very Short Introduction*, Oxford: Oxford University Press.

Trade Union Congress (1978) *TUC Report 1978*, London: TUC.

Uhr, J. (2005) *Terms of Trust: Arguments Over Ethics in Australian Government*, Sydney: University of New South Wales Press.

Vighi, F. (2010) *On Žižek's Dialectics: Surplus, Subtraction, Sublimation*, London: Continuum.

Walden, B. (2006) 'The White Heat of Wilson', *BBC News*, 31 March 2006. Available at: http://news.bbc.co.uk/1/hi/magazine/4865498.stm. Accessed 3 November 2013.

Walker, D. (1989) 'The First Wilson Governments, 1964–1970', in Hennessy, P. and Seldon, A. (eds) *Ruling Performance: British Governments from Attlee to Thatcher*, Oxford: Blackwell, pp. 186–215.

Watkins, A. (1998) *The Road to Number 10: From Bonar Law to Tony Blair*, London: Duckworth.

Watkins, A. (1992) 'Battling John Smith lacks a knock-out punch', *The Observer*, 1 October 1992, p. 23.

Watt, N. (2012) 'Ed Miliband the Leader Steps into the Limelight', *Guardian*, 2 October 2012. Available at: www.theguardian.com/politics/2012/oct/02/ed-miliband-labour-leader-limelight. Accessed 27 November 2013.

Westlake, M. (2001) *Kinnock: The Biography*, London: Little, Brown and Company.

White, S. (1998) 'Interpreting the Third Way: Not One Road but Many', *Renewal: A Journal of Social Democracy*, 6:2, pp. 17–30.

Williams, P. (1979) *Hugh Gaitskell: A Political Biography*, London: Jonathan Cape.

Williams, S. (2002) *Interview with Stephen Meredith*, 25 June 2002.

Wilson, G. (2009) *SNP: The Turbulent Years, 1960–1990*, Stirling: Scots Independent.

Wilson, H. (1963) 'Labour's Plan for Science' – Leaders speech to the Labour conference, 1 October 1963. Available at: http://nottspolitics.org/wp-content/uploads/2013/06/Labours-Plan-for-science.pdf. Accessed 18 November 2013.

Wilson, H. (1964) *The New Britain: Labour's Plan Outlined by Harold Wilson*, Harmondsworth: Penguin.

Wilson, H. (1971) *The Labour Government 1964–1970: A Personal Record*, London: Weidenfeld & Nicholson and Michael Joseph.

Wintour, P. (1998) '"Smug" John Smith was major factor in Labour's 1992 election defeat', *The Observer*, p. 21.

Woodward, N. (1997) 'Labour's Economic Performance 1964–70', in Coopey, R., Fielding, S. and Tiratsoo, N. (eds) *The Wilson Governments 1964–1970*, London: Pinter, pp. 72–101.

Woodward, W. (2001) 'What's New?', *Guardian*, 1 October 2001. Available at: http://www.theguardian.com/education/2001/oct/16/schools.uk

Wrigley, C. (2002) *Winston Churchill: A Biographical Companion*, Santa Barbara: ABC-CLIO Limited.

Young, H. (1994) 'Labour rides a tide of change, not a wave of sympathy', *The Guardian*, 19 May 1994, p. 26.

Young, H. (2008) *The Hugo Young Papers*, London: Allen Lane.

Ziegler, P. (1993) *Wilson: The Authorised Life*, London: Weidenfeld & Nicolson.

Index